GETTING INTO YOUR CUSTOMER'S HEAD

GETTING INTO YOUR CUSTOMER'S HEAD

8 Secret Roles of Selling Your Competitors Don't Know

Kevin Davis

TIMES BUSINESS

RANDOM HOUSE

The "Five Phases of Learning," on pages 206–208 was adapted from "The Five Levels of Competence," *Creative Training Techniques Handbook: Tips, Tactics and How-To's for Delivering Effective Training* by Robert W. Pike (Minneapolis: Lakewood Publications, 1989), pp. 5–6. Used by permission.

Library of Congress Cataloging-in-Publication Data

Davis, Kevin
   Getting into your customer's head : 8 secret roles of selling your competitors don't know / Kevin Davis.
        p.   cm.
   ISBN 0-8129-2628-5 (alk. paper)
   1. Selling.   2. Consumer behavior.   I. Title.
HF5438.25.D38   1996
658.85—dc20   95-46877

Manufactured in the United States of America on acid-free paper

9 8 7 6 5

To my wife, Dale, whose inspiration got me started on this project and whose love and support gave me the strength to finish it.

ACKNOWLEDGMENTS

My greatest appreciation is for the help of the thousands of sales-people with whom I have had the privilege of working. Through word and deed you have taught me much over the years, and I thank you for allowing me to learn from you.

Many people contributed their time and expertise in helping me complete *Getting into Your Customer's Head*. My special thanks go to the following professionals, who generously contributed countless hours of interview time, thereby helping the sales "roles" come to life: Jana Neuenschwander-Turns, PA-C and Thomas Tighe, M.D. (Doctor), Jerry Gabriel, AIA (Architect), Monte Vista High School Head Football Coach Rich Cotruvo, Barbara Berns, Ph.D., L.M.F.C. and Bea Davis, Ph.D., L.M.F.C. (Therapist), Scott Radovich, JD, MBA (Negotiator), Jane Ware, MS (Teacher), and Mimi Luebbermann, author of *Pay Dirt: How to Raise and Sell Herbs and Produce for Serious Cash* (Rocklin, CA: Prima Publishing, 1994) (Farmer).

Writing a book can be a lonely experience. Thousands of hours in seclusion, putting words on paper in the hope that some day someone will be better off as a result. During this challenging time, Nellie Sabin, my editor, was always there for me, offering suggestions and encouragement that spurred me on to the finish line. Nellie is a world class editor with a golden heart.

My work would not have been completed without the special contributions of the following talented and caring people: Ed Harbordt, whose copy editing throughout these many months provided rigorous quality control; Joe Kendrick, who provided extensive feedback that helped ensure that my message would apply not solely to sales professionals, but to all professionals who sell; and to Ed Bastarache, a fellow student of selling who has contributed significantly to my learning, and whose thoughtful suggestions helped shape the final manuscript.

Over the years, many authors have contributed to my knowledge and interpretation of sales effectiveness. Of particular importance were *SPIN Selling* (New York: McGraw-Hill, 1988) and *Major Account Sales Strategy* (New York: McGraw-Hill, 1989), both by Neil Rackham; *Why People Buy*, by John O'Shaughnessy (New York: Oxford University Press, 1987); and *Non-Manipulative Selling*, by Tony Alessandra, Ph.D., Phil Wexler, and Rick Barrera (New York: Prentice-Hall, 1987).

Many other experts from whom I've benefited include: Ken Blanchard, Peter Block, Michael Bosworth, James Champy, Stephen Covey, Edward de Bono, Peter Drucker, Barry Farber, Roger Fisher, Michael Hammer, Mack Hanan, Stephen Heiman, Jim Holden, John Katsaros, Donald Kirkpatrick, Robert Mager, Robert Miller, Geoffrey Moore, Earl Naumann, Kenichi Ohmae, Tom Peters, Robert Pike, Michael Porter, Al Ries, Allison Rossett, Richard Ruff, Brian Tracy, Jack Trout, William Ury, Richard Whiteley, Larry Wilson, Carl Zaiss, Ron Zemke, and Elaina Zuker.

I am grateful, too, to John Mahaney, executive editor at Times Business, whose insightful advice improved the book immeasurably, and to my agent, Denise Marcil, for her advocacy and counsel.

I wish as well to thank those who read this book as it was being written and who offered constructive comments: Sarah Caverhill, Jeff Gardner, Bob Ronchi, Chuck Novotny, Bob Nelson, and Pat Zigarmi. Thanks also to the many sales professionals who shared their personal experiences, thereby allowing me to share them with you.

Last but certainly not least, thanks to my children, Lauren and Kyle, who kept the noise down to a dull roar while Dad was writing.

FOREWORD

As a student of effective business behavior for the past thirty years, my goal has always been to take the B.S. out of the behavioral sciences. One of the maxims I've discovered at the core of every successful organization is an intense focus on the customer. This holds true of businesses of all types and sizes and for my own business as well. In my organization, I know that I am ultimately responsible for the satisfaction of every customer we have. I don't just preach customer satisfaction; I have to practice it like everybody else.

That is why I value *Getting into Your Customer's Head* so highly. Kevin Davis identifies how to sell effectively in a way that also greatly enhances customer satisfaction. He describes in detail how you can think and feel like a customer—that is, how to get into your customer's head. He then shows you exactly what you must do to meet your customer's needs better than your competition.

As you will read, Kevin has determined that today's buyers follow a predictable eight-step buying process, and he has created eight easily understood selling roles to match each step: Student, Doctor, Architect, Coach, Therapist, Negotiator, Teacher, and Farmer. It's a sophisticated sales approach made simple.

This book provides a blueprint for anyone who wants to attain a higher level of sales success. It is invaluable for anyone who has customers, including salespeople, small business owners, professional service providers, managers, and, yes, even corporate executives.

As we prepare to enter the next millennium, one thing is certain: To do more than survive—to thrive—you must add more value to your business relationships. I predict that those who heed this book's message will increase their sales and in the process gain a competitive advantage for the future.

KEN BLANCHARD, PH.D.
co-author, *The One Minute Manager*

CONTENTS

GETTING INTO YOUR CUSTOMER'S HEAD

INTRODUCTION

Buying is where selling should start. Every time you make a sale, someone buys. Do you know as much about buying as you do about selling?

In our rapidly changing world, selling is becoming more difficult because buyers are changing. The lives of your best customers, those who have known and valued you the most, have been changed personally and professionally. In today's fiercely competitive marketplace, buyers are slashing costs to get by, which means there's more pressure on them to make better buying decisions. For you to win the sale, you must be more persuasive.

Today's new buyers don't know you well and don't have the time to get close. Their competition is growing tougher; they have to do more with less. Yesterday's buyers were more likely to rely on your recommendations, particularly if you had a long-standing relationship. Today's new buyers are:

- More demanding.
- More price-conscious.
- More knowledgeable about buying.
- Less loyal to suppliers.
- Deluged by choices.
- More uncertain about the future.
- More at risk if a mistake is made.
- Much more **cautious.**

In some ways, buyers' caution makes selling more difficult. However, with caution comes predictability—and therein lies your opportunity.

Your title need not be "salesperson" for you to benefit from this book. All professional service providers, including independent consultants, architects, lawyers, accountants, advertising/public relations executives, and physicians, must sell their services to create and keep clients. Even corporate managers must sell their ideas to fellow managers and employees to gain influence and career advancement. Small business owners and entrepreneurs must either sell or die. Everybody sells *something.*

Because buyers have changed, salespeople must change to meet the new needs of their customers. Recently, the Forum Corporation, a Boston-based consulting firm, surveyed 342 Fortune 500 companies in a variety of industries to discover what traits in salespeople were the most annoying to their customers. The top five sources of customer frustration with salespeople were:

1. Difficulty in communication.
2. Salesperson's lack of knowledge of customer's company.
3. Overaggressive selling.
4. Slow delivery.
5. Salesperson's overpromising and then not delivering.

All these sources of frustration can be avoided if you use a sales approach that matches how today's new buyers buy. By applying the skills described in this book, you can greatly reduce, or even eliminate, customer–client frustration.

WHY SHOULD YOU LISTEN TO ME?

I have been in sales since 1979 and have sold both tangible and intangible products and services. I was an award-winning salesperson, major account executive, sales manager, and district manager for Lanier Worldwide, the office equipment division of the $3.5 billion Harris Corporation. As an independent sales consultant since 1989, I have helped many of America's finest companies to increase their sales effectiveness. These companies are engaged in a wide variety of businesses. They range from industry leaders such as ADP, BellSouth, BusinessWeek, Dresser Industries, F. W. Dodge/McGraw-Hill, Pacific Telesis, and Standard & Poor's Corporation to promising growth companies such as A.E.I. Music Network, Bay Alarm Company, and

Pinnacle Data Corporation. My specialty is the design and presentation of customized sales training programs to corporate clients.

The services I deliver provide me with a uniquely objective vantage point for observing both buyers and sellers. First, I work with each client's salespeople, studying carefully how they sell and how their buyers buy. In this way, I gain knowledge about the client's industry. I also draw on my knowledge of selling, gained from over 12,000 hours of personal research, which has included my reviewing thousands of books, seminars, videos, audio cassettes, and articles focused on sales, sales management, and buyer behavior. Then, by blending in-depth knowledge of my clients with leading-edge sales expertise, I am able to create customized training solutions. Thousands of salespeople have benefited from my workshops. This book is the result of my work to date and of feedback from thousands of sales professionals.

My entire professional career has been devoted to selling, studying selling, and working closely with salespeople to help them achieve more. I know what you want. You are reading this book because you want new skills and strategies that are easy to remember and apply—skills that will give you an edge over your competitors. If you're a sales professional, you're probably tired of so-called experts, some of whom have never sold before, who tell you *what to do* but not *how to do it*. Theory doesn't produce sales; skills do. This book was written to give you the skills you need to create satisfied clients during good times or bad.

BUY-KNOWING VERSUS BUY-LEARNING

People buy in two ways. When buyers feel they already know what they need to know, they quickly reach a decision to buy. I call this method of purchasing "buy-*knowing*." There's no great challenge in selling buyers something they already know they want. That's easy. However, most buyers today fall into a more complex category, one that involves acquiring knowledge and weighing alternatives to arrive at the best buying decision. I call this method of purchasing "buy-*learning*."

For businesses and consumers alike, the first-time purchase of a significant product or service is typically accomplished with a buy-*learning* process. People buy either to solve a problem or to take advantage of an opportunity. The increasing velocity of change means that many current needs—and their solutions—are new; buyers do not have experience in dealing with them. All this uncertainty adds up to today's new buyers, who are more cautious and, hence, more frequent users of the buy-*learning* process.

Two different research projects have been conducted at opposite ends of the buying spectrum, one on consumer buying habits (Columbia University School of Business), and the other on major account buying habits (Huthwaite Research). Interestingly, both studies arrived at the same conclusion: When buyers feel the need to buy but sense the risk of making a mistake, they will seek to resolve uncertainty with a rational buying process.

This rational buying process, what I call buy-*learning*, unfolds in a series of predictable steps that can be anticipated by salespeople. Your prospects' motivation to buy may be emotional, but how they buy is rational. Just as you have a selling process, buyers have a buying process. Your challenge is to shepherd buyers through each step of the buy-*learning* process until they are satisfied with what you have to offer.

After a product is purchased and put to use, your customers become more knowledgeable about it and, over time, rely less on the seller for information. This growth in your customers' knowledge, and their comfort in knowing what they are buying, gradually leads to repeat purchases using the simpler buy-*knowing* process. You can expect your initial sale, however, to be time-consuming, because you need to allow a fearful or skeptical buyer time to gain confidence that your offering is best.

For professional salespeople, the days of the three-martini lunch and order-taking are over. Today's new buyers expect more value; they demand that salespeople refocus their expert knowledge on identifying and solving new problems. If you sell to businesses, these problems can't be found in the purchasing department; they exist in the buyers' core business processes, such as product development, manufacturing, sales, and customer service.

A new sales approach is required to meet the demanding needs of today's new buyers. To meet customers' needs, you (the salesperson) must be more proactive by:

- Studying a prospect's business.
- Getting appointments with key executives.
- Diagnosing larger problems.

Once you're in the door and you've found a problem, you're only part way home. You also need:

- Excellent competitive selling skills to show why you're the best.
- Negotiation skills to reach a mutually beneficial agreement.
- Postsale satisfaction skills to enable your customer to achieve value.

The new sales approach described in this book will help you not only to make a sale but also to stay a key person in the life of your buyers.

CUSTOMER-FOCUSED SELLING

We see the world not as it is, but as we are conditioned to see it. Who we are influences what we see. Two people can look at the same thing and see something totally different. Yet each person assumes that the way he or she sees things is the way things are.

In the world of selling, we have been conditioned to see things through a salesperson's eyes, and our sales behaviors are based on these perceptions. But your buyers have a different frame of reference. They have their own point of view. The key to success in selling is your ability to get into each customer's head, to see things from a buyer's perspective, and match how you sell with how your buyers buy. I call this approach *customer-focused selling*.

As you probe your buyers' needs, going through each step of the buy-*learning* process with them, you will need to take on an entire sequence of customer-focused selling roles: student, doctor, architect, coach, therapist, negotiator, teacher, and farmer. To cover these roles in detail, each is given a full chapter in this book.

Because the mind retrieves pictures more easily than words, it's helpful for you to have a vivid image of how to match selling techniques with buying behavior. I created these selling roles so that you'll be able to remember and apply much more of what you read here.

My purpose in writing this book is to help you sell more effectively to today's new buyers. If you apply these new skills, I believe you will create more new customers, each of whom will be better satisfied with the products and services you provide. Isn't that what selling is all about?

1

CLASH!

Today's New Buyer Confronts the Traditional Sales Approach

The urgent question of our time is whether we can make change our friend and not our enemy.

President Bill Clinton
1993 Inaugural Address

Changing times have made today's buyer especially wary. The economic conditions of today are much more difficult to deal with than those of yesterday, and the conditions of tomorrow are harder to predict. Changes in jobs, businesses, competitors, products, information resources, and technology have profoundly affected not only how people live but also how people buy.

You can turn change to your advantage. When you get inside a buyer's mind, you can match how you sell with how and why a buyer buys. By keeping close to your customer in this way, you'll create more beneficial solutions that produce greater value for both you and your customer.

YOUR BUYER'S CHANGING PERSONAL LIFE

The future is less predictable because it's coming at us faster than ever before. In his classic book *Future Shock*, Alvin Toffler says, "If the last 50,000 years of man's existence were divided into lifetimes of approximately 62 years each, there have been 800 such lifetimes. Of these 800, fully 650 lives were spent in caves. Only during the last 70 lifetimes has it been possible to communicate effectively from one lifetime to another—as writing made it possible to do. Only during the last six lifetimes did masses of people see a printed word. Only within the last two has anyone anywhere used an electric motor. And the overwhelming majority of all the material goods we use in daily life today have been developed within the present, 800th lifetime." John Malone, head of Tele-Communications Inc. (TCI), the largest U.S. cable-TV system operator, said in 1994, "The overwhelming majority of revenues we get by the end of the decade will be from services and products not yet invented." The pace of change is clearly accelerating.

Change means that buyers are faced with an increasing number of situations in which their previous life experiences don't apply. Cellular phones, satellite TV, personal computers, laptop computers, digital video disks, and personal digital assistants are just a few examples of new consumer products. Technology is merging telecommunications, television, consumer electronics, computers, information services, and publishing into a single information industry, which ensures greater consumer uncertainty in the future. Buyers already are faced with myriad choices of products and services they know nothing about. Learning is how consumers cope with change and uncertainty.

YOUR BUYER'S CHANGING PROFESSIONAL LIFE

While your buyer's personal life is changing fast, his or her professional life is changing faster. Powerful forces are reshaping our business world and shaking the foundations of corporate America.

Competition

Seismic economic changes—including the transition from a national to a world economy, the ability to produce more products in less time with higher quality, and the convergence of markets—are dramatically increasing competitive pressures.

As our national economy becomes a world economy, U.S. companies face fierce competition from overseas. According to the

Federal Communications Commission, the number of international telephone calls quadrupled between 1988 and 1992, and the frequency with which people make these calls is increasing at a faster rate. Overseas companies with lower labor costs have lower production costs. This puts pressure on U.S. companies to reduce prices and costs.

Today's technology allows faster product development, which means that competitive advantages don't last as long as they once did. According to Dataquest, more than 1,200 new models of personal computers (PCs) were introduced in 1993. That's more than three new PCs every day! The average life cycle of a PC in the marketplace is just nine months. Motorola has been able to build a new microprocessor plant in eighteen months, a project that once required three to four years. Within a few weeks of opening, the plant set a new company record for quality. More products produced in less time at higher quality means that products are becoming more and more alike. It's more difficult to differentiate one product from all the others.

Markets that once were separate and distinct are now converging. This means companies will face competition in the future from major companies that haven't competed against them in the past. For instance, the airline industry's toughest competition in the year 2000 will come from the telecommunications industry as videoconferencing gains acceptance as an alternative way to hold a meeting.

Communications technology increases competition. The Home Shopping Network uses television to compete against department stores. Dell Computer uses telephone sales to compete with retail computer stores. Automobile pricing and buying services, many of which sell cars over the phone, are now providing stiff competition to car dealers.

Company Restructuring and Downsizing

Increasing competition forces companies and the people who work for them to make a choice: change or face elimination. Larry Farrell, author of *Searching for the Spirit of Enterprise,* says "of America's 100 largest companies in 1900, only 16 are still in business today." The message is clear: companies and people who are unwilling to change will fail.

To ensure survival, firms are downsizing to cut costs and to improve responsiveness and communications. Costs have had to be cut because overseas companies have lower labor and production costs. Responsiveness needs to be improved because time is crucial—delays in the introduction of new products can kill profits. Communications need to be improved to keep up with fast shifts in customer preferences.

This restructuring is paying off. *BusinessWeek* reports that the combined profits of America's 1,000 most valuable companies rose 34 percent in 1994 vs. 1993, while sales climbed a modest 9 percent. Profits in 1993, according to *BusinessWeek*, represented a 23 percent increase over 1992, while sales climbed 5 percent.

Technology allows companies to cut back on employees while still improving productivity and communication. Over the past few years, companies have substituted information technologies for labor, eliminating millions of jobs. Middle management has been particularly hard-hit. Judith Hamilton, CEO of Dataquest and a recent guest columnist for the *San Francisco Examiner*, writes, "Middle management jobs have disappeared and won't be coming back. Middle management jobs were created because we did not have sophisticated systems to manage all that information. They were necessary to filter, collate, summarize, forward, and act on information. Technology now does these functions for us." Frank Lichtenberg, an economist at Columbia University School of Business, has found that one information systems worker can replace six other employees without affecting output. Restructuring will continue as more technology makes more layoffs possible.

Continued technological developments make today's buyers more vulnerable to job loss. More than 85 percent of the Fortune 1000 Companies downsized their white-collar workforce between 1987 and 1991. A Harvard University study found that men aged 35 to 54 were twice as likely to lose their jobs in a permanent layoff in 1993 as they were in 1980. Joseph Cooper of the National Study Center said, "About 1 million men a year suffer this devastating midlife job crisis at a time when their financial and family responsibilities are the greatest."

You don't have to be a layoff victim to be affected by downsizing. David Noer, author of *Healing the Wounds: Overcoming the Trauma of Layoffs and Revitalizing Downsized Organizations*, studied the effects of layoffs on survivors—those who remained after others were let go. Noer found that those spared from layoffs live with feelings of fear and uncertainty for up to *five years* after the layoffs have occurred. In one survey cited by Noer, 70 percent of managers who survived corporate layoffs reported that they felt insecure about their future. For today's decision makers, there is greater risk and uncertainty than ever before.

Accelerated Change

Change has made the economic conditions of today more challenging and those of the future impossible to predict. The rising rate of change forces all of us to deal with problems we have never faced before. Buyers are more uncertain about their needs and the myriad options available to meet those needs. As a consequence, buyers are taking more time to decide on purchases. New problems and needs require buyers to learn more to ensure that they make the best decision, and learning takes time. This need for more information has led to a more frequent use of the buy-*learning* process I referred to earlier. By adjusting your sales approach to match the modern buying process, you can better meet your customers' needs and differentiate yourself from your competitors.

THE TRADITIONAL SALES APPROACH

For many years, salespeople have been taught a traditional sales approach, one that places great emphasis on the steps of selling, but gives very little attention to the process of buying. Yet every time a sale is made, a buyer is making a specific decision about a product or service. How can we begin to understand selling if we don't understand buying?

The traditional sales approach uses what I call *self-focused selling*. It was effective back in the days when buying was fairly simple. There were fewer choices, and limited information was available about those choices. Customers had fewer competitors to consult, and each product was easily distinguished from others. Sellers were able to simply raise the prices of their products to cover increasing costs. Today, products are less distinguishable, and a customer's customer is unwilling to pay higher prices.

Today's new buyers have changed. They have become better at buying. They play hardball with salespeople, not golf. Their customers and competitors won't allow prices to be raised so they want you to lower yours. Today's challenges demand more of them, so they demand more of you.

The traditional self-focused selling approach is no longer effective because today's new buyers are unwilling to follow you. They don't want to be "sold," they want to make educated buying decisions. To make a sale, you must join them on their buying path. That path does not end at the close of your sale. Your mutual destination should be *value*—a state of improvement for the customer.

Back in the late 1970s, I was taught a sales approach that focused almost exclusively on selling, not buying. Self-focused selling taught me to focus on my sales process and keep the prospect on my "track." This approach was based on control. Today, tens of thousands of salespeople are still being taught the same, or a similar, sales methodology.

The Old Sales Track

Just as a railroad track is a pathway to a destination, so too was my sales track designed to keep the prospect moving with me to my own destination—the close. The "sales track railroad," I was taught, had the following four stops on the way to a sale.

1. *Approach.* I was taught to get into comfortable conversation by identifying something that the prospect and I had in common. Communication experts call this "bridge building." By scanning the prospect's office, I was usually able to determine what he or she did with spare time: travel, golf, fishing, and so on. This step is still a good start on a new sales call today, provided your buyer has the time to chat.

2. *Needs.* I was taught to ask what I now call *self-focused questions* in order to gain and maintain control. One example of a self-focused question was called the "leading" question: any question to which both the buyer and seller already know the answer. For example, "Mr. Prospect, are you interested in saving money?" Another example of a salesperson-focused question was the "tie-down," a question designed to get the prospect to say "yes." For instance, "This is what you had in mind, isn't it?" The more times a prospect said yes (I was told), the more likely that prospect would buy.

3. *Presentation.* I was taught to memorize the perfect sales presentation, complete with my product's finest features and benefits. I used an almost identical script for every prospective buyer. In

my search for the best show, however, I frequently forgot the unique needs of my audience.

Some prospective buyers jumped off my track by coming up with objections. When this happened, my job was to overcome the objections and get the buyers back on track. With the "feel, felt, found" method, I was taught to say, "I understand how you *feel*. Others have *felt* the same way, but after they took a closer look this is what they *found*." (This is one traditional technique that can still be effective today.)

Another tactic I was taught was the "reverse wrench," in which I took an objection and instantly turned it into a reason to buy. Suppose the prospect said, "No way; your product is brand new, it doesn't have a track record yet." My response was: "Ms. Prospect, the fact that it is so new is the very reason why you should buy!" It was assumed that buyers would automatically want the latest and presumably the best the market had to offer.

4. *Close.* As my sales track approached the close, it was time to "turn up the heat." Here are some of the techniques I was taught:

- *Puppy dog close.* "Why don't you try this out for a few days and if you don't like it, bring it back."

- *"Let me make a note of that" close.* If my prospect asked whether my product came in blue, I said, "Let me make a note of that," and I would begin filling out a sales order.

- *The sharp angle close.* If the prospect said, "If we get this approved, we'll need delivery by the first," my response was, "If I could guarantee delivery by the first, will you sign the order today?"

- *The negative close.* If I expressed doubt about the buyer's ability to do something—for example, obtain the necessary financing—that buyer would buy just to prove me wrong. For instance, I might say, "By the way, are you sure you could qualify for this model if you wanted it?"

WHO'S IN CONTROL HERE?

The old sales track employed many variations of the same theme: *use controlling behaviors to get a close.* Have you been taught in the same way?

Today's buyers have become more resistant to traditional controlling-type sales techniques. When people feel that they are being controlled, they become resentful. For buyers, an emotional barrier springs up and the "fight or flight" response kicks in. Prospects either **fight** back with objections or **flee** to the competition. In my experience, buyers usually flee: it's less stressful and saves time. Buyers usually don't argue; they say, "I'll think about it," and then just go away.

Another shortcoming of traditional self-focused selling is that the sales pitch wraps up too quickly for today's buyers. In December 1993, *Sales & Marketing Management* magazine published the results of a study conducted by Dartnell Corporation, a Chicago-based business publisher. The study found that most salespeople finish selling before the prospect is ready to buy. Although 80 percent of purchases are bought *after* the fifth contact, 90 percent of salespeople quit selling *before* the fifth contact. This study supports my belief that the traditional approach to selling has taught most salespeople to sell too fast. They move rapidly through their sales process irrespective of where the customer is in the buying process, and they arrive at the end of their sales presentation with nothing more to say.

The destination of the traditional self-focused selling track is the close of a sale. The buyers' path has a different destination: value. Buyers want to be better off; they want results. They see your product as a means to an end, not as an end in itself. Buyers feel the sale *begins* when they take delivery. Most salespeople think delivery is the *end* of the sale.

Traditional Sales Approach	▶	Customer-Focused Selling
Present a fixed solution		Identify buyer's needs
Explain common features and benefits		Provide information on your product's uniqueness
Use an aggressive sales pitch		Give the buyer time to learn
Overcome objections		Help the buyer resolve fears
Close the sale and move on		Provide value and future results

BUYER/SELLER NEGOTIATING

A signed contract is the result of negotiation, between buyer and seller, that attempts to meet individual needs. The buyer's needs are for improvement; the seller's needs are to meet sales objectives.

Individual negotiating strength—both the buyer's and the seller's—affects the outcome. The stronger one is, the better one's needs are met. Negotiating strength is derived from several sources, some of which are:

- *Options.* The fewer options a customer has to meet a need, the stronger the salesperson's position.

- *Relationships.* A strong relationship with a buyer gives the seller relationship strength. People prefer to buy from people they like and trust.

- *Information.* A buyer who can obtain information from a third party has a stronger position because there is less need to rely entirely on the seller's knowledge.

- *Skill.* The more skilled a buyer is at buying, the more strength that buyer has.

Negotiating strength is discussed later in this book (see Chapter 8). The important point here is that the traditional self-focused selling approach was successful in the past because salespeople were in a stronger position than buyers were. Salespeople were able to form close relationships with their customers. Buyers had fewer options and limited information resources, and they frequently lacked skill at buying. Today's new buyers are in a stronger position. Here are the key reasons.

Downsizing and Reorganization Have Cut Short Many Relationships. Salespeople's strength in relationships has been significantly affected by downsizing and reorganization. Relationships with many of their best customers have been cut short. Some buyers have been laid off, and those who remain may have had changes in responsibilities. These are the people sellers have known and valued the most. Taking over are today's new buyers, who are expected to do more with less. Also, the downsizing of management ranks and the accelerating pace of business require managers to interact with more people during the course of each day. Relationships with salespeople are not a high priority.

Buyers Have More Options.   Never before have there been as many buying options for customers. Not too long ago, General Motors had 60 percent of new car sales. The number of new car introductions each year could be counted on one hand. Then along came Audi, BMW, Honda, Infiniti, Isuzu, Lexus, Mazda, Mercedes-Benz, Mitsubishi, Nissan, Porsche, Saab, Subaru, Toyota, Volkswagen, and Volvo with an unending number of models.

Buyers Have New Information Resources. A proliferation of industry-specific magazines keeps buyers fully updated on developments and improvements. For example, *PC World, Byte,* and *PC Magazine* help educate consumers about computers. Standard & Poor's and Dow Jones sell information that helps investors. Companies like J. D. Power, Datapro, and Dataquest research various products and services, then sell their information to businesses. On-line services such as CompuServe, America Online, Microsoft Network, and Prodigy give instant access to the World Wide Web, where information is updated around the clock. The result of all these resources is a more educated buyer who is less reliant on salespersons for information. For example, suppose you are thinking about buying a new minivan and want to gather information. Today, you can call a *Consumer Reports Magazine* 800 number at any time of the day or night, and input your credit card number and fax number. A nine-page competitive analysis is in your hands within two minutes for just $7.50. You now know more than most salespeople at car dealerships. Want to know how much the dealer paid for the minivan? No problem. Just call another 800 number.

Buyers Are Making More Decisions, and They're Getting Better at It. People are making more buying decisions today, which means they have learned more about effective buying. In the home-based business area, for instance, consumers are buying computers, modems, fax machines, pagers, and cellular phones. The more buying people do, the better they get at it because they learn from their mistakes. They learn to make more complex decisions and to achieve more favorable results. In fact, over 100 studies have found that if decision makers follow a systematic approach, they will have a better chance of achieving their goals than if they make choices because of "a gut feeling" alone. Buyers have also improved their skill by educating themselves about buying. The proliferation of negotiating courses, instructional videos, and self-help audio tapes is compelling evidence that buyers now recognize the value of empowering themselves with new skills and knowledge.

MAKING A COMMITMENT TO VALUE

Effective selling requires that salespeople join in the buy-*learning* process. Salespeople must travel on the *buyers'* path and help the buyers make the best decision, one that results in maximum benefit achieved. In Stephen Covey's book *Seven Habits of Highly Effective People,* habit number 2 is "Begin with the end in mind." For salespeople, this means making a commitment to **value,** in all its manifestations:

- *Value for your customer.* That's what the customer expects and demands.

- *Value for your company.* New competitors are pursuing your best customers, which makes the value of each loyal customer go up. It's easier and more profitable for companies to retain loyal, satisfied customers than to try to replace them.

- *Value for you.* By applying the skills described in this book, you'll enjoy less rejection, you'll have more repeat business, and you'll gain more personal satisfaction from selling.

I've explained how change has made today's buyers more cautious. *Your buyers* have changed, and *you* must change to meet their new needs. In this book, you will learn how today's buyers buy and what you can do to match selling with buying. By applying the skills in this book, you will turn the way you sell into a competitive advantage.

2

THE BUYING PROCESS

Getting Into Your Customer's Head

If passion drives you, let reason hold the reins.
Benjamin Franklin

Do you remember the movie *Patton*, in which General George S. Patton was up against German Fieldmarshal Erwin Rommel in the North African desert? Patton, portrayed by George C. Scott, looked at Rommel's tanks through his field glasses and said, "Rommel, you magnificent bastard, I read your book!" Patton had studied Rommel carefully and could anticipate the German's moves before Rommel made them. To Patton, this meant a competitive advantage.

I am *not* suggesting you look at your buyers as adversaries, but I *am* suggesting that you study your buyers carefully. When you know how your prospects buy, you can anticipate what they will do before they do it. This anticipation allows you not only to travel on the buyers' path, but also to stay one step ahead of both the buyers and your competitors.

People who buy have an emotional desire for improvement, a belief that their life will be better off as the result of a purchase. How they buy depends on many factors, including the magnitude of the purchase and how comfortable the buyers are with it.

When buyers already know as much as they need to know in order to buy, they make a simple choice. These buy-*knowing* decisions tend to be quick, made without deliberation, and primarily driven by emotional need.

The buy-*learning* process is more complex. It involves acquisition of knowledge and careful consideration of alternatives to ensure that the best selection is made. Selling to buy-*learning* prospects takes longer because learning takes time. Although the buyers' motivation to buy is still emotional, the process they use to reach a decision is sequential and rational. In the next millennium, possessing the skills to sell to buy-*learning* prospects will be the critical success factor for sales effectiveness.

ACCOUNT DEVELOPMENT

After a product is purchased and put to use, customers become more knowledgeable about it—and less reliant on sellers for information. Sometimes, this increase in customer knowledge results in customers who know as much about a product as the sellers do. In the telecommunications industry, for example, AT&T's loss of monopoly forced many large corporations to create the position of "telecom manager," an in-house telecommunications expert. Telecom managers know as much about basic telecommunications services as the salespeople who sell them those services. This growth in customer knowledge gradually leads to the simpler buy-*knowing* buying process.

Because buyers are becoming more self-sufficient, many companies are "reengineering" their sales organizations by creating inside order-taking positions to support basic customer needs—that is, servicing buyers who already know what they want—and refocusing telesales and outside salespeople on buy-*learning* prospects. With the cost per field sales call now in excess of $350, many sales organizations are concluding that it is inefficient for salespeople to call on customers who already know what they need. Knowledgeable customers can call in or fax their order. Valuable sales time is better spent on new account development activities. Therefore, the critical skill for successful salespeople in the future will be the ability to successfully sell to buy-*learning* prospects.

In the mid-1990s, IBM realigned its sales organization to cut its sales costs and better meet customer needs. In fact, 40,000 of IBM's 45,000 customers in Detroit are now covered by sales reps who work over the phone. IBM's outside sales force has been overhauled to emphasize industry-specific expertise; these salespeople have become more knowledgeable about their customers' businesses. IBM plans to have 80 percent of its customers reached by one of fourteen industry sales teams dedicated to areas such as health care, travel, and financial services. IBM recognizes that salespeople are not adding value to the buy–sell relationship unless they know more than the buyers. When buyers already know as much as the sellers, the natural focus will then be on the lowest price.

WITH KNOWLEDGE, FEAR OF BUYING DIMINISHES

The need to avoid taking risks is one of the strongest needs human beings have. Buyers know that it is possible to make mistakes, and that some of these mistakes can be costly, not only financially but also in terms of emotional regret. The increasing velocity of change constantly brings new needs and demands new solutions, but many buyers don't have experience dealing with these issues. These buyers become uncertain. Experienced buyers have learned that a systematic approach to decision making stands a better chance of achieving the desired results than "shooting from the hip." The buy-*learning* process is the buyers' cure for risk and uncertainty.

For businesses and consumers alike, the first-time purchase of a significant product or service is typically accomplished with a buy-*learning* process. In many other selling situations, uncertainty and risk will almost certainly be factors. All of the following sales situations will involve the buy-*learning* process:

- *There are many options to choose from.* Having more choices means experiencing more uncertainty. For example, there are now over 1,000 mutual funds to choose from, and this confusing array of choices causes uncertainty for investors who want to be certain that they are selecting the best fund for their purposes.

- *Buyers' perception of the investment required is high.* A major purchase to one buyer may be a minor purchase to another. Most people would consider a new car to be a major purchase, but a multimillionaire who owns ten other cars may not. When buyers perceive that they are making a "major purchase," they want to make certain they are making the right choice. With today's customers doing everything in their power to cut costs, what was considered a small purchase five years ago may now be perceived as a significant investment worthy of careful deliberation. In this way, cost cutting has forced a more frequent use of the buy-*learning* process.

- *Buyers are risking their credibility.* Many salespeople are finding that the senior managers to whom they once sold their product or service now delegate more of their authority. Downsizing has hit senior managers too, forcing them to empower subordinates to take on more responsibility. When authority to decide is delegated, the new decision makers have more at risk. The greater the buyers' perception of risk, the more they seek to avoid a mistake.

- *An "intangible" service is being considered.* When buyers can't see or touch what is being sold, they are likely to feel uncertain about what they will get. For example, when a builder "buys" architectural services, the building that is being purchased hasn't been created yet.

- *The decision is an infrequent one.* When a purchase is made infrequently, the buyer's knowledge of the product is relatively low. The decision to buy a home is made much less often than the decision to buy a new suit. Also, a product that is bought infrequently will be used for a long time. If a mistake is made, the buyer will have to live with disappointment or face expensive repercussions.

- *Buyers are not certain that the product will do what the salesperson says it will do.* The impact of some products and services is difficult, if not impossible, to measure. Consider a buyer of advertising who wants to increase awareness of a product in the marketplace. A seller assures this buyer that advertising in "Magazine A" will increase awareness, but the buyer wonders "When?" and "By how much?"

- *The product is brand-new and does not yet have an established track record.* When a technology company introduces a new product, its first customers are referred to as "early adopters." Early adopters take risks in buying new products that lack a proven track record. Many buyers choose *not* to be early adopters when a product's performance is unproven. Those who do buy a new product usually study it carefully to evaluate the risk involved.

- *Switching costs are high.* If buyers recognize in advance the difficulty of switching after a product is bought, they will take more care in its initial purchase. Think of someone considering whether an Apple or an IBM model should be purchased as a first computer. If this buyer spends $2,000 on an Apple now, then decides in two years to switch to IBM, the $2,000 computer is the least of the worries involved. New software will be required, documents must be transferred, and a new operating system must be learned. If the buyer recognizes these possible switching costs in advance, the initial $2,000 decision may be deliberated with the same care as a $25,000 investment.

Fears frequently resurface later in the buy-*learning* process. How to resolve these fears will be discussed in Chapter 7.

RESEARCH SUPPORTING THE BUY-*LEARNING* PROCESS

As I mentioned in the Introduction, two separate research projects have confirmed the existence of a buy-*learning* process. These projects, one on consumer buying and the other on major account buying, were conducted at opposite ends of the buying spectrum. Both studies concluded that when buyers feel the need to buy but sense the risk of making a mistake, they will engage in a rational and sequential buying process.

The first research project was conducted on more than 1,000 consumers by John O'Shaughnessy, Professor of Business at the Columbia University School of Business. After he recorded what consumers said before, during, and after buying, he interpreted those statements in terms of consumer buying behavior, and published his findings in his book, *Why People Buy*.

O'Shaughnessy found that when buyers feel uncertain about which product or service to buy, they will seek to resolve their uncertainty through a rational and deliberate buying process. First, consumers decide whether the anticipated benefits of buying a product or service outweigh the costs. This decision answers the question, "Do I really need this?" Then, consumers' focus shifts to selecting one choice among rival brands. According to O'Shaughnessy, the "consumer evaluates, ranks, or groups them on the basis of their fit to the choice criteria adopted." *Choice criteria* are defined as differences between alternatives that are important to the buyer. Furthermore, O'Shaughnessy says, "The process of evaluating rival brands is likely to be a process in which consumers come to know more precisely what they want. This is because the search and deliberation involved in evaluation is a process of education whereby wants and choice criteria become more refined and specific." The purpose of this process—what I call buy-*learning*—is to identify a preference.

The other study was conducted on over 35,000 major account sales calls by Huthwaite Research. Huthwaite's staffers traveled with more than 10,000 salespeople, watched each sales call, and counted how often buyers used certain behaviors. Their findings are published in the book *Major Account Sales Strategy* by Neil Rackham. Huthwaite found that in major account buying decisions "all people, whether influencers, decision makers, purchasing agents, or evaluation committees, normally go through distinct psychological stages when they make decisions." Huthwaite identified these stages to be recognition of needs; evaluation of options; resolution of concerns; decision; and implementation. These stages are rational, sequential, and predictable. Recognizing them enables the salesperson to "build a selling strategy that focuses on the steps the customer takes in making a decision, not on the steps the salesperson takes in making a sale."

O'Shaughnessy cites an example of a woman who bought a sewing machine. First, she decided she needed a sewing machine. Then she researched various brands and their features to identify her buying criteria. She asked the opinion of friends, and visited several stores to compare models, features, and prices. After several days, she identified a preference and almost bought, but had some last-minute reservations and decided to "think it over." She went home, discussed it with her husband, then made her purchase.

Rackham, in describing his findings, provides a case example of the purchase of a $500,000 industrial pumping system. First, one manager within the buying organization recognized that a new system was needed and would pay for itself in six months. This manager then convinced fellow managers of the need, and received approval to spend $550,000 for a replacement system. A buying committee was formed, buying criteria were identified, and a Request for Proposal was sent to various suppliers. The committee gradually eliminated alternatives, then had some last-minute concerns about the preferred choice. Finally, the company entered negotiations with the preferred choice.

The purchase of the sewing machine took days and the purchase of the pumping system took several months, but both decisions followed a similar buying process. I believe that today's buyer uses the buy-*learning* process not just for major account purchases, but when deliberating *any* purchase perceived as involving risk.

WHAT IS THE
BUY-*LEARNING* PROCESS?

The buy-*learning* process enables buyers to get their needs met. On the one hand, buyers have a need for improvement; on the other hand, they have a need to avoid taking risks. Using the buy-*learning* process, buyers achieve the greatest possible improvement with the least possible risk.

Join your buyers in this process. See their problems and opportunities as they see them. Make their hopes and fears yours. By identifying yourself with your buyers, you can, through *Customer-Focused Selling*, guide them step-by-step to the decision to buy your product.

The buy-*learning* process consists of four stages: (1) determining a need, (2) finding the best solution, (3) committing to buy, and (4) evaluating the outcome. For the sake of simplicity, I call these stages Need, Learn, Buy, and Value.

Each stage is made up of two steps. The buy-*learning* process comprises eight steps in all, as shown in Figure 2.1.

Stage One: Need

People buy products and services for their own reasons, not for yours. They buy your product for improvement—to be, have, or do more. This belief is the "need"—the prospects' mental image of expected future value. Examples of buyers' perceived needs are more money, more time, greater peace of mind, security, status, enhanced image, love, and so on.

Need is personal and subjective; it varies from person to person. Consider a couple deciding to buy a new car. To one of them, the new car represents greater safety and security during transportation. To the other, the new car represents enhanced status, the ability to signal success to others.

The Need stage consists of two distinct steps, Change and Discontent.

Step 1: Change

Think back to your last car purchase. Your decision to buy probably began with change. Perhaps the change occurred gradually—more

Figure 2.1 The Buy-*Learning* Process: The Four Stages and the Steps in Each Stage

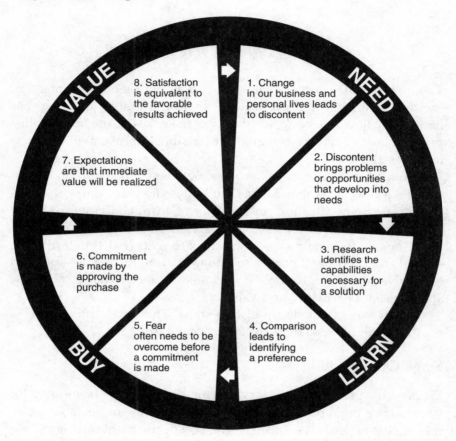

and more miles were being added to your odometer. Perhaps the change occurred rather suddenly—a job transfer or an auto accident. Or perhaps you anticipated a change—the arrival of a new baby. Change triggers discontent.

Step 2: Discontent

Discontent is a feeling of dissatisfaction with your current situation. Discontent can be caused by a problem (such as a wrecked car) or an as-yet-unrealized opportunity (such as when a new job pays more money and allows you to improve the quality of your life with a new car).

Often, early in the Discontent step, the problem or unrealized opportunity is not that pressing. Gradually, you become more and more dissatisfied until finally you decide you have a need—to buy a new car. You have now reached the end of the Need stage; you have decided to buy *something*, and your attention turns to considering which product will best meet your need. If you already know the answer, your buying decision is quickly made (buy-*knowing*).

Usually, however, the need that was identified is intangible; as a customer, you know you have a need, but you are uncertain how to fulfill it. The Learn stage is the answer to this uncertainty.

Stage Two: Learn

Let's go back to the car example. Suppose you need a larger car because of the birth of a baby. You first determine the essential capabilities of your new car. Do you want a sedan, minivan, or sport utility vehicle? You also identify budget limitations—your price range. Then you shop and compare various vehicles, all of which meet these essential requirements. By a process of comparison, you identify differences between options and select a preference. The end result of the Learn stage is an identification of the best choice.

The Learn stage consists of two distinct steps, Research and Comparison.

Step 3: Research

Buyers turn an intangible need into a tangible solution by researching their options and identifying the capabilities required for a solution. The capabilities identified by buyers are their buying criteria.

There are two types of buying criteria: "must-haves" and "nice-to-haves." A must-have is a specific capability or requirement that buyers absolutely must have. Must-haves are usually directly linked to need. For instance, suppose the change in your life is a new job that requires you to carry valuable demonstration equipment. Your current car is a two-door convertible. A must-have in a new car would be a large trunk for security. Other examples of must-haves could include four doors, automatic transmission, and an alarm system. If you live in the mountains, you may decide you must have four-wheel drive.

In the course of identifying must-haves, people typically identify some nice-to-haves as well. Nice-to-haves are acceptable options that would make the purchased item more attractive but are not essential.

Step 4: Comparison

Armed with your must-have capabilities, you proceed to the next step in the Learn stage. Options are shopped and compared. You begin this step by visiting dealerships and looking at only those cars that have your must-have capabilities. Then you start taking nice-to-haves into account. Gradually, you prioritize your nice-to-haves and reduce your options to a **preferred** choice. Major decisions are often made based on minor differences.

Your Comparison step, which began with many options under consideration, concludes when you identify a preference. Your focus then changes from "Which one should I buy?" to "What might happen if I buy Product C from Company XYZ?"

Stage Three: Buy

Thus begins the Buy stage, which consists of two distinct steps, Fear and Commitment.

Step 5: Fear

Often, when you make a significant purchase, you feel self-doubt just before you make the commitment. As a salesperson, can you recall working very closely with a potential buyer, feeling very confident of an impending order, only to suddenly have the deal turn upside down? Did your phone calls go unreturned? This is the Fear step in action.

Fear is emotional, not logical; it is the one step of the buying process that sometimes is skipped by the buyer. Fear seems to occur more frequently with large purchases because fear is caused by risk—the risk of making a mistake. The greater the risk, the greater the probability the Fear step will occur. The decision to rent a car, for instance, is much less risky than the decision to buy a car. Less money is involved, the rental is for a much shorter period of time, and if you don't like the rental car you can simply exchange it for another one.

Step 6: Commitment

Finally, you overcome your fear and commit to buying your new car. Usually, just before you commit, certain details must be ironed out through negotiations. After negotiations are completed, you have reached the end of the Buy stage. You have made a purchase.

Stage Four: Value

In the Value stage, customers ask themselves, "Did the results I achieved meet or exceed my expectations?" The Value stage consists of two distinct steps, Expectations and Satisfaction.

Step 7: Expectations

In the Expectations step, a buyer expects immediate value. The first thing you do after you buy a new car is to drive it home. Along the way, you try out all the new bells and whistles only to discover that you don't yet know how to operate them. You may feel a great sense of frustration because operating your new car is not as easy as you expected. Sometimes, the tremendous excitement felt immediately after a purchase descends into frustration, anger, and doubt as a buyer encounters the difficulty of change.

Step 8: Satisfaction

Eventually, you move on to the Satisfaction step. This is when you ask yourself, "Am I getting the value I thought I would? Does this car do what the salesperson said it would?"

Satisfaction usually varies over time. When you bought your new car, you felt it was the best choice. As time goes by, you may become aware of new alternatives that offer valuable improvements. Satisfaction may diminish according to your perception of the alternatives.

After a period of time, you're back in the Need stage and will once again go around the buying wheel. These steps are an ongoing cyclical process.

WHY PEOPLE BUY

Buying is an emotional need-satisfaction process that occurs when people believe that the results of buying will improve their lives in some worthwhile way. Every human being, either consciously or subconsciously, moves toward pleasure and away from pain.

Two types of needs—personal and social needs—cause people to begin the buying process. Personal needs are individual; social needs relate to how people want others to see them.

Examples of Personal Needs.   As individuals, we all want to be:

- Healthy, not sick.
- Physically safe, not threatened.
- Relaxed, not tense.
- Happy, not sad.
- In control of life, not controlled by others.
- Entertained, not bored.
- Free, not confined.
- Loved, not hated.
- Self-assured, not insecure.
- Rich, not poor.

Examples of Social Needs.   In a social context, we all want to be:

- Successful, not a failure.
- Admired, not snubbed.
- Beautiful, not ugly.
- Literate, not illiterate.
- Accepted, not shunned.

Your personal and social needs are what advertisers seek to serve when they paint a picture of how much better your life will be if you buy their products. Perfume makes you more attractive, fitness centers make you healthier, insurance gives you peace of mind, and a luxury car signals your success. Advertisers are attempting to convince you that the result of your buying will be a new, improved, and happier you.

Each of these needs can vary in importance as the buyer changes during life. A teenager may place entertainment needs over financial needs; later in life, the desire to become financially secure becomes of greater importance.

WHY ORGANIZATIONS BUY

Organizations, like individuals, buy for improvement. Every company has organizational goals it is striving to achieve: to increase efficiencies, cut costs, improve profitability, and gain competitive advantage. Standing between where a company is now (current situation) and where it wants to be (goal) are problems and opportunities.

Examples of Problems. Companies face immediate challenges, such as:

- Material or component shortages.
- Obsolete plant and equipment.
- Poorly performing suppliers.
- Competitors' activities.

Examples of Opportunities. Because they cannot afford to be complacent, companies must strive for:

- Increase in sales.
- Improvement in quality.
- Entry to a new market.
- Increasing efficiency of operations.

A business, using a logical process, buys to satisfy definable business needs. Management wants to achieve results for customers, employees, and stockholders.

Corporate goals, however, are achieved by individuals. Buying decisions are made by people who have personal emotional needs. Although these individuals have an interest in achieving their organization's goals, their motivation to buy is derived from their personal and social goals, including a conscious or subconscious desire to improve their status within the company.

Examples of Personal Goals.   Corporate buyers seek:

- More achievement, not less.
- More authority, not less.
- More money, not less.
- More job security, not less.
- More responsibility, not less.

Examples of Social Goals.   A business buyer desires:

- To be a leader, not a follower.
- To be a problem solver, not a problem ignorer.
- To be admired, not ignored.
- To have more influence, not less.
- To be valuable, not expendable.
- To gain more power, not less.

Most organizations tend to promote people who have proven themselves capable of exceeding the organizational goals for which they are responsible. Therefore, the best way to achieve a personal promotion is to achieve business results. Business results are achieved by solving problems or taking advantage of market opportunities.

There are some important differences between selling to businesses and selling to consumers. When a consumer buys, there are seldom more than two decision makers. When a business buys, there are often multiple decision makers, each of whom passes through the buy-*learning* process. These people are part of what I call a *Complex Buying Team*. Members of a Complex Buying Team fulfill different roles in the decision-making process and exert varying levels of influence on the final selection. In Chapter 11, we will take a close look at the Complex Buying Team and how you can sell effectively to multiple decision makers.

Today's buyers don't want to be "sold," they want salespeople to help them buy. To match selling with buying, you need a new sales approach that is based on the eight-step buying process. If you adopt the Customer-Focused Selling approach, you will increase your sales and enjoy greater customer satisfaction.

THE CUSTOMER-FOCUSED
SELLING SALES ROLES

Customer-Focused Selling is selling to customers the way customers want to be sold to. Throughout the buying process, you must change your sales approach to meet your customers' needs; that is, you must adopt the selling role that matches your buyers' current needs.

In the buying process, each step a buyer takes is firmly based on the preceding step. The more effective you are at meeting the buyer's information needs at each specific step, the better your chances of winning the sale.

The eight sales roles of Customer-Focused Selling are:

1. *Student:* Study the *Change* affecting your customers, and open some closed doors.
2. *Doctor:* Diagnose your customers' *Discontent* and uncover their big needs.
3. *Architect:* Design unique solutions that simplify your customers' *Research* and lock out your competition.
4. *Coach:* *Compare* your offering to the competition's and then implement a game plan to win.
5. *Therapist:* Draw out *Fears* and help to resolve them.
6. *Negotiator:* Discuss with a view to reaching a mutual *Commitment* to *open* a relationship (not *close* a sale).
7. *Teacher:* Identify *Expectations,* teach the customers to use your product, and test for the *Value* improvement achieved.
8. *Farmer:* Cultivate *Satisfaction* and grow the account.

As shown in Figure 2.2, each Customer-Focused Selling role is designed to meet prospects' changing information needs and to help them move forward in the buying process. The *Student* and *Doctor* roles help the prospect in the Need stage. The *Architect* and *Coach* roles help prospects in the Learn stage. The *Therapist* and *Negotiator* roles help the prospect in the Buy stage. The *Teacher* and *Farmer* roles help the customer in the Value stage.

Think of these roles as eight selling "hats." Which hat you wear depends on your customers' progress through the buy-*learning* process. With new prospects, determine where they are in the buying process and select the appropriate selling "hat." When a customer moves in the buying process (hopefully forward but possibly backward), change your selling "hat" to meet the new needs. The speed with which each buyer's wheel turns determines how fast you should change your selling role.

Why and How I Created the Eight Sales Roles

For the past several years, I have carefully measured the impact of my sales training services by mailing a questionnaire to individual

Figure 2.2   The Buy-*Learning* Process: The Roles of Customer-Focused Selling

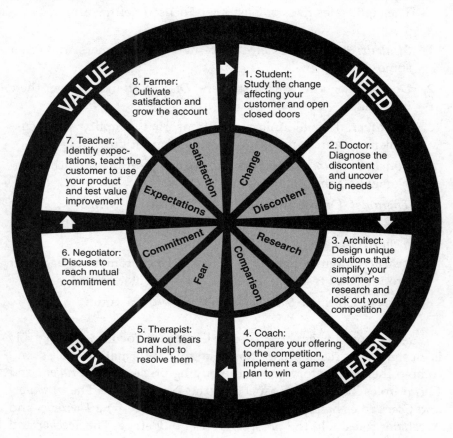

participants six months after the completion of a program. Responses have indicated that (1) my program contains valuable information that produces increased sales, and (2) participants have difficulty retaining everything they have learned during the program and are omitting some helpful approaches in their later sales efforts.

My solution was to create a labeled role for each phase of the selling process, to give salespeople a clear mental picture of the activities associated with each phase. With this device, the selling process can be easily recalled in a sequence that matches how people buy.

After reviewing everything I had ever learned or observed about selling, I selected eight roles that represent the eight phases of the new selling process. I then conducted in-depth interviews with several practitioners in each profession, to gain a composite image of Doctor, Architect, Coach, Therapist, Negotiator (lawyer), Teacher, and Farmer. My interviews confirmed my insight: the activities of these professionals match the activities that salespeople should be performing as the sales process unfolds. Labeling the sales roles simplifies a sophisticated sales approach, making it easier to learn, remember, and apply.

Together, these eight roles represent *Customer-Focused Selling: selling to customers the way they want to be sold to*—with honesty, empathy, and nonmanipulative behavior. The goal of Customer-Focused Selling is to nurture the buy–sell relationship. In this way, you create more new customers, each of whom will be more satisfied with the value you provide.

CREATING CLIENT/ADVOCATES

In the 1980s, Robert Miller and Stephen Heiman's book, *Strategic Selling,* popularized the concept of the sales "funnel," which compared sales activity to using a funnel. You move your various prospective buyers down the funnel at a steady and predictable rate (see Figure 2.3). Your commissions are then steady and predictable, and you are never left high and dry with no customers.

Originally, the goal of the sales funnel was to close an "order." In the late 1980s and early '90s, the goal of the funnel changed from "order" to "client." A client is a long-standing customer, that is, a sale that generates repeat orders. If your goal is to "close the sale," you will have a certain mindset to do what is necessary to close it, focusing on short-term features and benefits. If your mindset is to create clients, your behavior changes. Your plan then becomes: to work with

Figure 2.3   The Components of the Sales Funnel

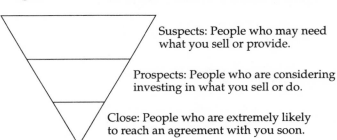

Suspects: People who may need what you sell or provide.

Prospects: People who are considering investing in what you sell or do.

Close: People who are extremely likely to reach an agreement with you soon.

each client over and over again. Your interest in what happens *after* each sale is made increases.

Over the past few years, many salespeople have once again changed their goal. Now they seek "client/advocates." A client/advocate is someone who not only continues to buy from you, but who also sings your praises and sells your services to others. When you shift your mindset toward creating "client/advocates," your behavior changes once again. Now you have a dual goal: to do long-term thinking about your client *and* to continually strive to add value over time. When your goal is to create a client/advocate, you go the extra mile, practice random acts of kindness, and genuinely give of yourself in the service of others.

If you're ready to commit to creating client/advocates, buyers who give you both loyalty and new client/advocates, then this book was written for you. Read the following chapters very carefully. And *don't* tell your competitors about this book.

3

Sales Role #1: THE STUDENT

Study Change and Approach Your Prospect

I will study and prepare myself and one day my chance
will come.

Abraham Lincoln

For years, salespeople have recognized the importance of a consultative sales approach, but have had difficulty defining what a consultative sales approach is. Mack Hanan, author of *Consultative Selling*, said recently, "Too many people say things like: 'A consultant is someone who is a good listener.' That's my definition of a bartender. A consultant is someone who's measured by the value that he brings to his customer."

In times past, the product or service you sold was itself of the greatest value to your buyers. Now, what is truly valuable is what you *know*—your knowledge of your customers, combined with your knowledge of the various applications where you can add value. To know more about your customers and to be seen eventually as a consultant, you must *study your customers*. This chapter will show you how.

YOUR CUSTOMERS' FIRST
STEP: CHANGE

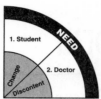

The first step of the buying process is Change. In the Change step, your prospects' business or personal life is altered by external and/or internal forces. External forces that affect businesses include changes in: customers, government regulations, competitors, technology, and the economy. External factors such as technological advances, politics, and the economy also affect the personal life of your customers.

Business buyers experience other changes from within their company. Internal changes made in reaction to external changes may include strategic planning/goal setting, quality initiatives, cost cutting, and reengineering. All buyers go through personal lifestyle changes—job changes, marriage, children, illness, separation, divorce, and retirement.

Change is constant. With change comes opportunity. If you seek opportunity in change, you will be rewarded with a constant supply of new sales opportunities.

SALES ROLE #1: THE STUDENT

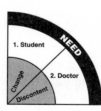

Change is a catalyst for realizing sales because it presents problems and opportunities. When your customer is at the Change Step, your Customer-Focused Selling role is the **Student.** As a Student, you will study how changes are affecting your prospects and find opportunities where you can add value.

To make larger and more profitable sales, you must find bigger and more significant needs. Whether you sell to businesses or to individuals, the prospects you call on in the future will be busier than the prospects you called on in the past. "Customers don't want to educate salespeople anymore," says Kevin Corcoran, Vice President of Marketing for Learning International, a training and consulting firm based in Stamford, Connecticut. "As a salesperson, you have to do a lot more homework today just to earn the right to talk about your products and services."

How much time you devote to studying each prospect depends on that prospect's potential value to you. For accounts with limited potential value, studying your prospect may be as simple as showing up ten minutes early for an appointment and reviewing a few brochures. For accounts with significant potential, your studying may involve several days, perhaps weeks, of analysis. The information in this chapter will help you lay the all-important groundwork for studying your prospects' needs and will also advise you on how to approach a new customer.

THE THREE LEVELS OF MANAGEMENT

If you sell to business, study the three levels of a business: (1) CEO, (2) Core, and (3) Support (see Figure 3.1). Each level has its own needs and opportunities. The higher the level to which you sell, the more dramatic the impact on your sales profitability.

The CEO Level

The executives at the top level of a business, including the CEO, president, ranking vice presidents, and chief financial officer(s), try to anticipate developments and steer the business toward greater profitability. The CEO-level executive looks for new approaches to cutting costs and gaining competitive advantage. The success of executives at this level is measured by the company's on-going profitability.

What Keeps the CEO Awake at Night?

When you study an executive at the CEO level, look for his or her specific concerns, such as shareholder satisfaction or a new company

Figure 3.1   The Levels of Management

vision. You can be sure this executive wants innovative solutions that cut costs or create a competitive advantage. The ever-present goal is to increase profits. You will get an appointment if you can connect your product or service to the CEO's anxieties. The CEO-level executive is always thinking about the competition. If you want to create interest, talk about things a competitor is doing and this company isn't doing. Fear of falling behind is a CEO's nightmare.

The competition isn't all that a CEO-level executive worries about. Recently, the Gallup Organization polled CEOs, presidents, ranking vice presidents, and chief financial officers of Fortune 1000 companies. The Gallup findings were published in a report titled *Hesitant at the Helm: American Executives in a Sea of Change*. The 400 executives who responded said the three changes that cause them the most concern are:

1. Cost pressures.
2. Rising customer demands.
3. Information technology.

The study also found that senior executives feel they are not very effective at handling change. A majority of the respondents (56 percent) admitted that their companies have no formal structure in place to handle change. Your job is to help your prospects do what they admit they can't do by themselves: respond effectively to the increasing rate of change.

Leading economists are predicting that corporate America is about to switch its focus from cost cutting to revenue growth. Strong corporate profits in the first half of the 1990s are the result of downsizing, not revenue growth. Sales tallied by S&P 400 companies increased just 3.1 percent per year from 1990 through 1994— less than half the growth rate of each of the previous four decades. With most of the fat already cut, profit growth in the future *must* come from sales increases. So, your customers' key question to you may soon be: How does your product or service increase our sales?

The Core Level

Beneath the CEO is the Core level, the beating heart of a business. The Core level consists of the frontline functions that are vital to providing goods and services to customers: manufacturing, operations, sales, and service. Core functions are to a business what heart rate, respiration rate, and brain wave activity are to the human body. If you lose just one of them, you're dead.

Core-level activities are connected to one another, like links of a chain. The Core functions of a McDonald's restaurant are shown in Figure 3.2. They connect to each other in this sequence:

Order taking. The customer gives the counter person an order from the available menu. As the order is taken, it is entered on an electronic keyboard and then communicated to the next function.

Preparation. The food is cooked and packaged.

Delivery. The food is delivered to the waiting customer.

Payment. The customer's payment is received and the transaction is complete.

The hoped-for results are:

1. The customer is satisfied.
2. McDonald's makes a profit.

Each of the preceding activities passes the test of what a core function is: each step is linked to functions that come before and after, and **if one step is removed, the business dies.**

What Are Core-Level Managers Concerned About?

The managers of Core functions want **problems solved** NOW, because a problem in any one function can affect all other functions in a chain reaction. When an order is taken at McDonald's, if the food

Figure 3.2   Core-Level Activities Are Closely Linked

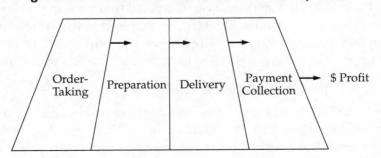

is not prepared, then delivery can't occur, payment can't be received, a customer is annoyed, and other customers are forced to wait while the problem is resolved.

To better understand a prospect's business, study the Core-level activities and learn how they are linked. Then, once you are face-to-face with the prospect and you find a problem (or opportunity) in one activity, you will better understand how that problem can affect other activities in the chain. When a prospect recognizes the "chain reaction" a problem creates or could create, the prospect's desire to buy intensifies.

Key Success Factors

By studying the Core level, you can quickly spot a prospect's *key success factors*—those two or three things that the organization must do extremely well in order to thrive. For Domino's Pizza, they are order entry and delivery. For the American automobile industry over the past decade, they have been quality production and price. In the Persian Gulf War, one key success factor was rapid deployment of equipment and personnel.

One of McDonald's key success factors is speed of transaction, achieved by combining the order-taking and order-entry functions. Burger King's Core level operates differently. At Burger King, the customer places an order, then the order taker speaks into a microphone, giving the order to the cooks, and the food is prepared. It takes longer to get food at Burger King, but customers can "have it your way," made to order. One of Burger King's key success factors is customized food preparation.

When you study a prospect's Core level, identify the two or three key success factors that drive the business, then look for ways you can add value to them. These factors are the constant concern of executives. If you can link your solution to one or more of them, the price of your product need not be an obstacle.

Core-level managers are also interested in **improving their operations.** Production would like to produce faster, sales wants to sell more, service wants to serve better. If you can help a Core-level manager improve operations, you will earn the right to an appointment.

Whom Should You Call On at the Core Level?

Your best Core-level prospect is the executive responsible for a specific core function: Vice President of Sales, Vice President of Manufacturing, Vice President of Customer Service. If you are unable to see the Core-function executive, your next best prospect is the person to whom the Core executive entrusts and delegates important business issues.

Some managers have *influence* and some have *authority.* There is a difference between influence and authority. Influence is a result of the ability to persuade; authority resides in a title. Some people have authority, but little influence, according to Jim Holden, the author of *Power Base Selling.* The Vice President of the United States is an authoritative figure, but there is no guarantee that he has any influence on the President. Other people have little official authority, but are very influential. The First Lady has often had tremendous influence but no official title. If you want to get your idea sold to the President, the First Lady may be the person to see.

If you want to sell to a Core function but you can't get an appointment with the Core executive, you need an "influential sponsor" to be your messenger. An influential sponsor is someone who will sell your ideas to others. Downsizing and reorganization have added to the responsibilities of many executives, forcing them to delegate more of their duties. Usually, there are one or two subordinates in whom a Core executive places the greatest reliance and trust. Your objective is to find out who these influential people are, and sell them on being your sponsors.

How do you find an influential sponsor? Influential sponsors are involved in key projects. They are effective communicators, they build trust with others, and they are committed to a mission. Sometimes they are recent hires brought in by a vice president to make a difference. Has the VP hired anybody recently? To whom does the VP delegate important business issues? Get that person on your side.

The Support Level

The bottom level of a business is Support, which provides assistance to both the CEO and Core levels. Examples of support functions include the purchasing, legal, training, and accounting departments. The Support level reacts to the needs of the Core and CEO levels. For example, the purchasing department, which buys replacements for products and services that already exist, usually wants the most product for the least amount of money. That's purchasing's organizational role; it's what others expect of that function.

The "Transactional Sale"

The transactional sale is price-driven and is often made to a purchasing department. Purchasing reacts to needs that already exist.

Figure 3.3   The Most Profitable Sales Are Made to the Higher Levels Because These Executives Have Other Priorities Besides "Lowest Price"

Those who work in purchasing are price-focused because their job is to get more product for less money. For a purchasing agent to "win," you must lose. To most purchasing agents, "value-added" simply means discount.

The purchasing department should not be ignored. It is an important cog in the wheel of a corporate buying process. When you sell to purchasing, emphasize your price/performance and availability. Purchasing is interested in hassle-free buying.

The "Consulting Sale"

To make larger, more profitable sales to business, you must call on prospects who are either struggling with today's problems or looking toward tomorrow's opportunities. Your sales effort moves up to the Core or CEO level, to people who have their hands on the pulse of the business and have some organizational authority to act. This is a move toward what is known as a "consulting sale" (see Figure 3.3). The simple truth is: *if you find big problems, you'll make big sales.*

HOW TO BE A GOOD STUDENT

To be a good Student, change how you think. Forget about your product and imagine that you work for your customer. In fact, imagine you are selling for your customer. If your customer sells financial services, you sell financial services. If your customer sells technology products, you sell technology products. What result(s) is your customer trying to achieve? How can you help toward achieving those results? How can your product or service help stimulate demand for your customer's product or service?

Sales trainer Barry Farber, in his audiocassette program *State of the Art Selling*, tells a story of a copier salesman trying to make a sale to an ice cream store owner who owned an old copier. At first, the salesman pitched the features of his new copier, but he got nowhere because the prospect didn't care about copy quality or speed. Then, by imagining *he* was selling ice cream, the salesman began asking revealing questions about the prospect's business. Soon he discovered that the ice cream store distributed its products to local retail stores, and that the owner wanted to expand his business to include the distribution of ice cream desserts to local restaurants. The salesman suggested that the owner go to local restaurants, get each restaurant's logo, and produce a customized menu of ice cream desserts that could be placed on dining tables. The hoped-for results were more desserts sold for the restaurant and more sales for the ice cream store owner. According to Farber, the prospect immediately "bought off" on the salesman's idea, and quickly ordered a new copier at full list price to implement his new marketing plan. The copier salesman had created a solution that stimulated end-user demand for his customer's product. By imagining that you sell for your customer, you will quickly understand your customer's business strategies. You will then be in a position to identify innovative sales opportunities that achieve value for your customer.

How Downsizing Helps Salespeople

The downsizing trend has hit the Support level very hard. In an effort to cut costs, many companies are cutting back on Support functions. In 1994, Xerox turned over all its worldwide computer and telecommunications networks to E.D.S., a unit of General Motors. Xerox "outsourced" the information and communications systems to cut fixed costs and focus on the company's "core business." As the number of internal Support people dwindles, there is less internal help for Core- and CEO-level managers, and they must look outside for assistance. This presents an opportunity for you to get to the heart of a prospect's business and add value!

Doing Your Homework

When you study your account, seek answers to the following questions.

1. What changes are affecting this prospect? Are there external changes such as new government regulations, new foreign competitors, or an increase in interest rates? Is the company experiencing internal change, such as a merger, downsizing, or a reengineering of business processes?

2. What are the Core functions and how are they linked? How does work flow within the business? If there is a problem in one function, how will it affect other functions?

3. What are the two or three key success factors for this prospect's company and/or department? Who are the customers? Is there a tough new competitor? How is this company different from the competition? If you were your customer's customer, whom would you buy from and why?

4. How is your prospect's job performance measured (i.e., what is he or she trying to accomplish?)? What motivates the prospect? What positions has the prospect held in the past? Where did the prospect go to college? What awards has he or she won? What are his or her professional memberships and affiliations?

5. How can your product or service help your customer achieve the targeted goals? What problems does your customer have that you can help solve?

Once you have answered all these questions, you will find a "hook"—a convincing reason why your prospect should agree to meet with you. Keep in mind that Core- and CEO-level prospects are busy people; scheduling an appointment with them can be difficult. When you get an appointment, it's important to be knowledgeable on a whole spectrum of relevant topics. Advance study is essential. You can access the information you need via an *on-line service* or a quick visit to your local *library*. The next sections take a look at both.

ON-LINE SERVICES

Perhaps the single most important step you can take to be effective in your sales role as a Student is to subscribe to an on-line service. Computer information services offer inexpensive, convenient access to a wealth of information. Subscribing to a computer service costs as little as $9.95 per month. For as little as $19.00 per month, you can get ten hours of research time *plus* your customers' and competitors' press releases sent daily to your computer. Wally Bock, author of *Getting On the Information Superhighway*, says, "On-line services enable you to get to know prospective customers before you meet them. In five minutes you can learn the basics of an industry. In ten minutes you can study the problems affecting a specific company. On-line services are the power tool of the decade."

On-line services enable you to:

- Study corporate business information, including a company's financials.
- Study industry information, such as revenue, market share, employment, and so on.
- Search and retrieve full-text articles from hundreds of industry publications.
- Have a clipping service scan publications and news wires and send information to you.
- Join a forum and receive answers to your questions from industry experts.

Currently, the two largest and most well-established on-line services are America Online (800-827-6364) and CompuServe (800-848-8990). Basic monthly service fees for both are less than $10 and each service offers optional information for various additional charges. All on-line services are engaged in fierce competition, and with powerful Microsoft, AT&T, and MCI recently entering the fray, future on-line users are sure to enjoy more and better information at reduced prices.

I subscribe to both America Online and CompuServe. I have found America Online to be the easiest to use and least expensive of the on-line services. CompuServe offers by far the most comprehensive business information, albeit at a higher price. Let's take a close look at both of these services.

America Online

America Online (AOL) includes access to Hoover's Business Resources in the monthly service fee. The Company Profiles database available from Hoover's profiles 1,450 of the largest, most influential public and private companies in the United States, and the 200 largest international companies with U.S. operations. Each profile provides a company overview, the names of key executives, business financials, and the names of key competitors. Hoover's Industry Profiles offers information on almost 200 industries: industry revenues, market descriptions, individual companies' market shares, forecasts, and information on changes affecting each industry.

If your company does business with the federal government, you will be interested in AOL's access to Commerce Business Daily (CBD). The CBD, published daily by the U.S. Department of Commerce, lists notices of proposed government procurement actions, contract awards, and other procurement actions that exceed $25,000 in value.

AOL enables you to search and retrieve articles from publications such as the *The New York Times,* the *San Jose Mercury News,* and the *Chicago Tribune.* Generally, you can get basic information free, but you must pay a little extra for the full text of an article.

AOL's Mercury Center NewsHound is a clipping service that searches over 2,000 articles every day and sends relevant documents to your e-mail box. NewsHound searches business articles from over 60 newspapers through the *Knight-Ridder/Tribune Business News, The New York Times News Service, The Associated Press, Kyodo News Service,* and *Scripps-Howard News Service.* You can receive press releases from your key account customers and competitors because NewsHound searches the *Business Wire* and *PR Newswire.* NewsHound is easy to use and inexpensive. Simply fill out a form with words and phrases that could appear in the information you want, and you have created a "profile." Current prices are just $9.95 per month (above the monthly AOL fee) for up to five profiles.

Forums

Forums are the clubs of the on-line world. They enable you to connect with experts, ask them questions, and discuss topics of interest in a wide variety of fields. Some forums are based on industries, such as computers, real estate, or travel. Other forums are based on professions, such as human resources and marketing/public relations.

There are two ways to gather information from an on-line forum: (1) message boards and (2) libraries. Message boards enable you to catch up on the latest news, post questions or comments, and contribute to current discussions. Forum libraries offer files consisting of past interviews with industry experts. You can copy the files and download them to your computer.

Regarding forums, America Online lags behind CompuServe. AOL lists everything chronologically, which makes it difficult to find current information. When you enter a forum on AOL, you arrive first at the oldest information entry, which may be several months or years old. This requires you to scroll forward until you find current messages. Because AOL's system never deletes entries, some information is extremely dated. Messages on CompuServe are more current because they scroll off after a certain period of time. The rate at which CompuServe drops off messages varies based on forum activity. On active forums, old messages are deleted after a few days; on slower forums, deletion comes after several weeks. AOL is a fairly new service. CompuServe is the granddaddy of the industry, having been born in 1980. The result is that AOL has fewer forums and less specialization. Let's look at CompuServe.

CompuServe

CompuServe offers a wealth of information resources, the best of which carry charges over and above the monthly fee. Some resources carry an additional hourly charge of up to $24.00. Other resources charge for each article you retrieve, and still others charge a combination of the hourly and per-article fees. Once on-line, check each resource for price and usage information.

There are three ways to gather information on CompuServe: (1) database searching, (2) clipping service, and (3) forums.

Database Searching

For the most part, CompuServe serves as a bridge between your computer and various databases offered by third-party suppliers. A database is a body of information made up of individual items organized so that they can be reviewed in a variety of ways. There are two ways to access databases on CompuServe. First, you can go through a service called I-Quest. Unfortunately, I-Quest is relatively expensive. A more economical option is through CompuServe's Knowledge Index. The Knowledge Index is available only from 6:00 P.M. to 5:00 A.M. in your local time zone, but it gives you access to a significant portion of the databases provided by DIALOG, a service that makes various databases available. DIALOG is the world's largest commercial database provider.

Through DIALOG, the Knowledge Index provides access to many databases. Among them are:

- **ABI/Inform** provides comprehensive information on business practices, strategies, and trends. It draws from over 800 journals on accounting, banking, data processing, insurance, marketing, real estate, and telecommunications. ABI/Inform enables you to get abstracts (shortened summaries of entire articles). Abstracts are helpful because they provide you with the most important information from the article, but take far less time to read. Full-text articles are also available. (Data Courier, Inc.)

- **Disclosure** provides information compiled from the 10Ks and other documents and reports that all publicly held companies file with the Securities and Exchange Commission. Of particular interest to salespeople will be each company president's letter, which typically discloses company goals and strategies, as well as new trends and market challenges affecting a company's business.

  When studying a customer's business, many financially savvy salespeople prefer 10Ks over annual reports. The 10Ks typically provide more factual information because they are written for federal regulators instead of individual investors. An annual report may be somewhat misleading if a "positive spin" has been placed on a negative event. In the summer of 1996, almost all corporate filings, including 10Ks, will be available directly from the SEC via the World Wide Web. The Web address is: http://www.sec.gov/.

- **Dun's Market Identifiers** offers a directory of over 6.7 million U.S. public and private establishments that have more than five employees or more than $1 million in sales. Dun's also offers access to a parallel Canadian database, consisting of 350,000 companies, and to an international database, a 90-country directory with over 2.1 million public, private, and government-controlled companies. This resource is also available in print. (Dun & Bradstreet, Westport, CT.)

- **The Marquis Who's Who** provides information on several hundred thousand key North American professionals, including the names of family members, education, positions held during career, memberships, awards, and other organizational affiliations. When you access this information before meeting with a new decision maker, you may discover something the two of you have in common, which can help you build trust quickly when the two of you meet.

- **NewsNet** is for you, if your field is specialized. It's the only on-line service that concentrates on niche newsletters. A few examples of its sources include *Pharmaceutical Litigation Reporter, Toxic Materials News,* and the *Asbestos and Lead Abatement Report.* Hard-to-find business information can be found here.

- **Standard & Poor's Register** contains important information on over 55,000 public and private corporations and 500,000 executives. Accessible positions include:

Chairman of the Board	Marketing Manager
President	Sales Manager
Vice President(s)	Operations Manager
Treasurer	Advertising Manager
Secretary	Public Relations Director
Comptroller	Purchasing Agent
Personnel Director	Data Processing Manager

In addition, the Poor's Register answers questions like: What products and services does a company provide? Who are its competitors? The Register is also available on CD/ROM and in print. (Standard & Poor's Corporation, New York.)

Searching within the Knowledge Index is both easy and economical. When I needed to gather information on the local access telecommunications market, I accessed ABI/Inform's database. The first search parameter I entered was "telecommunications," and ABI/Inform indicated it had 34,729 articles available! Next, I entered "local access"; 404 records were found. Finally, when I requested only those articles written in the previous twelve months, the titles of the 139 most recent articles were displayed. I scrolled through these titles, selected nine abstracts of pertinent articles, and downloaded them to my computer for reading off-line. My cost for this search and retrieval was $2.27.

Clipping Service

Executive News Service (ENS), CompuServe's clipping service, monitors many news sources, including *Dow Jones News Service,* the

Associated Press, and *The Washington Post,* to name just a few. You don't have to subscribe to these publications to have access to the articles and information you need. When you give a clipping service a description of your needs, it automatically will send relevant articles to your electronic mailbox. The cost for ENS is $10/month plus an hourly usage charge.

Forums

CompuServe offers the finest selection of forums of any on-line service. There are specialty forums for almost every interest and industry. In June 1995, *Selling Magazine*'s "Selling On-Line" began running on CompuServe. "Selling On-Line" is a forum that allows you to seek out the advice of other sales professionals by posing questions on the message board or participating in on-line conferences with a variety of experts. You can also retrieve highlights from *Selling Magazine*'s back issues. To access "Selling On-line," simply type "Go Selling" in the CompuServe main menu. Other professional interest forums on CompuServe include public relations, marketing, and law. Industry forums include computers, small business, education, and travel, to name just a few. Each of these forums is divided into sections with more focused interests.

Don't Overdo It

The ease of on-line information access may cause information overload for some salespeople. If you swamp yourself with information, you'll have less time to sell. Daniel Burrus, author of *Technotrends,* recently was quoted in *Sales & Marketing Management* magazine as saying, "There's a big difference between data, information, knowledge, understanding, and wisdom." Burrus says most salespeople are struggling at the lowest end of the information chain—data. The future for all salespeople, he predicts, lies in knowledge and wisdom, or being able to use information to benefit customers.

Here are a few tips for avoiding information overload and putting the power of information to work for you:

- Use a clipping service.
- When searching for an article or topic, narrow your search field to save time and money.
- If you search for an article, retrieve the abstract first.

- Learn to scan instead of read. Read titles, subtitles, and the first paragraph. Glance at headings within an article because headings announce shifts in the article's focus. Usually, the first paragraph after each heading will describe where the author is going.

- Use a highlighter on your hard copy to capture key ideas.

Remember, your goal is to put information to work *for* you, not *against* you!

USING YOUR LOCAL LIBRARY

If you can't get on-line, there's always the reference section of your local library. Here are a few resource tools for finding the information you need:

- **Business Periodicals Index.** In print form, the Index covers 375 business periodicals, listed either by subject (such as Accounting, Banking, Petroleum, and so on) or by company (such as Exxon, General Motors, IBM, and so on). (The H.W. Wilson Company, New York.)

- **Dun's Directory of Service Companies.** Information on 50,000 public and private companies in the service sector is offered. (Dun & Bradstreet Corporation.)

- **Dun's Million Dollar Directory.** The top 160,000 companies in the United States are profiled. (Dun & Bradstreet Corporation.)

- **Dun's Regional Business Directory.** Dun & Bradstreet publishes 54 regional directories nationwide. Your local directory includes brief company descriptions and names of key executives. (Dun & Bradstreet Corporation.)

- **International Directory of Company Histories.** You will find here in-depth two- to three-page descriptions of 1,800 companies. To be included, companies must have achieved $500 million in annual sales. Some smaller companies are included if they are leading influences in their industry. (St. James Press.)

- **On-line services available.** Many local libraries offer computerized information services free of charge. My local library provides access to **Prompt,** a database provided by Information Access Company of Foster City, CA. Prompt provides information access and full-text retrieval of more than 1,100 sources.

Users can obtain abstracts on new-product announcements, market research studies, general and business newspapers, trade journals, and other business publications. Your library may also carry the **Prompt Directory,** a printed version of a significant portion of Prompt's database. Check with your local library for the specific services it offers.

- **Seller's Guide to Government Purchasing.** This is a comprehensive history of federal, state, county, and municipal procurement contacts. It includes the names of purchasing agents and the products and services that each agent buys. (Gale Research, Inc.)

- **Standard & Poor's Industry Surveys.** These are in-depth analyses of all major domestic industries, including aerospace, automobiles, banking, building and forest products, chemicals, computers, electronics, food/beverage/tobacco, health care, insurance, leisure, media, metals, oil, railroads/trucking, retailing, steel/heavy machinery, telecommunications, textiles/apparel/home furnishings, and utilities.

  Industry Surveys examines the prospects for each industry and then gives an analysis of trends and problems. Of particular value to salespeople is the "Comparative Company Analysis," which compares leading companies' growth in sales and earnings and also tracks their profit margins, dividends, and stock price over a five-year period. (Standard & Poor's Corporation, New York.)

  Industry Surveys is also available through the Profound on-line service (800-270-9896), another new entrant to the U.S. on-line market. Profound is a division of Management and Information Database, a well-established European on-line service.

- **Standard & Poor's Register.** See the description given earlier in the section on CompuServe. The Register is a gold mine of information and is available in print form in your local library.

- **Value Line.** A two-page synopsis of industry trends is given for each of 96 industries. In the tire and rubber industry, for example, I learned that tire demand is strong, but increases in raw material costs have exceeded tire price hikes, so profits are down.

  In addition to industry analysis, Value Line includes a half-page synopsis of many companies within each industry, which enables you to compare a company's averages to industry averages. (Value Line Publishing, New York.)

OTHER INFORMATION SOURCES

Here are a few more ideas that you don't have to go to the library for:

- **Buy some shares of stock in a key account.** Quarterly and annual reports will be sent to your home, enabling you to stay abreast of important business issues. You might make some money on the stock, too!

- **Subscribe to industry publications.** Read what your customers read.

- **Subscribe to your local business journal** to receive in-depth articles on local companies, plus the latest executive appointments. Most business journals also sell a "book of lists," in hard copy or diskette, that contains information on the top 25 companies in many different categories—the top 25 real estate firms, the top 25 high-tech companies, the top 25 stock brokerage firms, and so on. A book of lists will include sales revenue, executives' names, and phone numbers.

- **Dun's Million Dollar CD ROM Disc.** Information is given on 180,000 U.S. companies with a net worth of more than $500,000. Most are privately held firms. The Disc also provides 400,000 biographical profiles on key decision makers. CD ROM technology allows you to quickly search and sort on key data elements. (Dun & Bradstreet Corporation.)

- **Public Register's Annual Report Service.** With one phone call, you can obtain the annual reports of any of 3,000 North American companies. This service is available *free of charge,* and you can request as many company reports as you wish. To obtain your first eight annual reports, call 1-800-4-ANNUAL. (Bay Tact Corporation, Woodstock Valley, CT.)

HOW TO APPROACH YOUR PROSPECT

After you have studied your prospect, it's time to *approach* him or her. The approach is the beginning of personal contact. Your objectives are: create interest and schedule a brief appointment. You create interest by communicating knowledge of your prospect's specific concerns and goals and projecting your ability to help in reaching those goals.

The most common methods of approaching a potential buyer are:

- Appointment letter.
- Telephone call.
- In-person "cold call."

The Appointment Letter

A well-crafted appointment letter, followed up with a telephone call, is my favorite method for approaching busy prospects. The letter saves your prospect time because it communicates the value that you offer. If the value you describe sparks interest, you will get an agreement to meet. Later, when you follow up your letter with a phone call, the executive's assistant may ask, "What is your call regarding?" You can respond, "It's regarding a letter he received. Mr. Jones is expecting my call."

Your appointment letter should be personalized to each prospect. When you write your appointment letter, think BIG. Be Brief, be Interesting, and be Gone. Don't waste your prospect's valuable time.

Figure 3.4 shows my Letter A, which I use to promote my sales training services. In Figure 3.5 is my Letter B, a well-crafted appointment letter for a salesperson selling a voice mail system.

Keys to an Effective Appointment Letter: An Analysis of Letter B

Composition.   There is a *you* viewpoint. The focus of attention is the reader, not the writer. Paragraphs don't start with *I*. The sentences are short and use simple language. The tone is conversational, not pompous. The words are active: *hot, cut, rapid*. Words that don't add value have been mercilessly deleted.

Knowledge You Gained from Your Studies.   Show that you have done your homework. As was mentioned in the Introduction, the number-two source of customer frustration with salespeople is a salesperson's lack of knowledge of the customer's company.

Figure 3.4   Appointment Letter A

4115 Blackhawk Plaza Circle, Suite 100 • Danville, California 94506
(510) 831-0922 • Fax: (510) 831-8677 • E-Mail: kdavissell@aol.com

Mr. Thomas Sorenson
Vice President of Sales
ANY Peripherals Corporation
One Disc Drive
Somewhere, CA 94506

Dear Mr. Sorenson:

Selling is growing more difficult because your customers have become more demanding. Sales techniques that once closed a large sale of data storage devices and software today are likely to push customers away. You can gain competitive advantage if you show your salespeople how to adjust their sales approach to match how today's more insistent decision makers buy.

Downsizing, reorganization, and change within your major account customer base have cut short several of your most valuable client relationships. New customers take time to cultivate and are becoming more difficult to satisfy. In addition to being more demanding, your customers are now:

- More price-conscious.
- More knowledgeable about buying.
- Less loyal to suppliers.
- Deluged by choices.
- More uncertain about the future.
- More at risk if a mistake is made.

We believe that knowing the buyer is where sellers should start. If your buyers are changing, shouldn't your salespeople change to meet their new needs? What if a competitor changes first?

In training workshops customized to the unique needs of ANY Peripherals, Inc., your salespeople will learn about today's new buyer and the adjustments they can make to strengthen their sales effectiveness. We have helped some of America's finest sales organizations to increase sales effectiveness, companies including *BusinessWeek, BellSouth, Pacific Telesis, and Standard & Poor's Corporation.*

Mr. Sorenson, perhaps we can help you, too. I'd like to schedule a brief appointment and let you be the judge. I'll call you in a few days to arrange a convenient time.

Sincerely,

Speaking/Consulting/Training • Sales & Sales Management

Figure 3.5   Appointment Letter B

VOICE MAIL TECHNOLOGIES

Mr. Edward M. Jones
Executive Vice President of Operations
M.B.I. Corporation
Two Corporate Center
Anytown, CA 94506

Dear Mr. Jones:

Two aggressive foreign competitors entered your market recently, in hot pursuit of your major accounts. From your customers' perspective, new options usually translate into more buying power—and rising expectations of your support capabilities. M.B.I.'s traditional method of handling customer calls, which once satisfied customers, may soon become inadequate. You can improve responsiveness to customers, strengthen customer loyalty, and cut costs by allowing technology to work for you.

Imagine incoming customer calls being instantly routed to the individuals most capable of resolving their needs. Service calls would go directly to the service desk, and user assistance calls would go immediately to your training department. This system would provide:

- Rapid response to customer needs.
- Reduction of workload for your customer support staff.
- Possibility of reassigning employees as you see fit.

Many service providers feel that if their customers are changing, they must change to meet their new needs. They are concerned that their competitors may change first.

Voice Mail Technologies has helped many successful companies similar to M.B.I. increase customer satisfaction. These companies include ABC, DEF, and GHI. New customer Sally George, Vice President of Customer Satisfaction for ABC, recently wrote: *"Voice Mail Technology's unique method of programming made for a simple transition. In no time at all, our expectations were exceeded."*

Mr. Jones, perhaps we can help you too. I'd like to schedule a brief appointment and let you be the judge. I'll call you in a few days to arrange a convenient time.

Sincerely,

Letter Organization.   Beginning with the Need stage (the company must improve responsiveness, strengthen customer loyalty, and cut costs), the letter follows the logical steps of a buying process:

1. Change—two new competitors pursuing major accounts, rising customer demands, need to cut costs.
2. Discontent—rising customer expectations. If the prospect doesn't act remedially, customers may leave.
3. Research—a specific description of how incoming calls would be processed. An intangible need for technology is turned into a tangible solution.
4. Comparison—a "unique method of programming," the competitive advantage.
5. Commitment—a request for a specific action, such as an appointment.

Letter Format.   According to Herschell Gordon Lewis, sales letter writing expert for *Selling Magazine,* indented paragraphs are more inviting than flush-left paragraphs. Use reasonably large type, and set wide margins to enhance readability. Bullet points help to "open up" the letter. Strive for contrast; sameness is dull. Lewis also advises against using the flush-right key.

Grammar.   Before you send your letter, have it proofed by someone who can be trusted to catch your mistakes. Misspellings or other errors in your appointment letter may cause prospects to question your attention to detail. Would you want to make a major purchase from a salesperson who neglects details?

The Tie-In to the Buy-*Learning* Process.   The first question to ask yourself as you compose your appointment letter is: "What buying step is this prospect on?" Write the letter to match the reader's needs. The voice mail letter is meant for a prospect who is in either the Change step or the Discontent step, and doesn't yet recognize the need for voice mail. That's why Letter B begins by clarifying how change triggers discontent. A letter to a prospect who already owned a voice mail system would be entirely different. It would focus more on the value of the system's unique capabilities and the problems those unique capabilities solve.

Mixing Graphics with Text.   As the saying goes, "A picture is worth 1,000 words." A graphic included with your text can be a real eye-catcher, so you may want to include one in your letter. If so, place the graphic on the left side of the page with text on the right. (The left visual field of each eye is processed in the brain where pictures are interpreted; the right visual field is processed where text is interpreted.) When you mix graphics and text, placing the graphics on the left will make your letter pleasing to the eye and more comfortable to read.

Building Paragraphs to Form a Strong Unit

- Paragraph one has got to be loaded with dynamite or your prospect won't bother with paragraph two. The first sentence should tie in to Change and hint at a specific reader benefit. The second sentence should suggest a significant problem. The third sentence should suggest that the problem will get worse if nothing is done. The fourth sentence should introduce the central selling point of the letter. Ask yourself, "Which single benefit is of greatest *value* to this specific prospect?" Build your first paragraph around that. Your goal for the first paragraph is *attention!*

- Paragraph two should deliver a persuasive description of the single biggest benefit, because specificity is necessary for reader *interest*. Customize your letter to your prospect's industry. Show you know something about this particular business.

- Paragraph three reinforces the buyer's need. Keep in mind that the fear of falling behind can be a more powerful motivation than the desire for gain. Ask yourself, "What is the potential cost to the reader if nothing is done?" You can avoid appearing as if you're preaching by attributing your point to a third-party source ("experts agree," "many service providers believe," and so on).

- Paragraph four builds reader *conviction*—a strong belief in your ability to deliver on your promises. Whatever you have said you can do for the reader, prove that you have already done it for others. Use customer testimonials to bolster your credibility, but don't be too wordy. A testimonial offers something unique about your offering and should be aimed at the most common objection you hear. In our voice mail example, the most common objection is, "Our employees are resistant to change."

- Paragraph five is specific about the action you want the prospect to take. A phrase like "You be the judge" suggests no pressure. The letter's close is a confident expectation of an appointment, not a plea for consideration. Don't beg.

The Telephone Call

Excellent telephone skills are important. The largest sales can begin with a single phone call. If you don't get an initial appointment, you won't make the sale. The more senior the executive you are approaching, the more difficult it will be to get an appointment. When you call a Core- or CEO-level prospect, you've got ten seconds to create interest, or you may hear a dial tone. That's pressure on you!

You face challenges when you approach busy executives. First, you usually must get past an executive assistant who is skillful at screening salespeople. Second, executive time is the most valuable time in an organization, so executives are less likely to give it away.

The ABCs of Telephone Approach

The three components of every telephone approach are:

1. Acknowledgment.
2. Benefit statement.
3. Commitment.

1. *Acknowledgment.* When your prospect answers the phone, acknowledge by name the person to whom you are talking. As your phone call proceeds, acknowledge your prospect's questions or objections.

Prospects are busy people. When you first call them, they are preoccupied. Therefore, your acknowledgment/greeting should consist of a question that grabs attention. For example:

> Hi, Mr. Jones. This is Karen Smith with XYZ Company. We have helped [name an industry leader] to dramatically improve their [state a big benefit]. Do you have just 60 seconds for me?

2. *Benefit statement.* Your goal now is to create interest. What is your central selling point? You need to customize it not only to your prospect's industry, but also to that person's self-interest. Remember, the CEO level worries about competition, cost pressures,

rising customer demands, information technology, and soon, perhaps, sales improvement. The Core-level executive wants to solve business problems and improve operations. When you're making a benefit statement, keep in mind the executive's self-interest. Make your benefit statement specific, because specificity builds interest.

> I know that cutting costs is critical to you in keeping your Medicare payments under control and maintaining profitability. We've discovered some new ways to help you cut costs, particularly in the area of wasted meals and medication.

3. *Commitment.* You must be clear and specific about the action you are asking for. What do you want your prospect to do? If you want an executive to agree to a specific time for an appointment, you might say:

> May I see you next Tuesday at 1:45?

Once you've obtained a commitment, stop talking. Get the appointment, say "Thank you" and hang up. Don't talk past the sale.

Responding to Telephone Objections

When you first ask for an appointment, be prepared to get an objection. Objections can be handled using the ABCs. Here are some common objections and recommended responses:

Prospect: I'm too busy.

You: *(Acknowledgment)* I understand your concern about time. If you agree to meet with me, I can assure you that I will be brief, be interesting, and be gone.

(Benefit) Again, my purpose for meeting with you would be to discuss new ideas that can reduce the costs of wasted meals and medication.

(Commitment) May I see you next Tuesday at 11:45?

Prospect: Send me some literature.

You: *(Acknowledgment)* I certainly could, but it would take more time for you to read and review my literature than the ten minutes it would take to briefly meet and cover the highlights.

(Benefit) So, by agreeing to an appointment you'll save time and perhaps discover a new idea that can help you cut costs.

(Commitment) May I see you next Tuesday afternoon?

Prospect: You need to talk to purchasing.

You: *(Acknowledgment)* I'd be pleased to speak with purchasing.

(Benefit) However, we offer a new strategy toward *[corporate or market goal]* that can help you cut costs. It's important for us to meet because strategy is your responsibility, not purchasing's.

(Commitment) May I see you next Wednesday at 1:45?

Prospect: I don't have the time to see you.

You: *(Acknowledgment)* I understand how busy you are.

(Benefit) If I wasn't convinced that I can really help you cut costs, I would have given up by now. All I ask is ten minutes, and you can judge for yourself.

(Commitment) May I see you Monday at 10:50?

Prospect: I'm not interested.

You: *(Acknowledgment)* I understand.

(Benefit) All I'm asking for is ten minutes to show you how we've helped other companies cut costs. If you're still not interested, I'll be on my way.

(Commitment) Can you allow me just ten minutes?

Do any of these telephone approaches seem a little high-pressured? Throughout this book, I describe a selling process that is a consultative, no-pressure sales approach. However, calling for appointments can be difficult. Prospects are tougher on you over the phone because it's easy to reject someone who isn't physically present. Therefore, you must be a little stronger in return.

Use the ABCs on every prospecting phone call, whether you're talking to a support person or an executive.

Going Over Someone's Head

Perhaps you want to grow an existing account where you have a relationship with a low-level Support person. How do you go over your contact's head without causing damaging irritation? One way is to ask questions that your low-level contact can't answer, then ask for a blessing to call on someone who *will* know the answers. If you ask, "Which competitors pose the greatest threat to your customer base?" a Support person probably won't know the answer, but the Vice President of Sales and Marketing will.

If you go over someone's head, do it at the beginning of a sales process, not the end. The key is your intent. When you go over someone's head toward the *end* of a sales process, as a buying decision is being finalized, your intent is to save a sale you think you are about to lose. This can be effective, but BEWARE. By questioning the Support person's competence at decision making, you make that person look bad. Your move will be seen as an intent to undermine and reverse the person's decision. Prospects will feel less threatened if you go to a higher level **early** in a sales process, during the Change or Discontent step. At that point, your intent is to help the account achieve greater value, not to undermine the credibility of your contact.

How can you persuade your Support-level contact to allow you to go up to the Core or CEO level? Your success is your contact's success. If your sale goes through, your contact will enjoy the following good results.

Increased Contribution to the Business.   As was mentioned earlier, the Support level has been particularly hard-hit by downsizing. Support-level people no longer have time to venture out to help Core- and CEO-level people solve business problems. When you offer to be the Support-level manager's "pair of hands," you are helping to make a contribution to improving operations.

Increased Recognition from Upper Management.   If you are successful in adding value for senior management, your lower-level contact will be noticed as well.

Increased Personal Knowledge.   When you keep them "in the loop," Support people learn about important business issues that drive buying needs.

Increased Financial Gain for the Department.   When a higher-level manager buys something, the money usually comes out of a different budget, thereby leaving more money available in the Support department's budget.

Getting Past the Gatekeeper

How do you get to speak to an executive when the inevitable assistant answers the phone? The first rule to keep in mind is: Treat every Support person as if he or she were a manager. Some salespeople see Support people as adversaries, and adopt a condescending tone. Beware! The executive's assistant is often the closest friend that executive has in the whole company. If you talk down to this person, you may get screened out forever. If you think of an executive's assistant as a manager, you won't make the mistake of talking down.

Here are two options for getting past the gatekeeper: the "top down" approach and the direct approach.

The "Top Down" Approach. Call the company president's assistant, briefly describe how you can help, and ask to whom you should speak. The idea is to have the president's office refer you down to "just" an executive vice president. If the referral is coming from the president's office, you stand a better chance of not being screened out.

Support Person: President Soandso's office.

You: *(Acknowledgment)* Hello, this is Jim Smith with XYZ.

(Benefit) I have been studying your company and believe we can help *[state specifically how you can increase revenues, gain competitive advantage, or decrease costs for this prospect; base your benefit statement on information gathered during your studies].*

(Commitment) Who in your company would you recommend I speak to? *[You are given the name of an executive vice president, whom you then call.]*

Support Person: *[Executive vice president's]* office.

You: *(Acknowledgment)* Hi, this is Jim Smith with XYZ. Is *[the executive vice president]* in?

Support Person: Yes. May I ask what this is regarding?

You: *(Acknowledgment)* Certainly.

(Benefit) I just spoke with *[the president's]* office regarding how *[restate your purpose/benefit]* and it was recommended that I should speak with *[give the name of the executive vice president].*

(Commitment) Can you put me through, please?

The Direct Approach. When you call the senior executive directly, expect some resistance from the Support person.

Support Person: *[Executive vice president's]* office.

You: *(Acknowledgment)* Hi, this is Sally Jones with XYZ.

(Benefit) I understand there is tremendous competition in your marketplace and know that a little more advantage can go a

long way toward *[increasing revenues/decreasing costs]* for *[core business function]*. The purpose of my call is to schedule a brief appointment with *[the executive vice president]* to share my findings and see if they warrant action.

(Commitment) Is *[he, or she]* available?

Support Person: *[The executive vice president]* is not the right person for you to talk to.

You: *(Acknowledgment)* I understand.

(Benefit) However, my research has revealed potential opportunities for significant profit improvement. Profitability is a primary concern of senior management; that's why I want to speak to *[the executive vice president]*.

(Commitment) Do you make *[his, or her]* appointments or would I need to speak directly with *[him, or her]*?

You may need to be persistent in trying to obtain an action commitment. First, request the specific action you want from the Support person—you want to be put through to the executive. If that doesn't work, use an alternative approach. ("Do you make *[his, or her]* appointments or would I need to speak directly with *[him, or her]*?") If you know you have something beneficial to offer this prospect, you won't be put off easily.

Dealing with the Voice Mail Screen

For years, my greatest frustration in approaching prospects came from difficulty in getting past voice mail screens. I left messages, but prospects didn't call me back. Then one day, on an airplane, I sat next to a vice president of sales (my typical prospect). She told me she got sixty voice messages *every day*. Suddenly, I felt more compassion for my prospects. That's when I decided to switch to an appointment letter. Why continue to beat my head against the wall, as one out of sixty, when I can distinguish myself in a letter?

If you do leave a voice mail message, listen carefully to your prospect's recorded greeting for clues about his or her personality. Then modify the message you leave, to communicate a similar tone.

With voice mail sales calls, you again use the ABCs:

You: *(Acknowledgment)* Hello, this is Sam Campbell with XYZ. My phone number is (800) 556-1232. I know you're busy so I'll get right to the point.

(Benefit) I realize that you're concerned about profitability, so the more you can prudently cut costs, the better. I'd like a brief appointment to show you how we've helped *[name another client]* cut costs, particularly in the area of *[cite an area of corporate interest]*.

(Commitment) I'd like to schedule a brief fifteen-minute appointment to see if perhaps we can help you, too. I'm sure you'll find it rewarding. Again, my name is Sam Campbell with XYZ. My number is (800) 556-1232, and the best time to reach me is *[give a definite time frame]*. I look forward to hearing from you.

Leave your phone number at the beginning and the end of the message so your prospect doesn't have to replay the entire message just to get your phone number.

If you're not satisfied with your message, press the pound key (#) *before* you hang up. Most voice mail systems will then offer instructions on how you can erase and rerecord your message.

What If You Don't Get a Return Call?

I have used two options when I don't get a return call. The first is to repeat the voice mail approach up to *"I'm sure you'll find it rewarding."* Then I add:

If you have no interest in meeting, simply let me know and I won't contact you again.

This important addition often gets an immediate reply. Sometimes I hear, "Don't call me again." At other times, I hear, "I'm sorry, I've just been so busy; call me Friday afternoon and we can talk."

Another option is to fax a brief letter such as:

Dear [name of prospect]:

I have been unsuccessful in reaching you by phone for the past month. I appreciate your busy schedule.

May I have the courtesy of a return call? I've attached a copy of the letter I sent you for your reference.

You can reach me by calling (510) 831-0922. Thanks for your consideration.

Sincerely,

Kevin Davis

The In-Person "Cold Call"

My first sales position, back in the 1970s, was selling dictation equipment for Lanier Business Products. My job was to walk into an office building carrying my product in a large suitcase, take the elevator to the top floor, and cold call my way back down. It was a lesson named "Selling 101." My daily activity goal was thirty in-person cold calls in an effort to get in to see four busy executives, from which I would secure one "trial." A trial occurred when a prospect agreed to take my dictation system on loan for a three-day evaluation. For three years I made a darn good living selling in this way, twice winning my company's annual "Chairman's Council" award, Lanier's highest award for peak sales performance. Then I moved into sales management, where, during the next seven years, I hired and trained 135 salespeople to make in-person cold calls.

One thing I know is that in-person cold calls aren't as effective today as they were when I began selling. People are *busier* today, there's more pressure on them now to get the job done. Plus, there are more salespeople calling on them, so prospects feel oversolicited. They've had to get better at saying "no." The days of walking in off the street and getting in to see a busy executive, in my opinion, are over.

While "cold calling" in an effort to see a busy executive may be dead, in-person information gathering calls are not. Chances are, when you're moving from one appointment to the next, you pass by prospects you haven't yet called on. You know the ones I'm talking about. If you've got a few minutes of spare time, why not get something of value out of it?

When you walk into a business, the first person you meet is usually the receptionist. Receptionists, who receive more visitors and phone calls than anybody else in the business, possess important information about their companies' day-to-day operations. Receptionists know who the decision makers are, and the best way for you to approach them.

Just walk in, introduce yourself to the receptionist, and say, "I'm not here to barge in and see anybody today. I would like to ask you a few quick questions, because you probably know better than most people how your business runs." This approach usually disarms the receptionist, and enables you to get the information you desire.

Your sales productivity is the result of two factors, the quality and quantity of sales calls you make. This book was written primarily to help you improve the *quality* of each call. It's up to you to motivate yourself to make a higher *quantity* of calls. Why don't you give in-person information-gathering calls a try?

FOR PERSISTENT STUDENTS, DOORS WILL OPEN

Time is precious, for both you and your prospect. As a Student, you study your prospect so you are better prepared when you meet with him or her. Salespeople who study their prospect in advance are more knowledgeable and professional, therefore more pleasurable to deal with.

Once you have studied your prospect, it's time to approach him or her. To schedule appointments with busy prospects, you need two things:

1. Excellent approach skills, as discussed earlier in this chapter.
2. A personal quality of persistence, which drives you to use your approach skills.

Salespeople who lack persistence give up too quickly. They're gone after the prospect's first "no" response. They don't give themselves enough of a chance to use their approach skills.

Persistence can't be taught from the outside; it must come from inside you. William Feather said, "Success seems to be largely a matter of hanging on after others have let go." Your ability to persist in the face of resistance, to refuse to give up, and to ask again for an appointment, is a vital ingredient for a successful approach—and for sales success.

4

Sales Role #2: THE DOCTOR

Diagnose "Little Problems" and Uncover BIG Needs

A problem well stated is a problem half solved.
Charles F. Kettering

In hundreds of sales training workshops delivered to thousands of salespeople, I have asked, "What are your prospects' most common objections to buying your product or service?" The answers I have received indicate to me that over 80 percent of the objections salespeople receive today are either identical to, or slight variations of:

"It's too expensive." (or, "I can't afford it.")
"It's not in the budget."
"I don't need it."

All of these objections are symptoms of a problem that can be traced to a single cause: your prospect's low perception of the value of your offering. In effect, your prospect is telling you that the problem your product or service solves is not serious enough to justify the investment you are asking. In your buyer's mind, the cost of buying is greater than the value that would be gained by ownership.

Over the years, salespeople have been taught that all objections are good for the sales process because they indicate that the buyer is interested. This maxim is incorrect. Value-type objections are *bad* for the sales process because they indicate just the opposite: the prospect is not interested.

How should you handle these value objections? The best way is not to handle them, but to prevent them. The objection is only a symptom of an underlying problem. You need to attack the cause (low perception of value). You can do this early in the sales process, during the buyer's Discontent phase, by helping your customer recognize that "little problems" are really BIG needs. If you apply the skills in this chapter, you'll be able to say good-bye to value objections!

YOUR CUSTOMERS' SECOND STEP: DISCONTENT

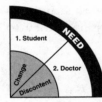 Your prospects' world is continuously changing. Change may occur gradually or suddenly. Change triggers Discontent, a feeling of dissatisfaction with the current situation. During the Discontent step, your prospects:

1. Recognize a problem or opportunity.
2. Ask, "How serious is the problem?"
3. Ask, "How much will the solution cost?"
4. Determine, "I need to buy!"

Let's take a closer look at the Discontent process.

Recognizing a Problem or Opportunity

Discontent occurs when prospects recognize that where they are now (actual situation) is not where they would like to be (optimal situation). Discontent can be caused by an awareness of either a *problem* or an *opportunity*. A problem relates to the past (for example, a photocopier has broken down, causing reduced productivity). An opportunity looks to the future (there is a possibility of entering a new market and increasing sales).

When attempting to diagnose prospects' needs, many salespeople make the mistake of asking questions to uncover only *problems*;

that is, they look exclusively at what has already happened. Salespeople who look only for problems are like drivers who look only in the rearview mirror. They are not focused on where their customers want to go. They should look for problems *and* opportunities.

Some prospects may recognize only a portion of a problem. My friend Marshall is a top salesperson for Stonhard, the world's largest supplier of industrial flooring products. He calls on the manufacturing managers of Fortune 500 companies in his territory, selling industrial floors that are chemical- and acid-resistant. Recently, Marshall met with a prospect who recognized a problem: a forklift had accidentally created a few divots in his factory floor. In the prospect's mind, the problem was relatively minor, appearing to be primarily an aesthetic issue. Marshall, on the other hand, saw other problems more serious than the divots. He saw an old concrete floor that was breaking down under spillages of acids, chemicals, and cleaning solvents. In Marshall's mind, the prospect had other problems with the floor besides the divots. In situations such as this, it's the consultative salesperson's responsibility to help the prospect recognize the entire problem.

How Serious Is the Problem?

Prospects usually have numerous problems but limited resources for solving them. For this reason, when prospects see a need, they ask themselves: "How serious is it?" They prioritize their problems and allocate their resources accordingly.

In Marshall's situation, the factory manager initially recognized a problem—a few divots in the factory floor. This divot problem was not serious enough to justify replacement of the entire floor. Marshall, by using the questioning process described later in this chapter, helped the manager to recognize that there were other, more serious problems with the floor. He also helped him recognize the consequences that might occur if these larger problems were ignored. As these problems and their consequences became apparent to the prospect, his buying desire grew.

Prospects' Discontent can vary in intensity, depending on whether a small nuisance or a major crisis is perceived. The more serious the prospects' Discontent, the greater the value of the solution, and the more resources the prospects will make available to solve it.

How Much Is Your Solution?

Prospects are very sensitive to price during the Discontent step. I'm sure you can recall a prospect asking you, early in a sales process, "Can you give me a rough estimate: *how much is your solution?*" By this time, prospects believe they understand the seriousness of their Discontent. Your "ballpark" figure allows them to balance the seriousness of the problem against the cost of resolving it.

Suppose Marshall had been unsuccessful at getting the manufacturing manager to recognize any additional problems besides the divots. If he quoted $20,000 for an entirely new floor, the prospect was likely to respond with a value objection: "That's too expensive" or "I can't afford that!" If, however, he quoted $1,500 to patch the problem, the prospect was likely to advance to the final portion of the Discontent process, "I need to buy."

The Need to Buy

Suppose Marshall's prospect believed that holes in the floor were forcing his forklift operators to slow down, and he estimated that this reduced productivity was costing his manufacturing operations $5,000 a year. If Marshall then quoted $1,500, chances are the manager would have thought, "*I need to buy!*" When prospects have bought off on the need, they see themselves as having bought your product or one similar to it. They form a mental image of its value, an expectation of the results that will occur as a consequence of buying. The greater your prospects' vision of value to be gained, the greater their desire to buy.

Marshall, however, knew this prospect needed a new floor. Later in the chapter, we'll see how he dealt with this challenge.

YOUR PROSPECTS' PRESENT CONDITION

Before prospects recognize the need to buy, they must feel dissatisfied with where they are now. Your focus early in a sales process, should be to ask questions that tell you where your prospects are now and compare that condition to where they think they should be. The difference that becomes evident through such a comparison is Discontent.

Your sales role for prospects' Discontent is Doctor.

SALES ROLE #2: THE DOCTOR

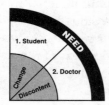 The Customer-Focused Selling role for your prospects' Discontent step is **Doctor.** A doctor is a professional who helps people achieve wellness through expert knowledge, questioning, and skill.

A doctor deals with three kinds of patients:

1. Sick patients.
2. Fairly healthy patients who want to be better off.
3. "In-Denial" patients who think they are healthy, but whose doctor knows that is not their true condition.

An example of an "in-denial" patient is someone who is overweight, smokes heavily, gets little exercise, and suffers from high blood pressure, yet still thinks of himself or herself as "healthy." You will meet sales prospects who have parallel characteristics: their companies are doing all the wrong things and could benefit from a salesperson's advice, but they are unwilling or unable to admit it.

"Sick" Prospects

These are prospects whose performance is not up to par at the moment. Usually, they function at an acceptable (or normal) level (Figure 4.1), but they perceive that lately their actual performance has been substandard. For instance, suppose interest rates have suddenly dropped. As homeowners rush to refinance their mortgages, mortgage banking businesses are swamped with loan applications, placing intense pressure on their processing system.

Figure 4.1   "Sick" Prospects Are Experiencing Problems

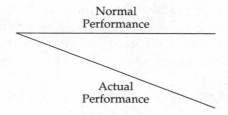

"Sick" mortgage banking prospects who want to cure their illness will be heard to say:

"We're spending too much time on overtime pay."

"We can't retrieve applicant records fast enough."

"Loan applicants wait far too long for approval."

"Healthy" Prospects

Healthy prospects' performance may be at an acceptable level, but they seek the *opportunity* to be better off and to achieve a higher level of performance (see Figure 4.2). These prospects want to thrive. Suppose a cellular telephone business has been growing at about 12 percent per year. That's a good growth rate for most businesses, but in the 1990s the cellular telephone industry has been growing at 30 percent per year, according to Hoover's Industry Profiles. Although the company is doing fairly well, it isn't growing as fast as the market. That lower growth rate is a source of Discontent. The difference between where the company is now and where it could be is the extent of the owner's dissatisfaction.

You will hear healthy prospects say:

"I want more customers."

"Our goal is to increase sales by 30 percent."

"We must increase our average revenue per user."

"In-Denial" Prospects

"In-Denial" prospects believe their performance is optimal, but they are mistaken. As a salesperson, you help others to change,

Figure 4.2 "Healthy" Prospects' Perception of a Goal

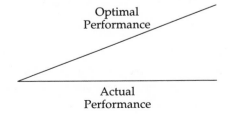

Optimal
Performance

Actual
Performance

Figure 4.3   "In-Denial" Prospects' Self-Deceiving Perception

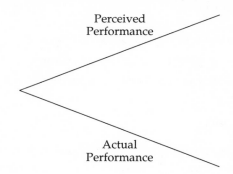

grow, and improve their lives or businesses. Unfortunately, some people prefer to hold on to the past. They don't want to change. These are the most difficult prospects to sell to because they are unwilling to admit a need (see Figure 4.3). Often, they say they want to be "left alone." It may take a crisis of some kind for this type of prospect to snap out of that attitude. The best strategy is to bide your time and keep in touch. Don't waste your valuable selling resources on prospects in denial.

You will hear in-denial prospects say:

"Business is wonderful." (Despite reports to the contrary.)

"We're hiring lots of people." (Many others recently quit.)

"Couldn't be better." (In reality, it's the worst it has ever been.)

When you are selling in the Need stage, **remember that you are selling against your prospects' inertia,** their desire to avoid change and to keep things moving in the same direction. You are *not* selling against your competitors until your prospects are in the Learn stage, which will be discussed in Chapters 5 and 6.

WHAT A DOCTOR DOES

Think back to the last time you visited a doctor when you were sick. A medical assistant took your blood pressure, temperature, and weight, and asked you a few questions. The doctor then read your chart, looking for any changes over time, reviewed your medical *history*, and asked questions about your current condition.

Next, the doctor asked questions about your *symptoms*. For any given set of symptoms, there are usually many possible *causes* or illnesses. By means of a physical examination, perhaps supplemented with lab tests, X rays, and so on, the doctor gradually diagnosed your illness. If you delayed your visit to the doctor, *complications* may have developed. Complications are negative consequences that occur if an illness is ignored. Often, we don't seek professional help until complications force us to take action. Finally, the doctor discussed what would be necessary for a *cure* and wrote you a *prescription* that restored you to health.

The Doctor of Selling

In the role of Doctor for the selling process, you diagnose "little" problems, uncover big needs, and share some information about how the product or service you are offering can meet those needs. As a "doctor of selling," you ask five types of questions:

1. *History questions* (to identify optimal vs. actual condition).
2. *Symptom questions* (to identify Discontent).
3. *Cause questions* (to define the true problem).
4. *Complication questions* (to clarify the seriousness of the problem).
5. *Cure questions* (to help you identify your prospects' expectations of value).

After gathering this information, you will offer your prospects *prescriptions* that prove your capabilities.

The Questioning Process

Earlier in this chapter, we were following my friend Marshall's efforts with a prospect, a manufacturing manager. When we left off, Marshall had persuaded the manager to spend $1,500 on a patch job. In the end, Marshall sold an entirely new factory floor for $20,000. Let's follow him through the questioning process as he performed the role of a doctor of selling.

History Questions

The purpose of history questions is to gather information about facts, situations, and backgrounds in order to determine the difference between optimal performance (what should be) and actual performance (what is). History questions may also verify what you already know or suspect. For instance:

- What are some of the changes going on in your business?
- What are your customers' expectations?
- Where are you now in relation to your company's goals?

Marshall, after discussing with the manager the divots caused by the forklift, began by asking a few *history* questions:

"When did you install your current floor? What types of chemicals have you been using here in your factory? Do you know what types of chemical resistance products, if any, were included in the concrete?" By asking these questions, Marshall learned that the existing floor was eight years old, several hazardous materials were being used in the manufacturing process, and the prospect was unsure what types of components had gone into the original concrete mixture.

After background information has been gathered, it's time to ask symptom questions.

Symptom Questions

The purpose of symptom questions is to identify your prospect's Discontent. Discontent occurs when your prospect recognizes a problem or missed opportunity that is preventing optimal performance. Symptom questions help the prospect to recognize problems. Examples of symptom questions are:

- Are you satisfied with _____?
- What barriers stand between you and your goals?
- Is your current level of _____ acceptable to you?
- Other customers of ours have had difficulty with _____. Has this been a problem for you?
- What would you like to see improved?
- Are you concerned about _____?

Marshall asked a few symptom questions, including: "Besides the divots, are you satisfied with the current condition of your factory floor?" The prospect told Marshall that the floor seemed to be holding up OK, although there were a few areas where the concrete had begun to break down, and these areas were becoming increasingly difficult to clean.

Cause Questions

The purpose of cause questions is to determine the specific origins of symptoms, with particular emphasis on those causes that you, in the role of Doctor, can treat. In business as well as medicine, there may be ten causes for a given set of symptoms. If you don't find the cause of a problem, your solution won't resolve it. You determine cause by asking:

- "What do you attribute that to?"
- "Any idea what's causing that?"
- "What factors bring about that problem?"

There is a difference between how a doctor of medicine and a doctor of selling diagnose cause. When you go to a medical doctor, you expect to be told what your illness is. You acknowledge in advance that the M.D. has specialized knowledge that you don't have.

As a doctor of selling, you too have specialized knowledge, but your relationship with your prospect is still in its infancy. Chances are, your prospect does not yet recognize your expertise. Also, some prospects mistakenly consider themselves experts in your field, even though they are not. If you take a direct approach by simply telling a prospect the cause of a business's illness, the prospect may not appreciate your style. Instead, ask participatory cause questions. Based on the answers you receive, gauge your prospect's expertise and personality type, and choose your approach accordingly. Gradually, proceed toward a diagnosis.

Many prospects are counting on you to diagnose their problems. They are good at describing their symptoms, but they look to an expert for an accurate diagnosis. To determine specific cause(s) of less than optimal performance, some salespeople seek information from others in the company, sometimes by means of surveys or interviews.

Determining the correct cause of your prospect's Discontent is vital. Doctors who fail to make an accurate diagnosis may be found liable for malpractice. If a patient reports headaches and the doctor prescribes aspirin, the patient may be dead in a week if the cause of the headaches is a brain tumor.

By asking what was causing the breakdown of the concrete, Marshall learned about various types of spillages that occurred during his prospect's manufacturing process. He also learned that the company's cleaning contractors were not effective at cleaning up these spills. Marshall asked a cause question, "Why?" The prospect said that because the texture of the floor was very rough, spills were not easily wiped clean. Marshall also learned that some spaces between the concrete slabs were damaged, possibly enabling small amounts of hazardous chemicals to leak into the ground. Gradually, this combination of factors was causing the floor to deteriorate.

Complication Questions

As we have already discussed, once prospects recognize Discontent, they next ask, "How serious is this problem?" When prospects are considering whether they have a need, they have a simple *value equation* in mind:

$$\text{Value Gained} = \frac{\text{Seriousness of Discontent}}{\text{Cost of Buying}}$$

All the studying you did in the Student sales role will help you uncover the extent of your prospects' need for your offering. Now is the time to apply the knowledge you gained and to help your prospects recognize a significant need. If you study your prospects' businesses in advance, you will be able to ask potent, targeted complication questions.

Remember our McDonald's example (Figure 3.2), illustrating how business functions are connected to one another, like the links of a chain? Many prospects fail to realize how a problem in their department affects other departments. If McDonald's has a problem with food preparation, you can predict how it will affect other functions within the business. A backlog of orders is sure to accumulate. Delivery and payment will be delayed, thereby reducing profit.

Complication questions help reveal the ramifications of a problem. Your goal is to help your prospects recognize that the problem is much more serious than was originally thought. This recognition of complications intensifies your prospects' desire to buy and justifies your solution. Examples of *complication* questions that you can ask include:

- "How does that affect _____?"
- "Does that lead to _____?"

- "That must cause real problems." (Pause and allow the prospect to elaborate.)
- "If you don't solve that problem, what might happen?"
- "What other problems does that create for you?"

At this point, Marshall's prospect was feeling mildly dissatisfied with his current factory floor because it had a few divots and was breaking down in a few areas.

If Marshall's prospect decides to solve his problem by replacing his factory floor, what are his costs of buying? One cost is, of course, money, but there are others. Let's take a look at the manufacturing manager's value equation:

Seriousness of Discontent	Costs of Buying
Divots in floor	$20,000 for a new floor
Concrete breakdown in a few areas	Time invested to shop and buy
	Less money to meet other needs
	Lost productivity during installation
	Risk of a bad decision

So far, Marshall's prospect had perceived the new floor as too expensive because the costs of buying outweighed the seriousness of his Discontent. Marshall anticipated a value objection, such as "It's too expensive" or "Let me think it over." Before the manager could put him off, he moved quickly to ask further questions that would help the manager see the full extent of his problem.

Uncovering Discontent is not enough. It's important not only to *diagnose* Discontent but also to uncover underlying problems and complications in order to clarify the value of what you offer. You do this by asking complication questions that explore a problem's financial costs and its effects on your customer.

From physics, we know that every action produces a reaction. The "ripple effect" is seen when one cause sets off a widening sequence of events. For example, shortly after the Clinton Administration came into power, the issue of survival of the Spotted Owl, an endangered species, was dealt with by preventing logging activity on tens of thousands of acres of forests. This action triggered an economic ripple effect in the logging industry. Sawmills were shut down, mill workers were laid off, government unemployment payments went up, income tax receipts went down. The price of lumber then went up because the supply of wood went down. The high cost of lumber caused housing materials prices to go up. Demand waned, so new home construction went down. Construction workers were laid off, and so on. This example shows that, even more than the initial problem, the related complications that the problem triggers can be painful. Helping your prospects to recognize the complications of a problem will intensify their buying desire.

Complications may have already occurred, or you may see them as a logical extension of a current problem if it is not solved soon. Suppose a doctor says that a patient's high cholesterol may lead to heart disease. Simply living with high cholesterol is not a difficulty. However, the possibility of heart attack or death from heart disease is a serious problem. The doctor will discuss potential complications with a patient in an attempt to motivate the patient to change.

As a salesperson, you can offer your insights, but you'll be more effective if you *ask* your prospects to speculate on possible complications. This approach allows them to take ownership. Although you're an expert in your field, prospects know more about their situation than you do. When you ask them to speculate on possible complications (rather than inform them yourself), they will be more committed to change. When prospects tell you what the complications will be, they are selling the remedies to themselves.

Complication questions help "sick" prospects to realize that their actual performance is even worse than they had thought.

Complication questions also put additional items on the Discontent side of the prospects' value equation. In Marshall's selling situation, the only Discontent items the prospect listed were divots and concrete breakdown in a few areas. Marshall then asked his prospect a few complication questions, including:

- "If you had a serious spill, what might happen?"
- "Might that create some health or safety concerns?"
- "How do hazardous spills affect your insurance coverage?"

By asking complication questions, you help your prospects recognize the impact of a problem on other areas of personal life or business. Complication questions also help your prospects to recognize likely future consequences if the problem is not solved. There is nothing artificial about these questions, and the consequences are (or should be) genuine concerns. Recognition of these consequences intensifies your prospects' Discontent. In Marshall's situation, the manager soon recognized that serious complications might occur if the floor was not replaced. These complications altered the balance of the value equation:

Seriousness of Discontent	Costs of Buying
Divots in floor	$20,000 for a new floor
Concrete breakdown in a few areas	Time invested to shop and buy
Potential worker safety issues	Less money to meet other needs
Potential liability	Lost productivity during installation
Legal fees, higher insurance premiums	Risk of a bad decision
Possible fines from the Health Department	
Possible negative publicity	

Cure Questions

The final type of question to ask is a cure question. Cure questions ask your prospects to speculate on the value of a solution. Examples of cure questions include:

- "Suppose you could _____. What would that enable you to do?"
- "How would that help?"
- "Would _____ have any other advantages?"
- "How much would you save if you could _____?"

The difference between complication questions and cure questions is that complication questions ask prospects to speculate on the negative effects and costs of a problem, while cure questions ask prospects to speculate on the potential value of a solution. Complication questions are bad news; cure questions are good news.

Cure questions are usually more effective when phrased as "open" questions, not "closed" questions—questions that can be answered only with "yes" or "no." Open questions ask for a conversational response.

For several reasons, open-ended cure questions are more effective. The answers you get will tell you what results your prospects expect. When your prospects tell you the desired results, they are, in effect, telling you which capabilities the solution must have. This is their "vision of value." For instance, suppose you are a realtor talking to someone who is considering a move. You ask: "What would a new home in a new neighborhood enable you to do?" The prospect responds, "It would allow us to get the extra bedroom we need, have a larger kitchen, and place our children into better schools." You now know your prospect's *expectations of value*, what the prospect wants to accomplish with a new home.

Often, a prospect you are working with will be one of many people involved in the buying decision. In "complex" sales—sales that involve several decision makers—the prospect you work with must sell to other people in the company, some of whom you may never meet. In big-ticket sales to businesses, most of the selling may be done internally by prospects who believe in what you have to offer. When you ask open-ended cure questions, your prospect rehearses the sales presentation in the actual wording that will be used to deliver your message to other decision makers on your behalf.

How your prospects answer cure questions tells you their perception of your product's value. Sometimes, their perceptions of your solution's value will surprise you. Unexpected benefits suddenly "pop out." When Marshall asked the manufacturing manager a few cure questions, the prospect suddenly recognized an important benefit. By replacing the current "rough-textured" floor with a smoother surface, spills would be easier for the maintenance people to clean. Smaller amounts of hazardous chemicals could be used during the clean-up, which would reduce both maintenance expenses and the prospect's potential liability.

Eventually, Marshall won the sale at $20,000, despite a competitor's bid of $12,500. Why? Marshall attributes his success to his questioning skills, which helped the prospect to recognize the value of his offering. Marshall's company used higher quality materials and had a better track record. Because the purchase was of major importance, the manufacturing manager was able to justify the added cost of Marshall's solution.

Asking the Right Questions

Here is an example of how the five types of "doctor of selling" questions were recently used on a particular sales call. This salesperson is selling automated mail delivery systems.

Salesperson: How are you currently delivering mail to the various departments within your company? *(history question)*

Prospect: George goes around the building twice a day delivering the mail to each department.

Salesperson: Are the departments satisfied with the level of service they are receiving? *(symptom question)*

Prospect: Actually, no. They complain that the delivery is inconsistent, and they never know when or if they will be receiving their mail.

Salesperson: What do you think is causing the inconsistency? *(cause question)*

Prospect: Well, it is probably two or three things. First off, we have a real problem when George is out sick. On those days, we are lucky to get the mail to the departments at all. The other thing is that George has a tendency to get a little talkative. He spends too much time gabbing with other people.

Salesperson: That must cause real problems. *(complication question)* *(pauses to allow prospect to elaborate)*

Prospect: Yes, it does. When George is out sick, I am the person who delivers the mail, so my work doesn't get done. Also, we get people from the departments coming down here interrupting us all day long looking for their mail.

Salesperson: How does that affect you? *(complication question)*

Prospect: I can't work on other important projects during the day, so I have to stay late. With a new baby at home, it's a big strain on my wife.

Salesperson: Have your departments ever missed deadlines for customers because they didn't receive their mail? *(complication question)*

Prospect: Yes, it happened last week with a new customer. It was very embarrassing, and we almost lost the customer.

Salesperson: If you are able to cure your inconsistent mail delivery problem, how will that help? Would there be any advantages to increasing the number of deliveries each day? *(cure question)*

In the above dialogue, the prospect freely admits that the department is not functioning well. This is a prospect who wants to improve, and feels comfortable talking about it. You may find some prospects are reluctant to open up to you in this way. If so, ask the Doctor questions *backward*. Begin by talking about the cure—how things could be better—then gradually work your way back toward the problem. In this way, you appear less threatening to a prospect who is somewhat closed-minded during the initial stages of your meeting.

Here is another example, taken from my own experience, of the importance of asking the right questions. I went on a sales call as a seller of sales training services, and assumed the role of a doctor of selling. My prospect was the Vice President of Sales for an outdoor advertising/billboard company. After establishing rapport, I asked him several *history* questions to discover his current situation. I learned that he had 20 salespeople who sold advertising space for 300 billboards in northern California. I asked him a *symptom* question and learned that he was dissatisfied because his sales organization was meeting only 75 percent of quota. I then asked him a *cause* question ("What's causing that?"). He responded, "Low prospecting activity." Next, I asked a *complication* question: "How is that affecting your sales?" He pondered for a moment, then responded, "It has probably cost us about $1,000,000 in sales so far this year." Then I asked him a *cure* question, "Suppose you could increase your sales force's prospecting activity to an acceptable level, how much of that $1,000,000 in increased revenue would go to your bottom line?" He said, "About $650,000."

The sales training solution necessary to meet his need required a $15,000 investment. Do you think my prospect told me "Let me think it over" or "I can't afford it"? No way! He recognized a critical need for sales training and turned his attention toward selecting the best sales trainer for his needs. By the time he arrived at Step 6 (Commitment), he was convinced I was his best choice. Then, he couldn't wait to get started.

As you begin to apply these kinds of questions during your sales calls, don't get bogged down trying to phrase them perfectly. This is a learning process for both you and your prospects. In order to learn, you must ask questions *and* listen. By focusing on what you want to learn, the questions will come naturally. The goal isn't to ask the perfect question, it's to learn about your prospects' problems and how those problems affect their companies' bottom line.

As a doctor of selling, your goal is to identify your prospects' degree of discontent, then intensify that discontent with urgent questions so your prospects are motivated to buy. History, symptom, cause, complication, and cure questions will help you accomplish this goal.

Selling is an urgency-creating process. The more momentum you generate early in the buy–sell process, the greater the probability that a sale will be made. The questions you ask in your role as Doctor will increase your prospects' perception of the value of what you have to offer and, therefore, will reduce the number of objections you hear. This is objection prevention rather than objection handling. An increased perception of value, combined with fewer objections, spells sales success for you!

Uncovering Financial Goals

You and your prospects need to arrive at a realistic appraisal of what your prospects could expect to happen to their business's bottom line if they do nothing. Occasionally, doing nothing means spending nothing, but if you have uncovered real needs, your prospects can't afford *not* to fix them.

At this step, you are not yet offering your solution or discussing the exact cost of your solution. Your area of interest is determining how expensive inaction would be for your customers.

As a doctor of selling, you diagnose problems and complications. Most of the problems and complications that you uncover will have a financial cost associated with them. If you identify these costs now, you will be in a better position to cost-justify your solution later. Following is a list of possible costs to consider during your needs analysis:

- Time lost.
- Money lost.
- Equipment repair.
- Lost business.
- Impact on your prospects' customers.
- Amount of work completed.
- Duplicated effort.
- Extra supervision.
- Training.
- Employee salaries and benefits.
- Overtime.
- Hardware and software costs.

If you don't know the true cost of a problem, you and your prospects won't know the value of your solution. To identify *all* the costs of a problem, refer to these cost items.

Later on, when you make a concerted pitch for your fully considered and customized solution, you'll refer to the hidden costs of doing nothing and compare them to the cost of your solution. If the equation is favorable enough to satisfy your buyers, you'll have a sale.

OFFERING A PRESCRIPTION

Once your prospects recognize a need to solve a problem, they will be immediately curious about your solution. Now, you must demonstrate that you can help to accomplish the stated goals. Your prospects must know that a solution is feasible, otherwise there is no reason to proceed to the next step (Research).

At this precise point, however, many salespeople self-destruct by presenting *too much* information. When a salesperson tells a prospect everything there is to know, there is no compelling reason for the prospect to continue discussions. When customers need information from you, they are easy to reach; when they don't need your information, they are almost impossible to reach. If you "spill the beans" too soon, your prospects may conduct the Research step without you—and with your competitor. You can meet this challenge by carefully pacing the information you deliver.

Just as a doctor prescribes no more medication than necessary, so too should a doctor of selling present only those features that achieve the specific result(s) that prospects desire. The results your prospects expect are revealed to you in the answers to your cure questions. By presenting the capabilities you can offer to achieve the desired results, you are showing your prospects that you listened.

Presenting only your features and benefits, however, is not enough. Many of the features of your product or service are also offered by your competition. That's why, when you present your capabilities, you must also differentiate yourself. By doing so, you get a jump on the next step of the buying process, Research. To begin to differentiate your solution, ask yourself, "How am I *uniquely* able to accomplish this prospect's goals?"

A salesperson selling automated telephone answering equipment may say:

> You mentioned that it is critically important to improve your company's responsiveness to your customers. Our EZ-Call processing system would enable you to meet this need because of our

unique Less-on-Hold capability. With Less-on-Hold, once a customer remains on hold past a certain period of time that you designate, that call is automatically call-forwarded to your other office. This capability ensures that your customers will make your company their one-call, first-call information resource. How does that sound?

The purpose of your prescription is not to outline a total treatment plan. It's too soon for that. Up to now, your prospects have been focused on *whether* to buy, not on *what* to buy. Your goals are to go forward with your prospects to Step 3 (Research) and to design a unique solution that meets their needs.

Going forward together is the next logical step in the buy–sell process. Specifically, where you go and what you do on your next sales call is your *sales call objective*, the goal you were seeking to accomplish from the moment you walked in the door. Let's take a closer look at call objectives.

SETTING CALL OBJECTIVES

If you are like many salespeople I work with, you've noticed recently that it's taking more time for your prospects to make a buying decision. Sales that once might have been consummated in one or two sales calls now take five or more. How do you keep the momentum going while your prospects deliberate?

When they are somewhere between "no" and "yes," prospects often seem extremely interested during your call, but nothing happens afterward. You need feedback, or you could end up wasting valuable time with low-probability prospects.

To determine how truly interested your prospects are, once again, examine what doctors do.

The Return Visit

At the conclusion of each patient examination, doctors always determine what must be accomplished next. Perhaps the next step is to discuss lab results, or to monitor the patient's response to medication. Doctors set up a "return visit," the next logical step in patient treatment. At the end of each appointment, as a doctor of selling, you too must determine what the next step should be.

In my seminars, I ask salespeople to list the next five sales calls they have scheduled and to specify what their call objective is. Typical responses include:

- "Build trust."
- "Close the sale."
- "Get positioned with a new decision maker."
- "Write a proposal."
- "Gather information."
- "Identify needs."

Look closely at the above objectives. How is "close the sale" different from all the others? It is the only objective listed that requires the *buyer* to take action. All the others are sales activities, things a salesperson does. They are means to the end, not the end itself. When salespeople set call objectives such as "build trust" and "identify needs," they are setting activities for *themselves,* not for their prospects. If at some point you're going to ask your prospects for a major commitment to buy, shouldn't you be involving them by asking for minor commitments along the way?

The secret is to set call objectives that specify something your prospects should do, an action they should take. I refer to these call objectives as **action commitments**—actions that customers agree to take that move the sale forward.

Suppose at the end of a sales call your prospect asked you to prepare a proposal. Would that be an action commitment? No, it would not, because preparing a proposal is something *you* do, not something your prospect does. If, on the other hand, you then ask the prospect, "Once I prepare the proposal, may I have an hour of your time to present it to you?" and the prospect says "Yes," you have achieved an action commitment. Your prospect has agreed to invest something of value—time—in you and your proposal. Now you know your prospect is truly interested.

How do you secure an action commitment? It's simple. Before each sales call, sit down and plan backward. Begin with your end result in mind. Determine the action commitment that you would like to achieve on the call, then plan your sales activities to accomplish that result. Here are a few action commitment objectives that may work for you:

- Prospect commits to another appointment.
- Prospect commits to conducting a survey.
- Prospect commits to attending a demonstration.
- Prospect commits to meeting with other decision makers.
- Prospect commits to getting you an appointment with another key person.
- Prospect grants you access to confidential company information.
- Prospect agrees to trial of your product or service.

As a doctor of selling, expect your "patients" to take some form of action to help themselves improve. The more involved your patients become in their own care, the faster their recovery will be.

When a sales call ends with a signed contract, you know you have succeeded, but because buyers today are taking more time to decide, you can't realistically expect to close a sale on every call. That's why you need a new method for determining success and failure on individual sales calls. Setting action commitment call objectives will not ensure the success of every sales call, but it will remove the frustration of uncertainty. In these increasingly challenging times, we need all the feedback we can get!

5

Sales Role #3: THE ARCHITECT

Design Customer-Focused Solutions
That Lock Out Your Competition

The best way to predict the future is to create it.
                                            Peter Drucker

Selling in today's marketplace reminds me of that line from ABC's *Wide World of Sports*: "The thrill of victory and the agony of defeat." Sometimes you win the sale, sometimes you don't.

Throughout my sales career, my most agonizing defeats have followed situations where I put a great deal of effort into creating a sales opportunity, only to eventually lose the sale to a competitor. One memorable sales situation, early in my career, began when I stopped by the radiology department of a medium-size hospital. From the receptionist, I learned that the department was using out-dated dictation equipment. A few days later, I sent the chairman of the department an appointment letter. After several attempts to reach him by phone, I was finally successful in speaking with him and scheduling an appointment.

Having been trained in the traditional four-step sales approach described in Chapter 1 (Approach/Needs/Present/Close), I began the sales call with comfortable conversation, which was successful in building trust. I then began questioning my prospect about his needs. During this portion of the call, I helped him recognize a serious problem with his current equipment. The solution—new dictation equipment—would enable his department to become much more productive. Gradually, over the next fifteen or twenty minutes, he recognized the need for new equipment. Next, as I had been taught, I began to present my product, emphasizing its most popular features and benefits.

What I know now—but didn't know then—is that once my prospect recognized a need, he had moved forward in his buying process from Discontent (Step 2) to Research (Step 3). His focus had changed from "Should I buy?" to "What should I buy?" He began learning, in an effort to identify the capabilities necessary for a solution. As I was presenting my product, my prospect was thinking, "Hmmm, which of these capabilities do I need? No, not feature A. Feature B looks interesting, but I'm not sure I would use it. Oooh, feature C would be nice. And, yep, I've got to have that feature D."

When I reached the end of my presentation, I went for the "close." My prospect told me he needed some time. He said he would check his budget figures later in the week, and he asked me to call him the following Monday. When I left my prospect's office, I knew he was interested, but I had no idea which capabilities he considered most important. I had done a good job helping him to recognize a need for new dictation equipment, but I had not worked with him to refine his needs. That day, I made the mistake that millions of salespeople are still making today. I had not joined him in his buying process. I had seen the sale through my eyes, not his.

I called him the following Monday and, you guessed it, he had already purchased dictation equipment from my competitor. I had been with him during Steps 2 and 3, Discontent and Research, but then lost contact. My competition had been with him during Steps 4 through 6, Comparison, Fear, and Commitment. Has anything like this ever happened to you?

If I had applied the custom-solution concepts described in this chapter, I would have won that sale to the radiology department chairman. If you apply these concepts with your prospects, you'll enjoy more thrills of victory and fewer agonies of defeat.

SALES ROLE #3: THE ARCHITECT

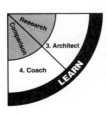 As a Student, you studied the changes affecting your prospects. As a Doctor, you diagnosed your prospects' "little problems" and uncovered BIG needs. When your prospects recognize a need to buy, they have completed the Need stage. If you have been involved from Step 1, you have successfully

communicated a mental picture of how your prospects will be better off as the result of buying. You are ready to fulfill the role of **Architect.**

In the second stage of the buying process, the Learn stage, the focus shifts to selecting the solutions that best meet your buyers' needs. If your buyers are afraid of making a mistake, they will take rational action to ensure that they make the best choice. Your job now is to make sure your prospects don't turn around and buy your competitors' products or services. You can avoid this outcome by assuming the role of an Architect and designing, for your buyers, solutions that showcase the unique capabilities you have to offer.

If you entered your account at the start of the need stage, you have an ongoing dialogue with your prospect. Frequently, however, the Change and Discontent steps occur before a salesperson makes contact. Prospects recognize their own need, then call in a salesperson when they are ready to start determining their buying criteria. Most buyers will conduct Step 3, Research, with one leading supplier because talking to just one salesperson saves time. If you are that salesperson, you are still not home free, however. Your buyers will soon move on to Step 4, Comparison, which involves shopping for other alternatives and talking to your competitors. Part of your job as an Architect is to design a solution that locks out your competitors before your buyers talk to them.

BUYING CRITERIA

Buying criteria are standards against which competing products are measured. Each criterion consists of a difference between alternatives that the prospect considers important. For instance, to a purchaser of a new car, seating capacity may be a criterion if one choice seats five people comfortably and another choice seats six. The one-person difference in seating may be important to the buyer.

"Must-Haves" and "Nice-to-Haves"

To translate an intangible concept into a tangible solution, buyers first identify the essential "must-have" requirements for their solution or purchase. By identifying must-haves, prospects are able to reduce the number of options being evaluated.

In the course of identifying must-haves, prospects typically identify some "nice-to-haves"—capabilities that would be nice to have but are not essential.

Buyers may want a nice-to-have but that does not mean they will insist on it. Unlimited budgets are rarities. Each nice-to-have has a cost factor that is weighed against its benefit. For *buyers*, nice-to-haves range in priority. For *sellers*, all nice-to-haves are important because each one can provide an advantage over the competition.

YOUR CUSTOMERS' THIRD STEP: RESEARCH

Your primary objective in the Research step of the buying process is to influence your prospects' buying criteria in a way that best meets the prospects' needs while simultaneously creating a competitive advantage for you.

Early in a sales process, your prospects' concept of what they need is frequently unclear. They may have a rough idea of the result they want, but they will be unsure of how best to accomplish it. To ensure that they make the best choice, they will begin gathering information.

You can meet your prospects' information needs and gain competitive advantage by helping to translate their intangible concept into more definite buying criteria. You should help your prospects to refine their needs in a way that not only ensures they will achieve the outcome they desire, but also takes advantage of product/service criteria that are your competitive strengths. Consider how advertising seeks to refine a consumer's intangible concept in a way that creates specific product needs. BMW's "Ultimate Driving Machine" ads translate the nebulous concept of a "luxury car" into the more specific capabilities of "high performance handling and quick acceleration."

Have you ever wondered why prospects are always asking you, "Why should I choose you?" They want you to give them reasons for choosing one supplier over another so that they can make the best decision. I believe, however, that just giving prospects reasons is not enough. I recommend that you take the selling process one step further: help prospects to define their needs by seeing the importance of certain capabilities your solution provides. Later, when your buyers compare alternatives, they will discover that certain important capabilities are strengths of your offering. Anticipate in advance your prospects' need for reasons why you should be chosen, and meet that need by refining your customers' concepts in a way that clarifies the value of your strengths. In this way, you design customer-focused solutions that lock out your competition.

WHEN PROSPECTS CALL YOU

When prospects call you and you have had no prior contact with them, you must find out where they are in the buying process. Was a competitor the first one in their door? If so, the competitor has most likely influenced their criteria. You are then entering the sale at Step 4, the Comparison step, and you'll need to assume a different selling role.

If you are the first supplier in their door, your buyers are probably in Step 3, the Research step. These prospects feel Discontent and want some idea of how much a solution would cost. Have you ever had a prospect ask you, during the first appointment, "Can you give me a rough idea how much a solution will cost?" The prospect is mentally balancing the seriousness of the problem against the cost of a solution. If the value exceeds the cost, the buy-*learning* process will begin. If not, the need will be dismissed or other potential solutions will be examined.

Regardless of whether you enter at Step 3 (Research) or Step 4 (Comparison), you must gain a clear understanding of each prospect's initial concept and criteria.

HOW SMALL FACTORS CAN AFFECT BIG SALES

Suppose you are a contractor who needs to buy a truck to move dirt from one side of town to the other. Your must-have criteria are related to what the vehicle must do:

1. Hold dirt.
2. Move dirt.
3. Dump dirt.

Each of these must-have criteria is necessary for solving the problem, and each allows you to eliminate hundreds of vehicles from consideration. In this way, you divide options into those that are acceptable and those that are unacceptable.

Suppose you identify two vehicles that meet your must-have requirements. One option is a large Mack dump truck (option A). The other is a small Chevrolet dump truck (option B). Both of these vehicles can hold dirt, move dirt, and dump dirt.

You now begin to notice nice-to-have differences between your two options. These include:

1. *Purchase price.* The large Mack truck costs $70,000; the Chevy costs $35,000. (Advantage: Chevrolet)

2. *Time necessary to complete the job.* The Mack truck will require half as many trips, so the job will get done faster. (Advantage: Mack)

3. *Labor costs.* With the larger truck, less time is required to do the job, so fewer work hours are involved. (Advantage: Mack)

4. *Maintenance costs.* These are lower with the larger truck because fewer trips are required. (Advantage: Mack)

Must-haves are usually linked directly to solving the customer's major problem or opportunity. Nice-to-haves are related to differences between options that the prospect feels are important.

In this case, because both the Mack and the Chevrolet meet your must-have requirements, your choice depends on which nice-to-have differences are identified and how you prioritize them. For instance, you would probably go with the Chevy if you ranked your nice-to-haves as follows:

Very important: Purchase price (Advantage: Chevrolet)
Somewhat important: Speed of completion (Advantage: Mack)
                          Labor costs (Advantage: Mack)
                          Maintenance costs (Advantage: Mack)

Suppose your contract to move the dirt contains a severe penalty clause if the work is not done on time. Under this scenario, your preference would be Mack because your nice-to-haves would be ranked differently:

Very important:	Time to completion (Advantage: Mack)
Somewhat important:	Labor cost (Advantage: Mack)
	Purchase price (Advantage: Chevrolet)
	Maintenance costs (Advantage: Mack)

Some of our major decisions are determined by small differences because we trade off some advantages we consider to have equal value, which leaves only minor differences. You would choose the Mack truck if your most important nice-to-haves cancel each other out:

Very important:	Time to completion (Advantage: Mack)
	Purchase price (Advantage: Chevrolet)
Somewhat important:	Labor and maintenance (Advantage: Mack)

This example shows how major decisions are sometimes made on the basis of smaller factors.

THE TOOLS OF THE ARCHITECT

In your sales role as Architect, you will need **creativity,** the talent for bringing something new into being and for responding to perplexing design problems. Like a professional architect, your skill in problem solving must result in innovative but dependable solutions.

Your second tool as Architect will be **expert knowledge.** A professional architect must be an expert in design, drafting, layout, site selection, building materials, building codes, and so on. Similarly, you must be an expert in all facets of selling and buying. Clients will retain your architectural design services if you can show them you have the necessary expert knowledge.

THE ARCHITECT'S FOUR-STEP DESIGN PROCESS

To move from a general concept to a specific plan, you use the same four steps that an architect uses in the design process:

1. Understand the client's intangible concept.
2. Determine the must-have requirements necessary to achieve the concept.

3. Refine the concept by identifying nice-to-haves.

4. Determine the relative importance of each nice-to-have to the client.

Let's apply these components of the design process to your sales role.

1. Understand the Client's Concept

Architects begin by clearly understanding the client's concept, or what their client wants to accomplish. The future building owners have a vision of the results they seek with a new building. Inherent in that vision is communication of the uniqueness of the company that will operate at that site. The new building is to be a physical expression of that company's uniqueness. A high-tech company may want a "leading-edge design," to make a statement about its commitment to research and development. A retail business may want an "inviting design" that draws shoppers in. A city government may want a "durable design" for a new city hall because 50 years may pass before the voters approve a replacement. The first thing an architect must do is clearly identify the client's concept.

If you have created a particular sales opportunity or have been with the buyer through Step 1 (Change) and Step 2 (Discontent) of the buy-*learning* process, you will already be familiar with the buyer's concept. The cure questions you asked in the Doctor role would have prompted the buyer to speculate about the design needs.

2. Determine Must-Haves

Once architects understand the client's concept, they begin to translate the client's vision into a specific plan by determining the client's must-have requirements. Usually, some vital requirements have already been identified by the client, but some have not. To uncover preexisting must-haves, the architect asks the client what capabilities the new building must have. For example, a hospital must have a reliable ventilation system capable of supplying clean air for patients. It must have auxiliary power systems that will respond if the area's utilities fail. It must meet or exceed strict seismic standards to ensure that the building will withstand an earthquake. Must-have requirements are essential; any design the architect proposes must include them.

Many must-have requirements are established well in advance. Often, they are what drives the client's need for a new solution. In your sales role as Architect, it is important for you to uncover your prospect's preexisting must-have requirements. Then you need to determine new "must-have" requirements that will be necessary for your solution to be fully satisfactory.

To uncover must-have criteria, simply ask, "Are there any capabilities that any solution absolutely must have?" It's that simple.

Once you understand the prospect's concept, you may realize that the prospect has not yet considered certain must-have criteria that are necessary to get the job done. For example, as a sales trainer, I work with sales executives whose concept (the results they seek) is increased sales force effectiveness. They believe that a two-day sales training program will achieve their concept. I then tell them that research has found that as much as 87 percent of selling skills taught are lost within 30 days of a training program when there is no follow-up coaching by sales managers. I recommend coaching training for the sales managers so they can continue to reinforce the company's initial investment in sales training. This is a "must-have" of which my clients are often unaware.

If the client is not aware of certain requirements, it is up to the professional architect to make sure they are discussed. For instance, a European company building a new factory in the United States may not be aware of the various approvals needed from governmental authorities: environmental impact reports for federal agencies, building code restrictions of local agencies, and so on. If your client is unaware of certain must-haves, it's up to you, as Architect, to identify them. This is one of the services the Architect provides for the client.

3. Refine the Concept

Professional architects who understand the client's concept will seek to refine it, to make it more precise. Most clients see a new building as an opportunity to make improvements, but they are not aware of all the specific ways in which a new building can help them improve their operations. Architects carefully question the client about how the company operates, what its culture is, and how the client wants the company to be positioned in the future. The architects' goal is to enhance the concept, to make it more specific and detailed, so that the office environment will be an expression of the company's unique culture. Moreover, relating a company's concept to its unique needs allows the architect to creatively customize solutions that meet those needs.

Carefully question your prospects about their operations, goals, and objectives. What unique needs does each prospect have? What unique capabilities does your company and/or product have and what potential problems do those capabilities solve? If you can refine a prospect's concept in a way that creates a need for your unique capabilities, you have gained competitive advantage.

It is vitally important that you do not show your product at this time! It's still too soon. If you show your product now, you may be seen as just another commercial vendor delivering one of hundreds of messages your prospect hears each week. Your prospect may perceive you as just another self-focused product-pusher with commission breath.

You should not need to provide a complete product presentation to build your buyers' interest. Recently, the CBS television network ran a program titled "The Greatest Commercials Ever Made." According to this program, the number-one television commercial in history is Apple Computer's Macintosh kickoff, a commercial that appeared only once—during the 1984 Super Bowl telecast. In the commercial, a large, somberly dressed audience was listening passively to a lecturer, shown on a large screen, who was instructing them on how to conform with society. A female athlete is outside the auditorium, running down hallways, being chased by serious-looking riot police. The woman, dressed in white, is carrying a large hammer, like those used in the Olympic hammer-throwing competition. The woman runs into the auditorium and hurls her hammer up and into the screen, destroying the image of the rigid conformist speaker. The commercial concludes with a voice that suggests nonconformance is good. Interestingly, this famous commercial did not show a product.

Instead of presenting the features and benefits of your product, focus on each prospect's needs. In effect, you are planting a seed called NEED. When you come back for your next appointment, the NEED seed has taken root and grown, and your prospect has taken ownership of it. It's not your suggestion any more, it's your prospect's need. If the NEED seed you planted leads to your unique capability, you have gained advantage.

Perceptions, once formed, stay with people. If you influence the perceptions of your prospects, helping them to become aware of certain aspects of the overall concept for the first time, those perceptions will affect your prospects' future buying decisions. Provided you know what you're talking about and you meet or exceed your prospects' expectations, the initial perceptions formed by your prospects will influence all future purchases. Perceptions live on after the sale.

How to Handle "Show Me What You've Got"

You may be wondering how to handle the prospect who says, "Show me what you've got" the moment you walk in the door. This is a very direct prospect who may have already spent considerable time analyzing his or her own needs, either alone (at the Step 3 (Research) level) or with your competitor (at the Step 4 (Comparison) level). There are two ways to handle this situation. One way is to say, "I've got fourteen different services and each service has multiple options. It would be a waste of your time to show you something you don't need. If you'll allow me to ask a few questions first. . . ." The second way to handle this situation is to show your product, to satisfy the prospect's demanding curiosity, then immediately back up to identify the problem or opportunity the prospect is trying to solve. Regardless of which technique you choose, you cannot make solution recommendations without knowing about the prospect's Discontent and Research steps.

How to Refine the Client's Concept

After the concept has been defined, nice-to-haves are identified. As Architect, you first uncover any nice-to-haves that the client has already identified. To identify a prospect's nice-to-haves, simply ask, "Are there any capabilities that would be nice to have?" It's that simple.

Then, recommend nice-to-haves that you feel the prospect should consider. To elicit nice-to-haves, professional architects use careful questioning and listening skills. For example, suppose an architect learns that a corporate client has had a problem with employees taking too much sick leave. The architect may then recommend, as a nice-to-have, a new workout facility to improve physical fitness and thereby reduce sick leave. In this way, the architect makes a helpful specific contribution to the client's initial concept.

4. Determine the Relative Importance of Each Nice-to-Have to the Client

It's important for you to help your prospects prioritize their nice-to-haves *before they begin shopping around*. Your strength during Step 4

(Comparison) depends on how the criteria are ranked by your buyers and how you match up against your competitors. Ask your prospects to rank their nice-to-haves. Which one is most important, next most important, and so on? Your goal is to obtain the best match between your product's strengths and your prospects' criteria.

When You Are the First Salesperson in the Door

When you are the first supplier in the door, you must take advantage of your opportunity and influence prospects' must-haves and nice-to-haves in your favor. Because you won't know exactly against whom your prospects will be comparing you, you must be aware of your strengths in the marketplace in general.

Early in my sales career, I sold centralized dictation systems to hospitals. These were high-usage systems that doctors used to document their treatment of patients. The dictation systems consisted of recorders that doctors spoke into (typists then typed transcripts of the recordings) and a management computer that tracked each report. The management computer allowed individual patient reports to be instantly retrieved and processed.

One of my prospects was a large government hospital that had my competitor's system. I had kept in close touch with key medical record personnel and was able to be the first sales rep in the door when hospital management allocated funds for the system's replacement.

I knew in advance that I was at a significant disadvantage against my competitor because my system was not large enough to handle all the hospital's work. The only way I could handle the volume of work was to provide *two* management computers—in a sense, two different systems. My competitors had systems with much larger capacity and could provide one system that would meet the hospital's needs. This gave my competitors a significant price advantage.

I decided that just *presenting* the buyers with a reason would not be compelling enough. Instead, I questioned the director of medical records carefully about her problems and needs. I discovered that, because of government red tape, it sometimes took several days to get authorization for replacement parts for the current system. With the older system, this delay wasn't much of a problem, because that system was a collection of independent units. If one unit failed, twenty-three others continued operating. However, the new systems being offered by both my competitor and me were totally integrated. This "advancement" meant that a problem with one component could put the entire system down. A problem not immediately resolved could shut down the hospital.

I then suggested that it would be in the prospects' best interests to have two independent systems: if one went down, at least they had the other one. They agreed wholeheartedly. When their request for proposal came out several weeks later, the most important must-have was "two independent systems." This put my competitor at a major price **disadvantage** and I won the contract.

To turn a disadvantage into an advantage:

1. Understand how your product or service is different.
2. Determine what potential problems those different capabilities might solve.
3. Focus on those problems.

Here is an example of what you might say:

"How often does your present system break down?"
"What difficulties does a breakdown create?"
"If your entire system went down, how would that affect _____?"
"How would that affect you personally?"

After your prospect's needs have been refined, you must present a compelling reason why you are the best choice. *Inc.* magazine recently listed "failing to give customers a compelling reason to switch from competitive products" as the number-one reason businesses fail. A firm handshake and a warm smile are not compelling reasons. To determine a truly compelling reason why your prospect should buy your product or service, imagine the prospect presenting your concept to the CEO. What if the CEO says, "So what?" Does the prospect have a good answer?

YOUR STARTING POINT: THE MARKET ASSESSMENT

Identifying how your product or service is different from others that are available is a two-step process. First, list typical must-have and nice-to-have criteria used by prospects when they are considering your product or service. Then, compare your offering to others that are available. The market assessment does *not* look at specific competitors. Instead it addresses the entire collection of market alternatives. At this phase of the sale, you do not yet know who your competitors will be. By comparing yourself to the marketplace in general, you clarify your strengths and are able to look closely at your customers' needs to determine if they match. If so, you gain competitive advantage *before* the competition arrives on the scene.

Suppose you sell copy machines. Here are some typical musthaves and nice-to-haves that customers identify when buying a copy machine.

Must-Haves

- *Copier capacity.* A business that averages 10,000 copies per month would be best served by purchasing a 35-CPM (copies per minute) copier.

- *Document feeder.* The quantity of original pages that can be fed automatically into the copier varies from model to model. Companies that handle long documents on a regular basis need a large document feeder capacity.

Nice-to-Haves

- *Sorter* (a series of output bins that separate completed copy sheets). The cost of the sorter and the number of pages each sorter bin holds will vary.

- *Double-sided copy capability* (from single-sided or two-sided originals). Some smaller machines don't offer this capability. Midvolume machines with this feature suffer some loss of machine speed when making two-sided copies. How much each machine's speed drops varies.

- *Automatic stapler* (staples the copies that are output). The number of pages that can be stapled varies.

- *Paper supply.* The amount of paper stored varies from one machine to the next. Also, the number of paper trays can vary. Two trays are better than one because the copier can continue to operate while reloading paper.

- *Reduction/Enlargement.* Where this feature is available, the percentage of reduction and enlargement can vary.
- *First copy time.* The amount of time someone must wait for the copier to generate its first copy varies.
- *Photo mode.* This feature enhances the reproduction quality of photographs.
- *Account codes.* Inputting codes allows the number of copies per user to be tracked.
- *Price range.* Copier prices vary, depending on the configuration of individual units.
- *Service capability.* Everyone offers service, but the quality of service varies.
- *Service cost.* In the 35-CPM market, the cost of service varies between $.010 and $.015 per copy, per month.

How does your copier compare to other models available in the marketplace? In Figure 5.1, your 35-CPM copier is compared to other 35-CPM machines. For each criterion listed, your product has one of these designations:

SS	Significantly superior
S	Superior
A	Average
BA	Below average
SBA	Significantly below average

The market assessment shown is based on your typical must-have and nice-to-have criteria. For the 35-CPM mid-range copier market, your assessment rates your product against all other market alternatives.

Criteria that are significantly superior (SS) or superior (S) are your product's and/or your company's marketplace strengths. Any criteria that you designated below average (BA) or significantly below average (SBA) are your marketplace weaknesses.

Remember that each customer has individual needs and, therefore, each customer's must-haves and nice-to-haves will vary. Customer A may consider automatic double-sided copy capability an essential requirement, thereby making it a must-have. Customer B, who only occasionally makes two-sided copies, may consider two-sided copying simply a nice-to-have.

Figure 5.1   Sample Market Assessment Form

Typical Must-Haves	Your Product's Rating (SS, S, A, BA, SBA)
10,000 copies per month, 35 copies per minute.	Average (A)
50-sheet document feeder	Average (A)

Nice-to-Haves	Your Product's Rating (SS, S, A, BA, SBA)
Sorter	Average (A). You offer two sorters. Your large sorter has 20 bins, each of which can hold up to 50 sheets of paper. Your small sorter has 10 bins, each of which can handle 30 sheets of paper. Most of your competitors offer similar options.
Double-sided copy capability	Superior (S). Your machine produces double-sided copies in 90+ percent of normal machine speed. Other machines vary between 60 percent and 90+ percent.
Automatic stapler/sorter (Option 1) is compatible with your large sorter (20 paper bins, each holding 50 sheets of paper).	Significantly below average (SBA). Your stapler can't staple more than 25 sheets of paper. Many other competitors' staplers can staple up to 50 sheets. The cost of your stapler is also high, at $1,400. Other automatic staplers vary between $600 and $1,500.
Automatic stapler/sorter (Option 2) is compatible with your small sorter (10 paper bins, each holding 30 sheets of paper).	Significantly superior (SS). Your competitors do not offer automatic stapling capability on their smaller sorters. Your small-sorter stapler is capable of stapling up to 15 sheets.
Paper supply	Superior (S). You offer two paper trays as standard equipment, one with 250 sheets, another with 1,300 sheets. Many competitors offer 1,000 sheets or less, and some offer only one paper tray.
Reduction/Enlargement	Average (A). Your machine offers 50 percent to 200 percent reduction/enlargement range, a variance matched by many competitors.
First copy time	Average (A). Your time is four seconds. Most machines vary between three and five seconds.
Photo mode	Average (A). Most of your competitors have photo mode.

(Continued)

Figure 5.1   Continued

Nice-to-Haves	Your Product's Rating (SS, S, A, BA, SBA)
Account codes	Superior (S). You offer up to 100 account codes. Most of your competitors offer 50 or less. Some competitors do not have this capability at all.
Purchase price for a typical 35-CPM copier configuration, including double-sided copying, large sorter, and a 1,000-sheet paper supply.	Average (A). Your list price is $11,586. Competitors vary between $11,500 and $13,000, but they are eager to discount to match your price, resulting in little or no price differentiation.
Service capability	Significantly superior (SS). You have a highly competent service staff that responds quickly to customer problems. You offer the industry's most comprehensive total satisfaction guarantee: if for any reason your customer is not satisfied within the first three years of ownership, you will replace the customer's machine, no questions asked. You offer a twenty-four-hour service help line and a seven-year parts guarantee. Also, if your customer's machine is down for more than eight hours, your company provides a free loaner.
Service contract cost	Below average (BA). A typical customer making 10,000 copies/month pays you $.015 per copy, which is $150 per month. The average cost of your competitors' service contract is $.013, and some are as low as $.010.

In your sales role as Architect, it is your responsibility to identify your buyers' needs, and help your buyers recognize important capabilities that are necessary to get the job done. If your buyers consider your strengths to be important capabilities, you have achieved competitive advantage in the sale.

MARKET ASSESSMENT FORM

Figure 5.2 provides you with a blank market assessment form. Use it to complete your market analyses. To get some practice on your market assessment, think of one customer who recently bought

Figure 5.2   Your Market Assessment Form

Product or Service Being Assessed: _____

Must-Haves	Rating (SS, S, A, BA, SBA)

Nice-to-Haves	Rating (SS, S, A, BA, SBA)

(most important)

(least important)

from you and two prospects with whom you are currently working. Answer the following questions:

1. What are their must-have criteria?
2. How have they ranked their nice-to-haves, from most to least important?

If there is a consensus on the relative importance of certain nice-to-haves, then you can assume that, in general, these capabilities are going to be an important part of your sale. Write them down first, then follow them with less important criteria. After you have recorded and ranked typical must-haves and nice-to-haves, rate your product or service (SS, S, A, BA, SBA) in the rating column on the right-hand side of the form.

In my sales training seminars, I have found that many participants find it much easier to identify the criteria of customers who recently purchased their product or service than to list criteria for a prospect with whom they are currently talking. If you experience this same difficulty, consider it a sign that you have not been placing enough emphasis on the identification of buying criteria *during the buying process*. You should be very familiar with a prospect's buying criteria before a sale is made.

Low-Cost Competitors

I work with several clients that are experiencing intensifying competition from new, low-cost competitors. In some cases, these market entrants offer a competing alternative for *less than half* the price of my clients' product or service.

If you are experiencing similar difficulties, produce a second market assessment: Your offering versus low-cost alternatives. What do you provide your customers that low-cost alternatives do not? Next, ask yourself, "What problems would my customers be likely to experience if they were to choose a low cost-competitor?" In your role as an Architect, help your prospects to understand how serious these problems could be, and how your solution has been specifically designed to solve them.

When doing so, be careful not to mention these competitors directly. Remember, at this phase, competitors aren't yet involved. How do you do this? Perhaps your company offered an earlier version of your product that had problems similar to those that your competitors' offerings have now. If so, discuss the problems your customers had in the past with your older product, and how your new product has been improved to resolve these weaknesses. It's OK to cut yourself down, but unprofessional to speak ill of your competition.

CREATE THE BEST MATCH BETWEEN YOUR STRENGTHS AND YOUR BUYERS' CRITERIA

In your role as Architect of your buyers' best solutions, your job is to create the best match possible between your offering and your prospects' must-haves and nice-to-haves. There are two primary ways for you to do this:

1. Persuade your buyers to rank their buying criteria differently.
2. Change your solution to better match your prospects' buying criteria.

Reevaluating the Buying Criteria

How can you persuade your buyers to change their priorities? Either build up the importance of your strengths or diminish the importance of your weaknesses.

How to Escalate the Importance of Criteria in Which You Are Superior

Once you have identified your prospects' must-haves and nice-to-haves, you should emphasize the importance of criteria in which your product or service is superior. You want to help your prospects recognize the value of these criteria, especially if they represent an advantage you have over your competition.

Continuing with our copier example, you have a significantly superior (SS) service capability. To help your prospects recognize the value of your service support, you may ask questions such as, "You mentioned your current copier has been breaking down more frequently. What types of difficulties does that create?" Because you offer a free loaner after just eight hours of downtime, you might ask, "How often has your machine been down for more than eight hours?" In this way, you help your prospects to recognize the pain

of poor service and extended downtime. Notice that you don't simply tell the prospects the importance of these capabilities. Telling is
not selling. Instead, you ask questions so that the prospects come to
this conclusion unaided.

How to Diminish the Importance of Nice-to-Haves in Which You Are Weak

Don't put emphasis on nice-to-haves where you may be weak. Your
copier's Option 1 automatic stapler is significantly below average
(SBA). On the other hand, your Option 2 stapler is significantly superior (SS). You must be careful here. Depending on your buyers' preference, the pendulum could swing either in your favor or against you.
At this stage of the buying process, it's best to emphasize the importance of capabilities where you have a distinct advantage. In the next
chapter, we will take a close look at how to deal with weaknesses that
your buyers consider important.

Change Your Solution to Better Match Your Buyers' Criteria

Another way of matching your solution to your prospects' buying
criteria is to adjust your solution. Perhaps you can supply your
prospects with a stand-alone automatic stapler to make up for
your weakness in Option 1.

Adjusting your solution requires your creativity as a sales Architect. First, identify the desired result for a criterion that you can't
meet. Just ask, "What are you trying to accomplish?" Then, generate
a list of alternative ways that you can achieve that result. Creativity
is your tool for solving difficult design problems. Let's take a closer
look at the talent called creativity.

CREATIVITY IN SELLING

Creativity in selling means understanding your prospects' unique
problems and needs, then generating innovative ideas about how
those needs can best be met. In designing unique solutions, you
must anticipate clients' potential problems, then create innovative
solutions that will prevent those problems from occurring.

There are several reasons why creativity is vitally important
for salespeople. Just as no two people are alike, so no two customers

are alike. Unique customer needs require unique solutions. Your ability to customize your solution to the unique needs of each customer requires creative thinking skills.

If you commit to becoming creative, you will have a sustainable competitive advantage because your competitors won't know how you did what you did. Five years ago, the chances were that you could sustain a unique product capability for two or three years. Today, your competition can respond much faster because technology has shortened product development time. The Information Age has made product advantages much more difficult to sustain. However, your creativity at the point of sale can't be copied; it's an intangible. Through creativity, you generate "value-added" ideas that help your customers achieve their goals.

Creativity means doing for the customer what the customer can't do alone. By being creative, you can become "partners" with your key accounts by elevating your relationship to a new level of mutual trust and interdependence. The 80/20 rule says that 80 percent of your business comes from 20 percent of your customers, so the more value you add for your key customers, the more they will be willing to pay for your services. Your customers would rather deal with one salesperson who generates new ideas that help them grow than with ten salespeople who "hit and run," on their way to the next prospect.

Why Many Salespeople Have Difficulty Being Creative

For years, salespeople have been told that the key to selling is to "think fast on your feet" and to make lots of calls. This bias for quick thinking and a high activity level is exactly the *opposite* of what it takes to be a creative thinker. The key to creativity is to think slowly and to focus your concentration on a single issue. Highly creative people are not necessarily more intelligent than less creative people; they just take longer to study problems. To be concentrated means to focus completely on one aspect of a problem, not thinking of the next task to be done.

Some corporate salespeople have difficulty being creative because they think that creativity is the responsibility of their company's marketing department. The reality today is that the U.S. economy is a bundle of regional marketplaces, each with its unique challenges, workforces, and industry types. Marketing departments deal on a macroeconomic scale, but your sales territory is a microeconomy in itself. You simply can't rely on your marketing department to create innovative ideas that meet the needs of your customers. See yourself as the president of your own personal services corporation. The solution is local creativity, which is creativity directed at your customers by the person who knows them best—YOU!

Salespeople who have been trained to be self-focused will have difficulty being creative because they are too busy thinking about themselves. The key to being creative is to imagine that you sell your prospects' products or services. If a prospect sells financial services, *you* sell financial services. If a prospect sells insurance services, *you* sell insurance services. If a prospect sells consumer products, *you* sell consumer products. When you focus your concentration on growing a prospect's business as if it were your own, you will astound yourself with the number of your creative ideas.

Still another reason some salespeople have difficulty being creative is their self-limiting belief that they can't be creative. They identify creativity with artists, not salespeople. Study after study has found that creativity is a skill that can be learned. So, let's learn how to be creative.

How to Be Creative

Stop! Just for a little while, stop being a driver, which is being next-task-focused. Shift your mental gears into neutral and set your psychological parking brake. Go "into the silence" and focus your mind on a single issue. Assume there is a better way, and search for alternatives.

Brad sells office supplies—including toner cartridges, diskettes, and file folders—to corporate customers. A large bank in his territory wanted to purchase supplies for the lowest possible price, so they sent nearly every item they purchase "out for bid." Brad felt there had to be a better way besides simply responding to each bid, winning some and losing others, so he made a list of all possible alternatives. The right choice turned out to be the creation of a "Personalized Cost Containment Catalog." Instead of the bank's office managers getting multiple choices of all items—for example, six different types of file cabinets—he proposed that the bank choose one item in each category, which would enable Brad to offer larger quantity discounts on each item. Brad approached the bank's Vice President of Office Services with his idea. Besides saving the bank money, Brad's offer meant office managers wouldn't waste time evaluating multiple choices, and the purchasing department would have less paperwork. The benefit to Brad was winning 100 percent of the bank's business. Brad assumed there was a better way to meet the buyer's need for a lower price, and he searched for alternatives besides those that were obvious.

By Focusing on Quantity, Quality Will Follow

If you generate a high quantity of alternatives, some are bound to be high-quality choices. Begin by phrasing your challenge in the form of a question, such as, "How can our product be reconfigured to meet Client XYZ's needs?" Then list *at least* twenty possible answers. The first ten answers will be easy, the last ten will not. You may have to stretch your imagination, but that's when the most innovative ideas will materialize.

Look for New Ideas in Random Events

Many great discoveries have been made by people who looked for new ideas in seemingly unrelated events. Consider the example of Levi Strauss, a dry goods salesman during the California Gold Rush of the 1850s. One of Strauss's products was heavy canvas fabric, which he attempted to sell to miners for use as tents. Strauss was able to sell all his goods, except this fabric. Apparently, the "49ers" were not interested in shelter. Then, during a chance encounter with a miner in a San Francisco bar, Strauss learned that mining was very hard on pants. Looking for a way to dispose of his remaining inventory, Strauss invented Levi's jeans. Today, Levi Strauss is a $6 billion company. Strauss's story is an example of serendipity—an aptitude for making fortunate discoveries accidentally. The key is to be aware and look for new ideas in random events.

Turn a problem into an opportunity to improve your value to others. This book would not have been written were it not for a big "problem" in my professional life. I had a contract with a large corporate client to train several hundred salespeople—a contract that would require four months of continuous work. Suddenly, just a few days before the first training class, a new executive suddenly stepped in and pulled the plug. Once the shock wore off, I realized I had a four-month gap in my schedule, in a business that schedules three to six months in advance. Finding another client immediately just wasn't going to happen. I was looking at losing three months of productive time. Instead, I asked, "How can I turn this great loss into an even greater opportunity?" My wife suggested that I write a book, and the following day I began to write what you are now reading. This experience has proven to me that the bigger the problem you have, the greater the opportunity that lies beneath it. These great opportunities, however, almost always appear in disguise, so you must *search* for them. What perplexing problem are you facing right now that you can turn into a greater opportunity?

As an Architect, think of yourself as a designer of the future. Believe you are creative, generate a high quantity of new ideas, and commit to putting the best ones into effect.

Every human being has within himself or herself the capability to be creative. Creativity is like a dormant muscle; it's there waiting to be exercised. The more it's used, the stronger it gets. Creativity is like selling; if you make the effort, the results will follow.

EVALUATING YOUR BUYERS' LEVEL OF EXPERIENCE

The knowledge and experience that your prospects have with regard to your product are major factors influencing how and when they identify buying criteria. Prospects who are more product-knowledgeable tend to have more preexisting criteria than prospects who are less product-knowledgeable. The more knowledge your prospects have, the more specific their preexisting criteria will be when you meet with them.

If you were to rate your prospects' product knowledge/experience, you would find that some prospects deserve a beginner rating, some are intermediate, and some are expert. Your ability to influence the buying criteria depends on your prospects' knowledge and experience. Generally, the more knowledgeable your prospects are, the better defined their criteria are, and the less likely they are to be influenced by you.

- *Beginner* prospects have little or no experience with your product and therefore will have few criteria established before they reach Step 3 (Research). Joe Petrone, author of *Building the High Performance Sales Force,* began his sales career selling computerized scientific measuring equipment to corporate research laboratories. Beginner prospects that Joe sold to were people who used the equipment to run a few specific tests.

These prospects lacked in-depth knowledge of the equipment and needed to learn a great deal from Joe in order to identify their buying criteria.

- *Intermediate* prospects have some knowledge and experience about certain aspects of a purchase and usually have some criteria already established when they enter Step 3 (Research). Joe's intermediate prospects were users who needed more from the equipment than simple tests. One of Joe's customers, Kodak, used his equipment when there was a contamination during the production of film. These users were interested in more than a hard-copy printout. They wanted to adjust the equipment's sensitivity and isolate the contaminant.

- *Expert* buyers know almost as much, and sometimes more, about your product than you do. For Joe, the expert was a research chemist who stripped down his product into its component parts, then wanted to rebuild it into something new. Experts want to talk to your technical people in order to integrate your product or service with another "state-of-the-art" system they have recently installed. Expert buyers may have buying criteria you have never heard of before.

The Importance of Specialized Knowledge

Your ability to influence your prospects' buying criteria is directly dependent on how much more you know than your buyers do. Therefore, it is vitally important that you be an expert in your field. This means you must acquire knowledge of your customers' businesses, your product and service applications, your competition, your customers' competition, and so on. You also need to acquire advanced selling skills to use all this expertise persuasively. Your knowledge is the source of your competitive advantage, and the *faster* you gain that knowledge, the greater your advantage will be.

In the past, all you may have had to do was show a buyer how your product worked and process the order. In the future, salespeople will be more involved with integrating their product or service in the workplace and understanding how it interfaces with other systems. Your applications knowledge is becoming increasingly valuable.

Suppose a businessperson wants to buy a PC. He or she can shop price, buy individual components, and build a custom-made system. The alternative is to buy a system that you integrate. The customer will spend more money buying your system and having you integrate it, but the time saved can be put back into what he or she does best—what a business would call the "core" business.

In our information society, knowledge becomes obsolete at a faster and faster rate. This means that you must increase your speed of learning just to keep up. In 1993, Motorola provided every employee at least 40 hours of classroom training per year. Finding that 40 hours was not enough, Motorola announced in 1994 that training of all employees would be dramatically increased, to perhaps 160 hours of training each year by the year 2000. Motorola believes that the business battles of the future will be won with responsiveness, adaptability, and creativity. By investing $600 million a year in training, Motorola expects to provide the tools its employees need to compete and win. The future will belong to the knowledgeable— those individuals who commit themselves to becoming experts in their field.

In your sales role as Architect, your goal is to create unique solutions that meet your customers' needs. The solutions you design for your customers should include certain buying criteria that are competitive advantages for you. Then, when your prospects begin to shop in Step 4 (Comparison), the buying criteria will include unique capabilities available only from you. The result will be a customer-focused solution that locks out your competition.

6

Sales Role #4: THE COACH

Defeat Your Competition Without Slashing Price

> If you know the enemy and you know yourself, you need
> not fear the result of a hundred battles. If you know
> yourself but not the enemy, for every victory gained, you
> will also suffer a defeat. If you know neither the enemy
> nor yourself, you will succumb in every battle.
>
> Sun Tzu
> *The Art of War*, 500 B.C.

Is your industry becoming more competitive? Are your prospects taking a closer look at what your competitors have to offer? Are new, low-price competitors stealing important customers away? It's difficult when your prospects tell you, "Your price is too high," and your boss tells you, "You're practically giving it away!" This is perhaps the most challenging problem salespeople wrestle with today: how to defeat the competition without slashing price.

Never before have your competitors been as strong, as fast, or as agile as they are today. Never before have you faced as many *new* competitors as you do today. Yet, as effective as your competitors are today, they will be even more formidable tomorrow.

This trend of intensifying competition complicates your selling process, making it more intricate, difficult, and involved. Given these circumstances, it's dangerous to assume you will remain successful simply by doing the same things that once brought success. Good is no longer good enough. To consistently rise above all others and to win an even greater share of future business, you must master new rules of the game.

Most customers who demand a lower price have not recognized the unique value that your solution offers. If today's customers are to pay more, they must get more. You defeat your competition by getting the best possible match between the strengths of your offering and your customers' needs.

Step 4, Comparison, is the most competitive step of the selling process. Here, you will put into play all you have learned about your own product or service and the entire "package of value" you provide, your buyers' needs, and what the competition is offering.

PLAN, DON'T PUSH

Many salespeople get overeager during Step 4—a potentially fatal mistake. You do not want to lose communication with your prospects just as the competition arrives on the scene. Salespeople who follow the traditional approach to selling sell too fast. They thoroughly describe their product or service, only to lose touch with buyers just as the competition becomes involved. Sometimes this "sell too fast" problem is exacerbated by salespeople who mistake the prospects' first request for a price quote as a buying signal. When we discussed your Doctor sales role, we saw that a prospect first wonders "How much is your solution?" during Step 2, Discontent. The prospect's purpose is to balance the seriousness of the problem against the cost of resolving it, to determine whether a NEED exists. Salespeople who mistake this request for price as a buying signal may assume their buyer is further along in the buying process than is actually the case.

If you "spill the beans" by providing prospects with all the information they need in Step 3 (Research), there will be no compelling reason for the prospects to continue discussions. By carefully pacing how much information you deliver, you'll stay in touch with your customers at this vitally important juncture.

In today's saturated marketplace, the key is to *expect* that your competition will be involved in every sale, and to plan accordingly. Delay the delivery of your sales presentation by devoting more time to asking questions. If you adopt the Doctor and Architect sales roles and delay your formal presentation until the end of Step

4 (Comparison), you will keep in close communication with your prospects during all of Step 4, the most competitive portion of the buy-*learning* process.

WHY MANY SALESPEOPLE HAVE DIFFICULTY IN COMPETITIVE SELLING SITUATIONS

There are several reasons why so many salespeople have difficulty in competitive selling situations.

- *Many salespeople don't know how to handle competitive selling because little information is available on competitive selling skills.* Surprising as it may seem, virtually nothing has been written on the subject. If you have ten sales books on your bookshelf, chances are that none of them addresses competitive selling skills.

- *Some salespeople can't sell against the competition because they know about just one thing: their product.* To sell against competitors, you must understand not only what the competition is offering, but also what your customers need. Salespeople who lack in-depth knowledge of their customers are unable to distinguish themselves from their competition. Salespeople who haven't studied their customers will have nothing to talk about except themselves! Too much time is then spent talking about what the salespeople do have knowledge of, their own products. Not enough time is devoted to important customer needs. Customers don't buy products and services, they buy the results that products and services bring about. To truly understand what those results will be, you must have knowledge of your customers.

  In your Student sales role, you learned how to carefully study your prospects. For salespeople selling to business buyers, this means focusing on prospects' core business processes and key success factors. The knowledge you gained, and what you did with it in your Doctor and Architect roles, is what creates the difference between needs-based selling—identifying customers' problems and providing unique value-added solutions—and price slashing. The more information you have about your customers, the more value you are capable of adding, and the greater your edge over your competition.

- *Some salespeople lose out in competitive selling situations because they overlook minor differences between themselves and their competition.* What matters is not what the salesperson thinks is important, but what the customer thinks is important. For example, Dictaphone Corporation is the world leader in Emergency 911 Center voice recording systems. One small difference between Dictaphone and some of its competitors is that Dictaphone's recording system has been approved by Underwriters Laboratories, Inc. (U.L.). Little was made of this until one diligent salesperson carefully studied his prospect's cost components and discovered that installation of a U.L.-approved product would qualify a 911 center for a significant reduction in insurance premiums. This translated into a huge cost savings for the customer. Through customer-focused questioning, the salesperson matched a strength to an important customer need, giving him the advantage over the competition. Don't overlook anything! Differences that seem minor to you may be of significant importance to your customer.

- *To sell competitively, you need to prepare a game plan; that is, prepare well ahead.* As a sales manager and sales training consultant, I have personally observed over 500 salespeople selling in the field, face-to-face with customers. The first time I worked with them, perhaps half of these salespeople put little or no effort into preparation for a sales call. Your competition is making your selling process longer and more complex, so you must slow down and *think*. Take a few minutes to break down your offering into its component parts, compare it to that of your competition, and carefully analyze the situation to gain competitive advantage. (We'll discuss more about how to do this later in this chapter.)

Competitive selling is unavoidable, and you need to be able to handle the heat. On the other hand, certain scenarios make it almost impossible to beat the competition without cutting price. It makes sense to avoid simple price-war situations. To do this, focus on your prospects' needs.

In general, the higher up in an organization your customer contact is, the less competition there is. Most vice presidents don't have time to meet with six or seven vendors, but purchasing agents do. By using a solid sales approach from the start, that is, by applying the

Student techniques in Step 1 (Change) and calling on prospects whose primary concern is something other than price, you will reduce the number of competitors you face in Step 4, Comparison.

YOUR CUSTOMERS' FOURTH STEP: COMPARISON

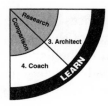

Today's buyers want to ensure that the best choice is made. Once buyers have completed Step 3, Research, they shop around. Of the eight steps of a sale, Step 4, Comparison, has the most competitive activity. When your buyers have arrived at Step 4, you may hear them say something like, "What's unique about your product/service?" or "Why should I choose you?" If you sell to businesses, your prospects may send out a Request for Proposal or ask you to make a formal presentation.

For your buyers, Step 4 of the buy-*learning* process consists of four activities:

1. Consider only options with must-have capabilities.
2. Request presentations.
3. Identify additional nice-to-haves in each option.
4. Identify a preference.

Consider Only Options with Must-Have Capabilities

Early in Step 4 (Comparison), your prospects will undoubtedly contact various suppliers. Options that do not meet the must-have capabilities are easily and quickly eliminated, thereby simplifying (at least somewhat) a complex decision.

Because one must-have criterion is usually price, all options being considered usually fall within an acceptable "price range." For this reason, price often disappears (temporarily) as an issue during the Comparison step. Instead, the buyers' focus is on identifying differences between alternatives in areas other than price. If the buyers fail to recognize a significant difference between acceptable alternatives, their buying decision will be based on the most obvious difference: lowest price.

Request Presentations

Next, your prospects will carefully evaluate different options by requesting presentations, or at least a clear description of your solution. The buyers' primary question is "What is the best choice?"

Identify Additional Nice-to-Haves in Each Option

As potential solutions are examined, additional differences between alternatives are identified. Buyers often perceive some of these differences as important. When nice-to-haves are added to the list, the customers' buying criteria change. As we have already discussed, nice-to-haves play a significant role in a buying decision.

Identify a Preference

Step 4 (Comparison) concludes when buyers identify their preferred option—perhaps yours.

SALES ROLE #4: THE COACH

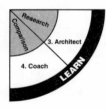

The Customer-Focused Selling role for the prospect's Step 4 (Comparison) is **Coach.** A coach's primary objective is to defeat the competition. A salesperson's objective in the Coach sales role is to defeat the competition without slashing price. A coach gains competitive advantage through analysis and insight, then executes a winning game plan on the playing field.

THE COACH'S THREE-STEP PROCESS FOR VICTORY

Imagine that you are a football coach preparing for a game next weekend. The steps you would take to win are:

1. Analyze your strengths and weaknesses in comparison to those of your competitors.
2. Develop a game plan to positively position yourself against the competition.

3. Demonstrate your superiority on the playing field with a great sales proposal and presentation.

1. Analyze Your Strengths and Weaknesses in Comparison to Those of Your Competitors

By the time a football coach begins to prepare to meet a specific opponent, he has already analyzed the strengths and weaknesses of his own team. To prepare for an upcoming contest, a football coach will analyze game films of the opposing team in action. The coach breaks down the opposing team position by position, identifying the players' strengths and weaknesses and comparing them with those of his own players. In the process of this competitive analysis, the coach identifies his opponents' tendencies or inclinations to move or act in a particular way in a certain set of circumstances. For instance, a competitor may tend to run the ball on first down and throw a pass on second down. By identifying tendencies, the coach attempts to predict what the competition will do *before* the competition actually does it.

How to Scout Your Opponents

In football, it's easy to determine who your competition is, but competing sellers don't have colored jerseys and large numbers on their backs. How can you identify the sellers you are up against? One way is to simply ask your prospects. Another is to ask someone on the inside, who has information. Still another is to pay close attention to your prospects' objections. At this stage of the sale, objections are often echoes of things a competitor has said about you. Street-smart salespeople are sensitive to these objections. They not only indicate who your competitors are, but often signal to you what your competitors' selling strategies are.

Another difference between football and selling is that your competitors don't have game films; even if they did, they wouldn't let you see them. So, how can you scout your competitors?

First, look at their advertisements and sales brochures. Write down in great detail their selling points. Call buyers who bought from your competitors and ask them what factors were crucial in their decision. Talk to your customers—those who evaluated your competition but bought from you—to find out why you were chosen. Are any of your company's salespeople recent defectors from competitors? If so, get them involved in your analysis. Write down the most common objections you hear regarding your product, and determine which of them are caused by competitors. Create a list of the selling points your competitors emphasize against you. These selling points are your competitors' *tendencies.*

The Competitive Analysis

As an Architect of selling during buyers' Step 3 (Research), you identified typical buying criteria by conducting a market assessment (see Figure 5.2). You used a market assessment form to measure your strengths and weaknesses against the marketplace *in general,* because buyers' Step 3 (Research) usually occurs *before* competition is involved. You then influenced your prospects' criteria to include your unique strengths. These criteria are the standards against which suppliers will be measured during Step 4 (Comparison).

Now, as a Coach, you will find out what your direct opponents are offering and use these same criteria to identify their strengths and weaknesses. I call this activity a **competitive analysis.** For simplicity, let's return to the copy machine example we used in Chapter 5. Remember that all must-have criteria are essential and that nice-to-haves, though important, are not.

Must-Haves

- Copier capacity.
- Document feeder.

Nice-To-Haves

(most important)

- Sorter.
- Automatic double-sided copy capability.
- Automatic stapler/sorter.
- Service capability.
- Price range.
- Service contract cost.
- Paper supply.
- Reduction/Enlargement.
- First copy time.

- Photo mode.
- Account codes.

(least important)

In looking at this list, you will notice that the buying criterion "service capability" has moved up in importance. Your customer doesn't divide service quality and product attributes into separate lists; these are all simply factors that influence this customer's decision. Service is an important issue—almost as important as an automatic stapler/sorter. Because the customer mentally considers one list consisting of both product and service differences, so too should you.

Now, compare your competitor(s) for fulfillment of each criterion, ranking them as: significantly superior (SS), superior (S), average (A), below average (BA), or significantly below average (SBA). Figure 6.1 shows how your analysis might look.

What You Learn from a Competitive Analysis

You must find out who your true competitor is. In football, it's easy to identify your competition: your opponents are listed on the season schedule. Selling is different. Several suppliers may be striving for the same sale. You want to make the most of the precious selling time you spend with each prospect. By identifying who your leading competitor is, you can focus your strategy on the specific competitor who threatens you the most.

The right-hand column of Figure 6.1 reveals that the number-one copy machine competitor is Competitor B because it is stronger than Competitor A in the more important buying criteria (automatic stapler/sorter and double-sided copy capability). Therefore, you must focus your game plan on Competitor B.

If competing alternatives are judged by a buyer as equal with regard to a certain capability, then the decision maker will shift focus to other criteria—the remaining differences between alternatives that are considered important. In our example, all three suppliers are judged as having equal sorters, so the sorter, as a decision criterion, now goes away. This feature is still important to the buyer, but it doesn't help the buyer make the right choice. Instead, the buyer shifts focus to differences between alternatives that are considered important. The differences that you must build your game

Figure 6.1   Competitive Analysis

Prospect: _____   Product or Service Offered: _____

Must-Haves	You	Competitor A	Competitor B	Advantage to
10,000 copies per month, 35 copies/minute.	Average (A).	Average (A).	Average (A).	—
Document feeder.	Average (A).	Average (A).	Average (A).	—

Nice-to-Haves	You	Competitor A	Competitor B	Advantage to
Sorter.	Average (A).	Average (A).	Average (A).	—
Double-sided copy capability.	Superior (S). Double-sided copies produced in 90+ percent of normal speed.	Below average (BA). Double-sided copies produced in 70+ percent of normal speed.	Average (A). Double-sided copies produced in 80+ percent of normal speed.	You.
Large automatic stapler/sorter (20 bins/50 sheets per bin).	Significantly below average (SBA). Your stapler only staples 25 sheets, yet costs $1,400.	Average (A). Staples 50 sheets of paper, and costs $1,100.	Superior (S). Staples 50 sheets of paper, and only costs $750.	Competitor B.
Service capability.	Significantly superior (SS). Competent staff responds quickly. "Total Satisfaction Guarantee" is best in the industry. Free loaner after eight hours of downtime.	Average (A). Good response time, but no guarantee of "lemon" machine replacement. Loaner after two days of downtime.	Average (A). Good response time, but no guarantee of "lemon" machine replacement. Loaner after two days of downtime.	You.

Figure 6.1   Continued

Nice-to-Haves	You	Competitor A	Competitor B	Advantage to
Purchase price.	$11,586.	$11,795.	$12,250, but vendor is willing to discount.	—
Service contract cost.	Below average (BA). $.015 per copy, per month.	Superior (S). $.010 per copy, per month.	Average (A). $.012 per copy, per month.	Competitor A.
Paper supply.	Superior (S). You offer two paper trays as standard equipment, one with 250 sheets, another with 1,300 sheets.	Average (A). One paper tray with 500 sheets, extra trays are $750 each.	Average (A). Two trays standard, one with 250 sheets, the other with 500 sheets. Additional 500 sheet trays are $850.	You.
Reduction/ Enlargement.	Average (A).	Average (A).	Average (A).	—
First copy time.	Average (A).	Superior (S). 3.4 seconds.	Superior (S). 3.2 seconds.	Competitors A and B.
Photo mode.	Average (A).	Average (A).	Average (A).	—
Account codes.	Superior (S). You offer 100 account codes, standard.	Average (A). Offers 50 account codes, maximum.	Significantly below average (SBA). Does not offer account codes.	You.

plan around are the differences between you and Competitor B. Those differences are:

Your Strengths vs. Competitor B	Your Weaknesses vs. Competitor B
Double-sided copy speed	Automatic stapler/sorter
Service capability	Service contract cost
Paper supply	First-copy time
Account codes	

Find More Advantage by Analyzing Intangibles

Don't limit your competitive analysis to a list of product features. Simply comparing your product against a competitor's product is like comparing a quarterback to a single pass defender: it doesn't take into account *all* the positions on the field.

Your objective now is to think "outside the box," to identify additional selling points that have, thus far, gone unnoticed. Remember, big decisions are often made because of small differences. To uncover these additional selling points, look at the entire buying process from your prospect's point of view, including not only your product but also less tangible aspects of your offering. This is your "package of value." Intangible customer/supplier interactions include:

1. Sales satisfaction (satisfying, nonmanipulative sales approach).
2. Ease of order placement/communication/payment.
3. Flexibility to meet rush orders and/or changing needs.
4. Quality of product/service.
5. Delivery (speed, accuracy, and method).
6. Installation (downtime).
7. Training (amount and methods).
8. Ease of operation.
9. Adaptability of product to changing needs.
10. Service responsiveness.
11. Obsolescence and disposal.

Taken together, these factors describe the customer's entire "process of ownership." Separately, each factor represents an opportunity for you. Imagine that each of these eleven factors is a position on a football team. Next, identify the factors of greatest importance to your customer. Then compare yourself to your competitors at each position, and determine potential advantages for you in each high-priority area.

Position 1, sales satisfaction, is becoming an increasingly important buying criterion. In the automotive industry, J. D. Power and Associates conducts extensive surveys to measure customer satisfaction. According to Power, an increasingly important factor affecting customer satisfaction is how competent and accommodating a salesperson was during a transaction. J. David Power, founder and president of the research firm bearing his name, was quoted in *USA Today* as saying, "As quality differences among nameplates become less distinguishable to the consumer, the fight to attract and retain customers is shifting to dealers and their salespeople." What Power calls sales satisfaction is what you call your relationship with the customer—your ability to establish credibility, build trust, identify needs, and present winning solutions.

Position 8, ease of operation, is always an important criterion, because simplicity is something everybody wants. Now, as the demonstration of our copier draws near, ease of use will become an important issue. Remember, though, that ease of use is an intangible. What one person considers easy, another may not. The salesperson whose product or service is considered easiest to operate is usually the salesperson who helps the customer see it as so. Before your presentation, carefully compare your product or service's operation to that of your competitor, then build your case around that.

Thoroughly analyzing yourself in comparison with your competition highlights both your strengths and weaknesses. Now let's turn our attention to the game plan, which is how you use this information to win the sale.

2. Develop a Game Plan to Positively Position Yourself Against the Competition

Once you have completed your competitive analysis, it's time to formulate your game plan. The goal of a game plan is to take advantage of your strengths (double-sided copy speed, service capability, paper supply, and account codes) and diminish the impact of your weaknesses (automatic stapler/sorter, service contract cost, and first copy time). The more effective you are at accomplishing this goal, the stronger your position and the less you will have to discount later.

At this point in the selling process, your prospect is considering many buying criteria, some of which are strengths for you, others of which may be weaknesses. Because your overall competitive position is determined by the sum total of your various strengths and weaknesses, a winning game plan consists of several strategies, not just one. **You need a strategy for each criterion.** Which strategy you choose depends on your relative position. General George Patton, a brilliant strategist, said, "Make your plan fit the circumstances, not the opposite." If the circumstances of one criterion are different from those of another, two different strategies are required.

In the following sections are several strategies for you to choose from when formulating your game plan. Some readers may find a few of these strategies to be too involved or too complicated for their typical selling situations. That's OK. The extent to which you apply any strategy should be determined by the complexity of your prospect's buy-*learning* process. The more complex your prospect's buying process, the more complex the sales strategy necessary to win. One goal of this book is to help you become more effective in the most difficult selling situations you face. Salespeople whose most difficult selling situations are complex will probably find all of these strategies helpful.

How to Take Advantage of Your Strengths

Always aim to match your strengths with your prospects' needs. If a prospect's most important nice-to-haves complement your strengths, you have established a formidable competitive position. Frequently, however, this is not the case. To take greater advantage of your strengths, you can choose from the following sales strategies.

Bolster Your Strengths.   In our copy machine competitive analysis (Figure 6.1), "double-sided copy speed" represents a competitive strength and "large automatic stapler/sorter" represents a weakness. Some salespeople mistakenly ignore their own competitive strengths (in this case, double-sided copy speed), choosing instead to focus all time and attention on damage control for criteria that represent weaknesses (here, the stapler/sorter). If you ignore your own competitive strengths, they may actually become less important to a buyer. To bolster the importance of a criterion where you have an advantage, ask your prospect, "Why is that important to you?" When your buyer tells you why a certain criterion is important, reinforcement of the importance of it occurs in his or her own mind.

Another reason to play up your competitive strengths is that your prospect may assign them more importance than during the initial product comparison. If, for instance, your buyer moves "account codes" (a strength of yours) up the list, you have improved your chances of winning the sale.

The examples above describe how a salesperson can bolster the strength of a *product*. You can use this same strategy to bolster the strength of your *company*, by emphasizing to the customer that

buying from the right *company* should be an important consideration. If you sell for an industry leader, you are probably experiencing increasing competition from new, low-cost providers. These
providers can copy your product (known as *benchmarking*), but they
can't copy the resources of your company. By bolstering the strength
of your company, perhaps by emphasizing your depth of resources
or your low-risk position, you shift the customer's focus to an issue
that is one of your advantages.

As a district sales manager for Lanier Worldwide from 1984 to
1989, I was responsible for sales and service of Lanier dictation
equipment and business telephone systems in San Diego. Our telephone system product line was manufactured by Toshiba, relabeled
with the Lanier name. Dozens of smaller business telephone suppliers also operated in the San Diego market, at least six of whom also
sold Toshiba telephone systems. These competitors sold the same
product as we did, yet charged 25 to 35 percent less.

To sell effectively against these competitors, we focused on the
resources of our company. With sixty district offices nationwide,
spare parts were, at most, one phone call away. Many of our competitors offered telephone systems produced by several different manufacturers, so we emphasized to the customer that our company sold
and serviced Toshiba equipment exclusively. This meant that many of
our parts in stock were interchangeable, and our technicians had to
learn only one system. Our company offered "in-house financing,"
which meant that if a customer leased a phone system for, say, three
years, each monthly payment was made to Lanier, the same company
responsible for servicing the system. Our low-priced competitors did
not have our depth of resources, so they financed the sale of their
equipment to customers through outside leasing companies. If a customer leased a phone system from Telephone Company A, monthly
lease payments were made to Leasing Company B. Leasing Company
B would pay off Telephone Company A in one lump sum on the day
the customer's phone system was installed. Telephone Company A
was therefore not financially tied to its customers the way we were.
When many of the smaller companies began to exit from the market,
our single-company contact was an important consideration and
helped us sell many more systems.

Study your leading competitor carefully and identify the differences between the two of you and the problems your unique capabilities solve. Then, do as coaches do: craft your game plan based
on these differences.

Add Favorable Criteria to the List.   During your competitive analysis, you may identify additional strengths that your buyer is not, as yet, aware of. Through careful questioning, you may discover a way to add more nice-to-haves to your buyer's list of criteria. In the mid-volume copier market, for instance, some machines offer a new capability called "chapterization." Chapterization enables users to separate each section of a document by ordering the machine to insert different types of paper from one of the alternate paper supply trays. If your copier has chapterization and you are able to develop a need for it, your position is strengthened. How to develop a need for your unique capabilities was described as part of the Architect's role (see p. 111), so be willing to backtrack in your sales process to gain more competitive advantage.

Turn Intangible Strengths into Tangible Ones.   Tangible criteria (such as price) are easily measured and understood by your prospects; intangible criteria (such as quality) are not. For example, with a photocopier, how do you determine what "good quality copies" means? To one prospect, the term might mean "clear background"; to other prospects, it might mean "fine print resolution," or "good solids," or "consistency" (the 1,000th copy looks just like the first).

If more than one individual is involved in the buying decision, there may be confusion regarding the relative importance of intangible criteria. The decision makers may not agree on what each of them means, and if there is a misunderstanding over an intangible criterion, the buying decision will be based on other, more tangible factors. However, when the decision makers focus exclusively on tangible product-oriented criteria, you are more likely to end up in a price war. Therefore, part of your game plan should address how to help your prospects define your intangible strengths in tangible terms so they can be easily explained to others.

Suppose one of your prospects cites "service responsiveness," which happens to be one of your strengths, as a buying criterion. First, ask your prospect, "What does 'service responsiveness' mean to you?" By asking how your prospect will judge service responsiveness, you discover how this criterion will be explained to others.

If your prospect's definition is somewhat lacking, you can then expand it by saying, for example, "You're right, two-hour response time is important. Would a free loaner unit be important as well? In the event your machine was down, what do you feel would be a reasonable time for a loaner machine to be delivered?" (Your service guarantee, the best in the industry, includes a free loaner after eight hours of downtime.)

Your objective must always be to help your prospect see what value will be received for the investment. This represents a total package, "the big picture," the intangible benefits and long-term payoff resulting from your solution.

Link Your Solution to Your Customers' Existing Equipment.   Look carefully at equipment your customers already have in place. Can you link your solution to the equipment better than your competitors can? (This strategy does not apply to copy machines. Copiers are "stand-alone" units that aren't required to integrate with other products.)

All customers prefer to buy products that will be compatible with others to be purchased in the future. For instance, if you need to buy a laptop computer and your desktop computer is an Apple system, chances are you will look only at Apple portables. You can gain an advantage by proving a link between your customers' existing systems or equipment and your offering.

How to Diminish the Impact of Your Weaknesses

The most important strategy for diminishing the significance of your weaknesses is: **Don't challenge the importance of your opponents' strengths,** because if you do, it will have an effect opposite to the one you desire. The criteria at issue will move *up* in importance to your prospect, not *down*.

Suppose a prospect wants a copier with the most rapid first copy time available. If you argue, "You don't need that," how do you think your prospect will respond? First, you'll be given all the reasons why the prospect *does* need this feature, and the desire to have it will intensify. Second, you'll lose credibility because the buyer's needs are being ignored.

Instead, when faced with important buying criteria in areas or features where you are weak, choose one of the following strategies.

Repackage Your Weaknesses.   You can't make all your weaknesses go away. You can, however, diminish their importance by showing how your strengths fill your buyers' needs. With repackaging, you uncover your customers' underlying concept—what they are trying to accomplish with a certain criterion that represents a weakness for you—and then show how certain strengths of your offering help fulfill this concept.

In the copy machine example, the greatest weakness is the *large auto stapler/sorter*. A stapler that is compatible with the 20-bin/50-sheet sorter staples only 25 sheets of paper, which means that on jobs with 26 to 50 sheets of output, the user must staple finished sets by hand. Competitor B's stapler can staple up to 50 sheets.

The repackaging would begin by saying to the prospect, "I understand your concern about our stapler. But, I was wondering, *what are you trying to accomplish?*" Suppose the prospect answers, "I want to complete large copy jobs as quickly as possible, and your stapler will slow me down." Now, look carefully at the competitive analysis sheet (Figure 6.1). Can any other criteria that are strengths be associated with "finishing large copy jobs as quickly as possible?" Yes; two can (see Figure 6.2). First, the *automatic double-sided copy speed* is the fastest available, which means large two-sided copy jobs will be completed faster. Another strength that affects speed on large copy jobs is the 1,550-sheet paper supply. Competitor B offers only 750 sheets standard, and additional 500-sheet trays are $850 each. In addition, many buyers consider four trays a hassle because, when they are making sets, they must constantly check the paper level in each tray. The more trays to check on, the greater the hassle. Repackaging helps the salesperson to better understand the customer's needs, and helps the buyer to better understand how the seller can help toward achieving those needs. Basically, the impact of a weakness is

Figure 6.2 How Repackaging Diminishes the Impact of Your Weaknesses

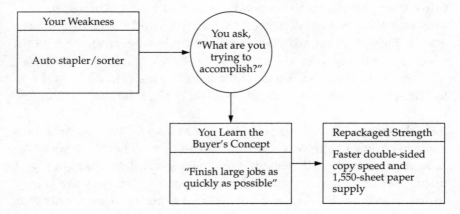

reduced by going around the immediate problem and focusing on other capabilities that meet the same need.

Purchase price is a frequent candidate for repackaging. By asking "What are you trying to accomplish?" you discover the buyer's concept of "lowest cost." You then ask the prospect to consider other factors that affect cost, including adaptability of product to changing needs (longer life expectancy), reliability, absence of downtime during installation, and flexible financing. Purchase price is only one aspect of total cost. So, while you may be higher priced, you can win the sale by proving that you are the lowest cost overall.

To get started on repackaging scenarios, look at the market assessment you created. Select a criterion that you rated yourself as BA (below average) or SBA (significantly below average). Now, on the same page, look at the other criteria that are your strengths. Can any of these strengths be repackaged with your weaknesses?

Correct Your Customers' Misconceptions.   Some customers may wrongly think your product or service is weak in a certain area. They may simply be confused, or your competitors may be saying things about you that aren't true. When this happens, educate your customer about the way things really are. Use customer testimonial letters or expert articles, if available, to reinforce your point.

Look for Weaknesses in Your Competitors' Strengths.   For years, IBM dominated the mainframe computer market. IBM's strength was its tremendous depth of resources and breadth of product line, which allowed application of integrated solutions to any computing problem. IBM's family of computers ran exclusively on IBM operating systems, so a customer who bought an IBM computer was locked in to IBM for years to come. IBM's proprietary product line prevented many smaller competitors from entering the market.

Upstart competitors saw a weakness in IBM's strength. The weakness was that customers didn't like being locked in to IBM, especially when they considered that IBM's computers were not price/performance leaders. These smaller, aggressive firms led the move to "open systems," centering on a nonproprietary operating system called UNIX. The UNIX system is compatible with many different hardware vendors' components. UNIX enabled customers to declare their independence from a single computer hardware vendor. Smaller computer companies could then compete more effectively—they had found a weakness in IBM's strength.

Customers shifted in droves to open systems, and IBM, for a while, suffered huge losses.

"Back to Square One."   This strategy is most applicable when you determine that, based on the customer's current criteria, you cannot win the sale. Your objective is to take the sale "back to square one"—the Need stage—and identify a different, and usually much greater need. This technique is most applicable in a situation where your competitor was the first supplier in the door and the ground rules have been set against you. In this case, you are entering your prospect's buy-*learning* process at Step 4 (Comparison), but going back to Step 1 (Change).

Dave, a senior account executive for BellSouth Business Systems, received a call from the Director of Management Information Systems at a hospital. The call was to request a presentation on one of BellSouth's phone systems. This customer had previously bought many products and services from BellSouth, and was now interested in a new phone system for all hospital rooms and administrative offices. Upon meeting with the customer, Dave was handed a copy of his competitor's bid for a new phone system. The bid contained the Director's buying criteria for a new phone system. They included 55 Direct Inward Dial trunks, 75 analog trunks, a certain number of executive phones with multiple programmable buttons, a certain number of speaker phones and single-line sets. Dave saw that the criteria were generic and primarily product-related. He knew that meeting these criteria point by point would mean a price war with a small local vendor—a war that he knew he couldn't win. Dave chose the "back to square one" strategy.

During the initial meeting with the Director, Dave asked a lot of questions and learned a few interesting things. He discovered that, in addition to a new telephone system, the Director had a few other major system purchases on her "wish list" for the future. She wanted an optical disc storage system, which is a digital system that stores patients' records electronically. She also planned on purchasing a computerized lab system that would allow completed lab reports to be automatically added to a patient's file. Both of these systems, once on-line, would transmit information back and forth to one another via phone lines. Dave told the Director he needed one more appointment before he would be able to bid, and they agreed to meet again the following day.

That night, Dave carefully studied both the customer's criteria and his competitor's bid. Dave noticed that the competitor had bid a low-cost battery back-up system, which, in the event of a power outage, would be unable to sustain the phone system for more than three minutes—not near enough time for most hospitals' needs. Armed with this information, and being careful not to offend the prospect, Dave questioned the hospital's original needs. He sincerely doubted that the solution prescribed by the prospect's buying criteria was broad enough in scope. Dave's case was compelling, and he was successful in raising doubts in the Director's mind that her telephone needs had not been carefully identified.

To properly identify his customer's needs, Dave offered the Director a free consultative survey—what he calls an "information flow analysis." Dave pointed out that the intelligence he would likely uncover would not only help identify the hospital's telephone system needs, but would be beneficial in purchasing an optical storage system and computerized lab system, too. The Director accepted Dave's offer for the survey.

The following day, Dave, with the Director's blessing, began meeting with hospital department heads. These interviews gave him a basic understanding of the hospital's information flow, and allowed him to build credibility with key figures, but Dave wanted to learn more. So, the Director set Dave up with a conference room, and, over the next three days, Dave conducted a series of 30-minute interviews. These interviews turned up many new issues, many of which were unrelated to phone systems, and Dave dutifully noted all points of interest. But still, Dave was not satisfied with his knowledge of the hospital's needs.

During these interviews, Dave came up with another idea. He received approval from the Director and hospital administration to pose as a hospital patient. Dave felt it was important for the hospital's customers' needs to be considered, too. A member of Dave's account team actually wheeled him into the hospital in a wheelchair, and he was admitted as a patient.

While in the hospital, Dave noticed an empty patient room that had just received a hot lunch. The patient had checked out earlier, but the hospital's kitchen had not yet been notified. Further questioning disclosed that when a doctor discharged a patient, a delay in paperwork processing postponed notification to other departments. As a result, the food service, pharmacy, housekeeping, and admissions departments were all unaware that a patient had been discharged. The result: a vacant room, uncleaned, with food in it, while sick patients waited in the emergency room or admissions area. It turned out that the hospital was losing over $80,000 a year to meals and medicine wasted in this way.

Dave had struck pay dirt. He had identified a new, greater need—one that BellSouth's phone system could solve. By dialing a simple two-digit code from the patient's room, a hospital orderly could immediately notify other departments of a patient's status, thereby avoiding paperwork delays.

After completing his needs assessment, Dave delivered his report to the Director and several department heads who, by this time, had become very interested in Dave's findings.

Included in Dave's report were recommendations on new criteria for the phone system. Some of these criteria included a beefed-up uninterrupted power supply. He also recommended a PBX telephone switch that contained "dual online processors," one of his system's unique strengths. Both of these processors are "hot processors," which means that both are performing redundant functions at all times. If one processor fails, the other is already working, so there's absolutely no downtime. Dave also recommended a complete disaster recovery system that would, in the event of a switch-room fire that destroyed both processors, transfer the hospital's telephone switch duties to BellSouth telephone switching equipment located at a nearby central office.

The customer was so impressed with Dave's thorough consultative approach that the plans to go "out for bid" for a new phone system were canceled. The original criteria were thrown out, and Dave was awarded the contract. Dave had won the order because he had demonstrated his enduring commitment to uncovering and meeting his customer's needs.

Keep in mind that "back to square one" is a risky strategy. Many customers are reluctant to start over because it means acknowledging that their buying process has been faulty. To some business buyers, this may be painful politically. As a sales professional, however, your intent with this strategy is positive and customer-focused. You are attempting to determine precisely your customer's real needs. If you present your approach to your prospect in this way, you may be successful (as Dave was) in turning to your advantage a seemingly hopeless selling situation.

Make a Small Sale First.   Suppose you have identified a prospect who has high potential but is currently buying from your competitor. Your first goal should be to make a small sale. Find a small piece of business, preferably in an area where you have a distinct advantage over your entrenched competitor. In this way, once you make the sale, you should be able to defend your position against your competitor's counterattacks. By gaining a foothold in the account, you demonstrate your capability and prove yourself worthy of consideration for much larger sales.

3. Demonstrate Your Superiority on the Playing Field with a Great Sales Proposal and Presentation

If you have applied the Customer-Focused Selling process as described thus far, you should now be in a strong position to win the order. As a Student, you studied your prospect's critical issues. As a Doctor, you uncovered problems and helped your prospect recognize a big need. As an Architect, you translated your prospect's intangible concept into a plan consisting of buying criteria, some of which are your strengths. So far, as a Coach, you have implemented a competitive strategy and influenced your prospect's criteria in a way that matches your strengths to them better than your competitors. It's now time to present your winning solution.

There are two methods for presenting your solution: (1) a written proposal and (2) an oral presentation. Most customers require both and, to save time, want the proposal delivered in conjunction with the presentation. Proposals and presentations should be customized to each prospect's individual needs. Using "boilerplate" for proposals or a "canned pitch" for a sales presentation reduces your credibility and serves as a barrier to winning the emotional trust of your prospect.

In most selling situations, a proposal should be more comprehensive than a verbal presentation. Why? In an oral presentation you know to whom you're talking, so you can tailor your presentation depending on your audience's needs and the time that has been made available. A written proposal, on the other hand, is often passed among several executives, many of whom do not attend your oral presentation but will nevertheless have an impact on the final decision. Because you may have no idea where some of these decision makers are in the buying process, your proposal must address the entire buying process, not just a single slice. In a copy machine sale, for example, the presentation is typically made to an office manager, but there are usually several other decision influencers behind the scenes. A finance executive may examine payment plans; a company president may make the final decision. Your proposal is your sales presentation to these busy executives.

You will want to finish reading this book before you tackle a full-fledged proposal or presentation. In the chapters ahead, we'll examine the remaining steps buyers must take before they can commit to your solution. However, at this point in the Customer-Focused Selling process, you communicate understanding of your customers' needs and demonstrate your capability to meet those needs.

WHAT ABOUT PRICE?

Money is always an issue for buyers, but it varies in importance during the buying process. Prospects are sensitive to price in Step 2 (Discontent), as they balance the seriousness of the problem against the cost of resolving it. The "ballpark" figure you provide your prospects in Step 2 helps them recognize their need to buy. At that point, the importance of price recedes as your buyers attend to other issues. When they enter Step 3 (Research), they are most concerned with learning about the capabilities necessary for a solution. During this learning process, they are attracted by features and benefits of various solutions—and distracted from costs. As D-Day (Decision Day) approaches, particularly if multiple proposals are received from you and your competition with varying prices, price will emerge again as a crucial issue for your customers.

During this decisive time when price is not so important, follow your buyers' lead by focusing not on price but on areas where you can make a difference. In doing so, you are building a case for why your solution is best. Later, when everyone's prices are on the table, your buyer will recognize why your solution is worth more.

As the customer's Step 4 (Comparison) comes to an end, there is a shift in focus from benefits back toward costs. Sometimes this shift causes Step 5 (Fear), a feeling of doubt just prior to commitment.

In anticipation of your buyers' renewed interest in price, now is the time to do your calculations. You may need to add components or change the configuration of your solution to accommodate all the needs you have now identified.

Prospects get emotionally attached to benefits, but then reality sets in. Some customers will ask you, "Exactly how much are we talking about?" Other customers will request a written proposal. At the end of Step 4, you must be ready to give a full accounting of the benefits and costs of your solution. The formal way to do this is with a sales proposal (in writing) and a sales presentation (in person).

WINNING PROPOSALS

A well-written and professional proposal will greatly improve your chances of winning the sale. For many salespeople today, as much as 90 percent of a buy–sell process takes place behind the scenes, without the salesperson being present, as corporate decision makers talk and decide among themselves. Frequently, salespeople are unable to meet some of these decision makers. In situations such as these, your success often hinges on the quality of your proposal.

There are two steps to creating a winning proposal. First, you plan it. Then, you write it. Let's discuss these two steps.

Plan Your Proposal

In planning your proposal, assume that the reader of your proposal is at Step 1 (Change) in the buy-*learning* process. To get approval, the people you have been selling to may have to present your proposal to another individual who has not been involved in your selling process and, therefore, may not recognize a need to buy. By assuming that the reader of your proposal has not been involved in your selling process, you will remember to highlight the importance of your prospect's need.

Talk to your sponsors, those decision makers who want you to succeed. Get their advice on key selling points. They often know the final authority's hot button and how you can push it.

Get Into Your Customer's Head

Answer the following questions before you begin writing your proposal:

1. Why am I writing this proposal?
2. Who will read it?
3. What do they need to know?

4. What questions will they have?

5. What problem(s) do my customers need to solve, and why are these problems serious?

6. How will my solution help solve my customers' problem or achieve their gain?

7. What are my competitive strengths?

8. What are my competitive weaknesses?

9. How will I emphasize my strengths and diminish my weaknesses?

10. If I met my prospect's CEO in the elevator, what would I say?

Proposal Components

Proposals vary in complexity from short one-page letters to comprehensive, sophisticated, booklike documents. Despite these differences, all proposals have certain things in common. Proposals should:

• Communicate your understanding of your clients' needs.
• Describe how your solution meets those needs.
• Prove why you are the best choice.
• Specify the investment required.
• Cost-justify your solution with a profit improvement analysis.
• Detail your delivery and implementation commitment.

Figure 6.3 gives you a checklist to use when outlining multi-page proposals. Shorter two- or three-page proposals, such as those communicated in a letter, can follow the same format, excluding the table of contents and executive summary. Note how the proposal outline matches your prospects' buy-*learning* process.

To keep these outline components in mind, refer to Figure 6.3 often. In your sales role as Coach, you are completing four of the eight sales roles. You've come a long way from your Student role. The elements in the outline make sense and you've begun some creative planning for fleshing out the crucial information you need to prepare your own winning proposals.

A completed, detailed sales proposal, based on the copier example we have been using in these early chapters, appears as an Appendix to this book. When you are informed about all of your sales roles and comfortable with their interrelationships and contributions to

Figure 6.3   Outline and Explanation for a Sales Proposal

1. Cover Letter

2. Table of Contents

3. Executive Summary
This summation of what you have to offer is usually the most important page of the proposal. It is often the only page key executives read. It should convince your prospect to select you and should provide a glimpse of what is to come. Write the executive summary last.

4. Opportunity Analysis

   a. Describe the changes affecting your prospect. You pinpointed these in the Student role.

   b. Show that you understand your prospect's problems and missed opportunities. You diagnosed these in the Doctor role.

   c. Quantify the cost of each problem's consequences, which you learned by asking "complication" questions in the Doctor role.

   d. Describe the financial improvement provided by your solution, as well as the "cost of delay." This is the financial loss that will occur if the decision to buy is delayed.

5. Goals and Objectives
Focus specifically on your prospect's expectations of value, which you learned by asking cure questions in the Doctor role.

6. Customer Requirements and the Proposed Solution
Show how you will meet your prospect's needs. Break each need down into buying criteria. You already did this as an Architect. Tie important features and benefits of your solution to specific needs.

7. Why This Is the Best Proposal
Show why you are the best choice. Include success stories as evidence that you are capable of exceeding your customer's expectations of value. Describe specifically how your strengths will benefit your prospect.
   If, by proposal time, you are still unaware whether your prospect is looking at the competition, be careful here. You do not want to write this section in a way that introduces your competition, thereby encouraging your prospect to look around. Use your best judgment here.

8. Financial Particulars and Profit Improvement Summary
Assume that the final decision maker will read only this page and the executive summary. Reiterate any important financial particulars from your opportunity analysis. Link prices to specific ingredients of your solution. Provide prices and profits on the same page. This helps your prospect to see the purchase as an investment, not a cost.

9. Implementation
Prepare an implementation plan that describes a timeline for the activities that will begin once the sale is approved. Affix responsibility for each activity. This should allay your prospect's fears and describe how you will teach your customer to exceed earlier expectations.

your success, you'll be ready to study the model and imitate it. Meanwhile, we'll continue with the particulars of being a Coach and the demands that will be placed on you in the remaining sales roles.

Writing the Proposal

Write in executive-focused, nontechnical language. To make your proposal easy to read, refer back to the writing tips provided in Chapter 3 (see pp. 56–61). In addition:

- Begin each section with a one-paragraph summary.
- Use bullet points and lists to open up the text.
- Use subtitles when shifting topics.
- Include visuals to reinforce each section's most important point.

To people whom you may never meet, your proposal says a lot about who you are. To proposal readers, spelling errors mean the salesperson has poor detail skills. Too much boilerplate material indicates the salesperson hasn't taken the time to identify the prospect's situation. A well-written, professional proposal says you understand your customer's needs and are committed to meeting them.

EFFECTIVE SALES PRESENTATIONS

The presentation necessarily repeats much of the proposal's contents. The difference is that you adapt your presentation to the needs of your audience.

People judge you by what you say and how you say it, so it's important to communicate effectively. You want your presentation to work *for* you, not against you. Lee Iacocca has said, "You can have brilliant ideas, but if you can't get them across, your ideas won't get you anywhere."

To communicate effectively with others, you must first communicate with yourself. *Plan* each sales presentation, don't just "wing it." Break it down into three component parts:

1. The opening (tell them what you will tell them).
2. The middle (tell them).
3. The conclusion (tell them what you told them).

Here are some points to keep in mind when planning your presentations.

Find Out in Advance How Much Time You Will Have.   Have you ever had a key decision maker leave in the middle of your presentation because he or she was out of time? You aren't holding the attention of a prospect who is looking at the clock! One consultant I have worked with solves this problem by asking at the beginning of the call how much time has been set aside. She then adjusts her presentation to take no more than 60 percent of her allotted time. For a one-hour meeting, she delivers a forty-minute presentation. Because her prospects' decisions to act typically occur at the end of a meeting, she wants to allow enough time to resolve any remaining issues and reach an agreement. Sometimes, she has to think quickly and cut back on her delivery time because the meeting turns out to be shorter than she expected. This is still preferable to having to stop halfway through a presentation!

Plan Your Presentation Backwards.   Start by determining the action you seek from your prospect, something your prospect will do. For example, the goal of most copy machine salespeople when making a demonstration is to secure a trial—the prospect's commitment to take the machine on loan for a few days and evaluate its capabilities. Once you know your destination, the path to get you there should be clear.

Plan What Your Prospect Should Do Immediately After the Meeting. Many salespeople are finding that prospects are less inclined to make a final buying decision with the salesperson present. When you request some form of immediate action to be taken after the presentation, you will benefit in two ways. First, you have a reason to continue communicating with your prospects, which is extremely important because your buyers' Step 5 (Fear) comes next. Second, the action you seek becomes your early warning signal. If your prospect fails to follow through, you have an indication that all is not well. With a follow-through, you are that much closer to your goal.

The action you request of your prospects should be a logical next step. For the sale of a copier, that step is usually a trial. For the sale of a telephone system, the buyers might need to supply you with a copy of the new office floor plan. You might ask a buyer to set up a future meeting, send you some information, or approve a small part of your plan. The immediate action you request should not be too involved. If you ask for extensive activity at this point, your prospect may freeze.

Plan an Opening That Will Grab Attention.   Begin by drawing your audience in with a strong opening line. Then, in one or two minutes, state your prospects' "big picture" goals and the impact they want to achieve. Next, describe the prospects' Step 2 (Discontent). What is the problem and why is it serious? What happens if the problem is ignored? Why is it important to solve it now? By focusing on your buyers' needs, you will get greater attention. For instance,

> Productivity. Performance. Prosperity. That's why I'm here.
>
> Your goal is to grow your business, to increase your value to your clients. But your current copier is holding you back. Frequent misfeeds and extended downtime hamper productivity and raise costs. Deteriorating copy quality is inconsistent with your high-profile corporate image. To attract larger clients now, you will soon begin a major new marketing plan, and that means a 25 percent increase in copies per month. If you don't take action soon, the problems you are experiencing will become much worse. By investing in CPC's Model 3500 copier now, you will enhance your image, increase your productivity, and take an important step toward growing your business.

Present a List of Your Customers' Goals and Objectives.   What are your customers trying to accomplish? (See Section III of the proposal presented in the Appendix.)

Plan to Review the Buyers' Criteria in the Middle Portion of Your Presentation.   Your primary objective in the middle portion is to help your prospects to understand how your copier will achieve their goals. Prove that you understand the buyers' needs by presenting a list of buying criteria. Review the list and ask whether anything has changed since you last met. (If they just met with your competition, the criteria may have changed.)

Here is a list of the capabilities that you said were important:

- Greater capacity and speed.
- Excellent copy quality.
- Consistent copy quality.
- Larger sorter.

- More reliable document feeder.
- Automatic double-sided copy capability.
- Outstanding service and support.
- Account codes.
- Larger paper supply.
- Reduction and enlargement capability.
- Faster first copy time.
- All at a reasonable price.
- Paper supply.

Has anything changed since our last meeting, or should anything be added to the list?

Rehearse How You Will Present Your Solution for Each Customer Criterion. Show how your offering meets or even exceeds the buyers' needs. For each criterion, do your prospect a FAVOR. Explain the specific Feature you offer, the Activity performed by that feature, and the Value Obtained as a result; then stop for Reaction.

Criterion   *"You mentioned that it would be nice to have someone to call with questions in the event of a malfunction."*

Feature   *"Our 24-hour Customer Assistance Center . . .*

Activity   *". . . provides answers 24 hours a day, 7 days a week. You need only call an 800 number."*

Value Obtained   *"This will improve your responsiveness to your customers."*

Reaction   *"Is that what you had in mind?"*

Build in reaction time from your prospects throughout your sales presentation. Do not present a monologue! Allow time for both open-ended and closed-ended questions. An open-ended reaction question cannot be answered "yes" or "no," nor can it be answered in a single word or two. For instance, *"How* would this be an improvement over your present system?" When you ask for reaction, you gain confirmation that you're on the right track. You also keep your prospects more involved, more alert, more interested, and more committed to your solution.

Differentiate Yourself to Win. Make sure your prospects are aware of your unique strengths. If you applied the Architect and

Coach roles, your prospects' criteria will already include your strengths, so you should be in good shape. If you have your proposal with you, you may want to present the page that states why your company is the best choice. Remember, the prospects' number-one question in Step 4 (Comparison) is, "Who is the best choice?" If you can't answer that question, you'll soon be in a price war.

Visuals: A Picture Is Worth a Thousand Words. Support an important idea with a picture, shown on an overhead, flip chart, or portable computer. Keep your visuals simple. If you mix graphics and text, place the graphics on the left and the text on the right.

Present the Investment Figures Together with a Profit Improvement Summary. By presenting purchase price on the same page with the financial benefits of buying, you help your customer to see the value of making a decision. (See Section VI of the proposal presented in the Appendix.)

Present Your Delivery and Implementation Timeline. (See Section VII of the proposal presented in the Appendix.)

Plan a Convincing Conclusion to Your Presentation. Studies show that what you say last, your prospects will remember most. Your conclusion should be a short summary. It should begin with a restatement of (1) the prospects' most significant problem and need, and (2) what the costs would be if nothing is done. (You clarified your prospects' costs of procrastination in Step 2.) Succinctly summarize your recommendations and restate the main value/benefit(s) that the prospects will enjoy. Remember to include emotional benefits as well as concrete ones. Finally, recommend the next step(s). Your two-minute conclusion to your presentation should go something like this:

- Restatement of discontent/need: *"As we have discussed, your existing copy machine is unable to generate 9,000 copies per month, which is the quantity you need to attract larger clients. Also, copy quality on your large jobs is inconsistent, which means that some copies may look good while others don't."*
- Cost if nothing is done: *"If this continues, you won't be able to ensure that all the mailers and promotional materials you distribute will be of the same quality. Also, the time necessary to verify quality could*

run several hours per month. In addition, you can expect to keep making emergency expenditures for outside photocopying."

- Summary of solution: *"As I have shown, my recommendation is to invest in our model 3500 copier."*

- Value/Benefit: *"This will enable you to promote larger special events, propose and implement more elaborate retail marketing plans, and aggressively pursue larger clients."*

- Action commitment: *"My goal is your complete satisfaction. That's why I'd like you to evaluate our copier for the next few days, to help you become comfortable with its unique performance capabilities. I'm sure, after you've used it, you won't want to be without it. Would you like to give it a try?"*

Involve your prospects in your presentation. Don't talk for more than a few minutes without some form of audience involvement. Ask open-ended questions to generate discussions, such as: "How would you utilize this?" Ask closed-ended questions to ensure you're on the right track. An example of a closed question would be: "Would this capability achieve that for you?" Let your prospect touch, feel, or operate your product or service, if at all possible.

Last, but not least, have fun and be yourself. Bert Decker, author of *You've Got to Be Believed to Be Heard*, says that if you want to persuade others, you must connect on a "gut level" first. Decker says that's why John Madden, the famed football coach turned TV commentator, is so successful. Madden makes emotional contact with his audience by just being who he is. To put impact into your sales presentations, connect with your prospects on a personal level by just being you.

A FINAL WORD ON BEING THE COACH

Coaches say that when two teams are evenly matched, the winner will be the team that executes its plays the best—the team that makes the fewest mistakes. That's why coaches spend a lot of time on the practice field, improving old skills and learning new ones. To win competitive sales, you must do the same. Coaches also know that, despite all the time and energy invested, you "can't win 'em all." Everyone who competes has, at one time or another, suffered defeat. When you lose a sale, look for the lesson, adjust your activities accordingly, and move onward toward your goals.

7

Sales Role #5: THE THERAPIST

Understand and Resolve Your Buyers' Fears

> Progress always involves risk; you can't steal second base
> and keep your foot on first.
>
> Frederick Wilcox

One day years ago, when I was a district sales manager for Lanier Worldwide, I was out making sales calls when I noticed a new tenant who had just moved into an office building. It turned out that the office was the new headquarters for a start-up company planning to provide medical imaging services. This company would operate outpatient centers where physicians refer patients for X-ray diagnosis.

I was successful in getting in to see Peter, the company's Vice President of Facilities and Engineering and, after just a few minutes, I recognized that I had stumbled across a huge sales opportunity. Peter's company was planning several imaging service centers nationwide. Each center would require a $60,000 digital dictation system.

Over the next four months, I met several times with Peter and his fellow decision makers as they endeavored to equip their first center. Throughout this period, Peter and his coworkers were easily accessible. Appointments were quickly arranged, and information was flowing back and forth between us.

I knew that Peter was talking to my competitors, too, but I had a game plan in place designed to win the sale. Finally, Peter came to my office for a product demonstration and to receive my formal proposal. The demo went great. Peter was excited. He felt we were the best choice, and he told me that, in a few days, the sale would be ours.

A few days went by without word from Peter, so I called him. His assistant said Peter was "in a meeting," so I left a message. Another few days went by, still no response. My subsequent phone calls also went unreturned. Peter and his fellow decision makers had suddenly become unreachable. A strange sense of numbness settled into my stomach as I realized these "sounds of silence" had a message for me—my "sure thing sale" was anything but. Peter had arrived at Step 5, Fear. How often have you experienced "sure thing" prospects who go silent on you at the last minute?

Having completed the Need and Learn stages of the buy-*learning* process, your prospect now enters the Buy stage, which consists of Step 5, Fear, and Step 6, Commitment. The Buy stage begins with your prospect putting on the brakes, but ends with him or her stepping on the gas.

SALES ROLE #5: THE THERAPIST

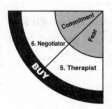 The buyer's Step 4 (Comparison) begins with many options under consideration but concludes when a preference is identified. The buyer then focuses more intently on that single solution. In the buyer's mind, the question changes from "Which choice is best?" to "What happens if I buy Product C from Company XYZ?" Expect a prospect to develop doubts and other mental pressures at this point. The prospect needs you to be a **Therapist.**

Occasionally, buyers skip Step 5, Fear. This is the only step of the buy-*learning* process that may not occur. If your buyer is fearless, you have reason to celebrate. Most people start to worry, and some panic. To close the sale, you must assume the role of a Therapist and resolve their fears.

YOUR CUSTOMERS' FIFTH
STEP: FEAR

 Your prospects' Step 5, Fear, occurs when they sense that they may regret a buying decision after the purchase is made. Up to this point in the sale, concrete issues, known to both the buyer and the seller, have been dealt with. In the Need stage, the customers' focus was on whether a change was needed. In the Learn stage, the focus was on specifying "must-have" capabilities, comparing options, and selecting a preferred solution.

Now, as the Buy stage begins, the prospect's fear of future regret emerges. Fear is a form of negative imagination that a prospect creates in his or her own mind; it produces a mental picture of possible negative consequences. Fear causes worry and stress. Very often, the prospect does not share these inner concerns with the salesperson. These concerns are not so much fact-based as emotion-based. They are perceived risks, not hard issues. Sometimes, even the prospect doesn't know why fear is present.

As a sales Therapist, you cannot "fix" these concerns through traditional objection-handling techniques. All you can do is help your prospects resolve the concerns themselves.

When buyers are making repeat purchases from existing suppliers, they usually don't experience fear because little or no risk is involved. On the other hand, a prospect who is about to spend a lot of money on an untried supplier (you) has reason to be nervous.

WHY BUYERS GET SCARED

The closer people get to making a major commitment, the more they focus on the future consequences. What if they regret the outcome of their decision? The **risk** of change causes fear of future regret just before a commitment is made. Following are some reasons why buyers can get nervous.

Major Dollar Investment.   The larger the financial impact of their purchases, the more likely your prospects will feel fear. A $100,000 decision will cause more heart palpitations than a $100 decision.

Long-Term Impact.   The greater the future impact of a buyer's decision, the greater the likelihood of fear. The decision to relocate an entire company to a new city would be of more concern than a decision to send two executives to an overseas conference for a few days.

Significant Changes in Operations.   The more change necessary to implement your solution, and the more people your solution affects, the more difficult the transition will be. Suppose a company buys a new voice mail system with operating commands that are completely different from those of their old system. Using the new system will require retraining, which takes people away from their jobs. A decision that affects many people carries more visibility than a decision that affects only a few people. Increased visibility makes decision makers politically vulnerable if the implementation doesn't go well.

Lots of Competition, or Zealous Competition.   If your prospects have consulted several salespeople from different companies, they may still be wondering whether they have made the correct selection. The larger the sale, usually, the more competitors go after it. If you are the "preferred choice," your competitors may roll out the "big guns" and try to reverse the sale.

New Product/Concept.   If you are selling a "new idea," your prospects may be reluctant to change or may doubt that your solution will work properly. New products or concepts require a shift in attitudes, a new way of thinking. For example, a new service being offered to hospitals is disposable medical gowns. Rather than wash used gowns, as has always been done, hospitals can now use them once and throw them away. This new concept may not be acceptable to certain decision makers.

Several Decision Makers.   The more decision makers involved in a sale, the harder it is for all of them to agree. Sometimes, late in the buying process, a new decision maker gets involved who hasn't yet bought into the Need. Everyone else has just completed Step 4 (Comparison): they have selected what they feel is the best solution. Then the new decision maker begins to question the original need, causing everyone else to backpedal. We will take an in-depth look at selling to multiple decision makers in Chapter 11.

You can see that most of these scenarios are not serious enough to stop the buying process altogether, but they can throw a wrench into your selling strategy. If you *expect* your buyers to experience a certain amount of anxiety, you won't be taken by surprise when they suddenly come up with new objections and seem reluctant to move forward. Their fears actually present you with an opportunity: the chance to solidify your position and show again, in another way, why your offering will be helpful.

WHY TRADITIONAL OBJECTION-HANDLING TECHNIQUES WON'T WORK

The traditional model of selling holds that when prospects express reluctance to buy, salespeople should treat this reluctance as an objection. Traditional sales approaches attempt to overrule objections by using logical arguments. However, for the reasons discussed in this section, traditional objection-handling techniques are not effective when dealing with fear.

You Are Dealing with Emotion, Not Logic.   Suppose you are engaged to be married, the wedding is scheduled for next weekend, and you are feeling fearful. Your best friend calls to see how you're doing. A traditional objection-handling technique would go something like this:

You: I'm scared stiff.

Friend: Why?

You: I'm afraid [he, or she] is not the right person for me.

Friend: Fear is typical for someone about to be married, but keep in mind that marriage has many advantages. Besides, you've already sent out the invitations, your guests have made travel arrangements . . . and your mother is so excited! You will go ahead with it, won't you?

Instead, your friend might say:

Friend: Can you tell me how you are feeling?

You: I'm scared stiff.

Friend: Anything in particular that's making you feel afraid?

You: I'm afraid *[he, or she]* is not the right person for me.

Friend: I felt the same way right before my marriage. It's perfectly normal to feel afraid. Is there anything I can do to help?

You: I guess I'm just totally nervous.

Friend: What can you do about it?

You: Actually, I'm always nervous before I do something new. Usually, I'm fine once things get started.

A traditional objection-handling technique is not effective when dealing with emotions because there is no "magic answer" that will make fear disappear. Traditional objection handling doesn't give prospects a chance to express their emotions. It moves too quickly past emotion on its way to a logical solution. When you encounter a prospect in Step 5 (Fear), think of what you would say to a close friend, and say that. The best way to handle fear is to encourage open expression of concerns, so the prospects can move past them.

Remember my "sure thing" sale to Peter, which suddenly had gone awry? Here's how I handled it. First, I let a few days go by without calling. Then I called our Research and Development Department and picked up a few choice morsels of information. Then, late one afternoon, after 5 P.M., I called Peter's direct line. Support people had already gone home for the day, and I got lucky—Peter answered. My goal in calling Peter was not to close the sale over the phone; it was to get an appointment. I explained to Peter that I had some new information regarding some upcoming software enhancements for his system. I asked Peter whether he could spare me just ten minutes the following day. He sounded somewhat reluctant, but agreed to an appointment.

The following day, as I was explaining the new software enhancements to Peter, I noticed that he seemed strained and uptight. I was attempting to get Peter engaged in conversation, but he kept responding with short, one-word answers. "Peter," I said finally, "You seem very quiet. I don't know how to read your silence." After a long pause, Peter said haltingly, "We can't buy your system." I asked Peter to tell me more.

"Jim Smith, the executive director of Children's Hospital, has agreed to join our firm as chief executive the first of next month," Peter said. "He told me you guys messed up an installation there several years ago, and ever since then his hospital has been dealing exclusively with [Competitor A]. Personally, I think you have the best system, and I know you've got your service act together now. But I'm concerned that if I buy from you, I'll upset my new boss."

"I understand," I said. "So if you stand firm for our system, that might be somewhat risky for you. However, you still believe our system is better, so there's got to be some way to resolve this. Do you have any ideas?"

Peter then came up with the idea to call a few friends at Children's Hospital to get the inside story on our supposed bad installation. He asked me to find out what I could, and we agreed to meet again the following day.

When I showed up to meet Peter the next day, I was ushered in—to see Jim Smith. For the next half-hour, Jim grilled me about our new system and service. I felt like a witness under cross-examination. I left that meeting without a clue of how I did or what Jim and Peter would do. The next day, though, I had my answer. Peter called, inviting me to stop by and pick up the purchase order. Apparently, I had passed the test with Jim. Yea!

Fear Often Develops When You Are Not in Front of Your Prospects. The longer your prospects take to make a decision, the greater the possibility that fear will develop when you're not there. Therefore, to effectively handle your buyers' fears, you need to find out how your prospects are feeling about the sale while you are talking to them. The previous chapter suggested that, at the conclusion of your sales presentation, you request some form of action, such as another meeting. This ensures that you get face-to-face with your prospect at the time when fear is most likely to become a factor.

THE THERAPIST'S FOUR-STEP TREATMENT PROCESS

A therapist is someone who deals with the emotional processes of others. A therapist dedicated to treating emotional processes helps patients to figure out for themselves what their problems are and to resolve what to do about them. This therapist's four-step process for understanding and resolving a patient's fears is:

1. Be sensitive and observe.
2. Explore concerns.

3. Empathize with feelings.
4. Discuss alternatives.

When a couple goes to a therapist, the therapist carefully observes the way they interact. What they *do* speaks as loudly as what they *say*. One person may dominate the conversation while the other watches the clock. Not listening, interrupting, sudden slumping in the chair, or reacting with a pained facial expression are all signals—verbal or nonverbal signs that indicate unrecognized feelings.

Many people have been conditioned by society to deny their feelings. They may feel angry, fearful, anxious, or happy and yet not realize those feelings until someone asks them a question or they take the time to get in touch with themselves. Usually, people do not try to contain joy and happiness, but they do try to hold in dark feelings like anger, envy, hatred, and fear. Unfortunately, holding them in does not make them go away—in fact, it can make them worse.

Therapists are **sensitive** to both what is being said and what isn't being said. Something is always happening even if it's not being discussed. Therapists **observe** how their patients behave and interact. Therapists have learned that underneath seemingly minor issues are often major problems.

When they sense repressed emotions, therapists **explore concerns** by asking: "Can you tell me more about that?" or "What concerns do you have?"

Therapists **empathize** with their patients' feelings in order to understand the patients better. They show empathy by saying things like, "I understand how you feel" or "I can see why that would be disconcerting." They realize that feelings are not right or wrong, they just *are*. Therapists have learned that helping people realize what their feelings are and why they have those feelings is often all that's required to help them become comfortable and move forward. Patients often discover that when their negative feelings are brought out into the open, they suddenly don't seem all that significant.

Finally, therapists help resolve patients' fears by **discussing alternatives**—how the patients think they should proceed. Therapists ask questions like: "What can be done to relieve your concerns?"

The goal is for patients to leave therapy knowing what their problems are and what needs to be done to resolve them. The therapist does not solve problems. The therapist helps patients to solve their own problems.

SELLER, BEWARE!

Suppose you have just completed a major proposal presentation. You were the first salesperson in the door, you diagnosed the prospect's discontent, influenced "must-have" criteria in your favor, and implemented a competitive strategy that resulted in your offering now being the preferred choice.

How are you feeling right now? Chances are you are very confident because you are expecting a sale. Perhaps the customer told you that a "rubber stamp" from one more executive was all that was needed to make the purchase order yours. Mentally, you are calculating your commission.

Overconfidence often leads to complacency, and complacency inevitably leads to disaster. The overconfident salesperson can easily overlook seemingly "trivial" issues that indicate the sale is in jeopardy.

The Coach role requires the salesperson to do a lot of "telling," that is, presenting information to interested prospects. Now, it's important for you to shift out of the Coach role and into the Therapist role. A "telling" approach is not effective at resolving another's fears.

HOW TO DETECT FEAR

You should anticipate that Step 5 (Fear) will probably occur in your *major sales opportunities*. Be on the lookout for indications that a prospect is getting nervous. Prospects often present a serious concern in a casual or joking way. They make it seem that it's not a big deal when, in reality, it is just the "tip of the iceberg." Be very sensitive to any "small concerns" at this step of the sale.

Detecting fear boils down to a "gut feeling" you have that something isn't right. To detect fear, you must be sensitive and observant. You may find this difficult because, in your role as a Coach, you were the expert. You did a lot of talking while your prospect did a lot of listening. Now, in the Therapist role, you must shift gears and be more intuitive.

Take time to review how things are going. What is happening that is out of the ordinary? What isn't happening that should be? There are no surefire ways of detecting fear, but chances are good that when one of the following occurs, fear is a factor:

- Negative, nonverbal body language.
- Unreturned phone calls.
- Inappropriate delay.
- Reluctance to meet.
- "One minor detail remaining. . . ."
- Unrealistic demand (price, delivery, etc.).

Now is the time when the strength of your trust bond with a prospect, which you have continuously nurtured, comes into play. Get face-to-face with your prospect and ask: "How do you feel about going ahead?" or "I get the feeling you are concerned about something." You are trying to get your prospect to open up to you. You must keep the lines of communication going. As mentioned in Chapter 6, never leave a major presentation or proposal without an appointment to meet again. Create a reason to go back: additional information, specifications, installation guidelines, delivery options—anything that may be a valid reason for meeting again.

HOW TO RESOLVE FEAR

You cannot resolve a buyer's fear until you understand its source. Therefore, *exploring your buyer's concerns* is the first step to resolving them. Ask: "Can you tell me more about that?" or "Why do you feel that way?"

Therapists frequently sense that a patient is feeling a negative emotion but is reluctant to admit what the emotion is. Salespeople frequently encounter this same challenge in identifying a prospect's true concerns. In your Therapist sales role, do what a therapist does and take a risk. A therapist will guess out loud what concerns a patient—for instance, "I sense you are reluctant to be here." Therapists report that this kind of leading statement, even if the guess is incorrect, often gets the patient to open up. The patient may respond, "No, I'm not reluctant to be here. I'm just frustrated about _____." What emerges is the *real* issue.

Realize that the first concern that is verbalized is often a "smoke screen." Neil Rackham, in his book *Major Account Sales Strategy,* reports on a study of lost sales where the customers had turned the sellers down because of price. Rackham's research found that, in 64 percent of the cases, price was *not* the most important factor. The real issues were "risks and penalties which the customer feared would come from making a decision in the seller's favor." Keep asking open-ended questions until both the prospect and you recognize the real concern.

Sarah, an account manager for AT&T, was proposing three telephone switching systems, consisting of 300 telephones, to a title insurance company. She had worked diligently to identify the company's needs and cost-justify her system, and was very optimistic because her sales presentation had gone so well. She left the presentation confident that the sale would be hers the following day. Two days went by without word from the prospect, so she called. When the prospect told her that her system "cost too much," Sarah knew she was in trouble. The cost justification that she had prepared earlier in the sales process indicated that the customer would break even on the investment in just six months. "Costs too much" just didn't make sense.

Throughout the sales process, Sarah had nurtured her relationship with this key prospect and, as a result, she was able to schedule an appointment with him. Through careful questioning during the meeting, Sarah found the *real* concern. The prospect was worried that the changes in branch operations required by the new system would cause the branch managers to turn against him. The real issue was a fear that the powerful branch managers would think he had made the wrong buying decision.

Sarah suggested that she and the prospect visit each branch, share the proposed changes with employees, and brainstorm ways to minimize disruption. These sessions resulted in the users and branch managers becoming excited about the new system. The prospect's fear was calmed and the sale went through.

To uncover the real issue, Sarah *empathized with her prospect's feelings*. She mentally placed herself in her prospect's shoes in order to understand him better. She knew he was hoping for a promotion. She also knew that, in order to get that promotion, the prospect needed sponsorship from branch managers. Sarah discovered the real issue by saying, "I get the feeling that there is some other issue besides price." In Step 5 (Fear), an empathic statement such as this is far more effective than a hard-nosed closing technique.

Help your prospects to resolve their fears for themselves by *discussing alternatives*. Ask: "What possible alternatives do we have?"

First, ask the prospect to tell you what the possible solutions might be. If your prospect can't think of any, you ought to suggest one.

If you have a solution, suggest it as an alternative, don't present it as a solution. Ask the prospect: "In your opinion, what is the best way to go?" If the prospect selects the alternative, he or she will be more committed to taking action. Your goal right now is to help the prospect explore alternatives so that you move forward, not backward.

HANDLING BACKWARD MOVEMENT IN THE BUYING PROCESS

Recently, I was involved in a consulting project with a client to design a new sales training program. As part of that project, I contacted thirty prospects who, I was told, had bought from the competition. I discovered that eight of these prospects had *never bought anything.* Apparently, the prospects had told the salesperson they had bought from the competition just to get the salesperson to go away. This finding shows that sometimes, just before a buying decision is made, prospects may move backward in the buying process.

If your prospects tell you they have bought from someone else, there's not a lot you can do. If what they say is true, you lost the sale. If it's not true, chances are the prospects won't listen to you now, anyway. What you can do is call all *lost sales* back sixty days later. You might be surprised at how many of them never actually bought from your competitor!

Most prospects who move backward in the buying process do so for one of two reasons:

1. They are deciding not to decide.
2. They may be changing their decision and buying from your competitor.

If your prospects are deciding not to decide, chances are they are returning to Step 2 (Discontent) and questioning the original need. This move may be the result of a competitor's "back to square one" strategy. Sometimes it's caused by a new decision maker who has "caught wind" of what is going on and is not providing the proverbial "rubber stamp." In any event, you must match selling with buying. If a prospect goes back to Step 2, put your Doctor hat on.

If your prospects are moving toward your competition, they are returning to Step 4 (Comparison). They have probably reevaluated and reprioritized their buying criteria, a situation that presents a challenge to you. Reexamine your competitive analysis form (Figure 6.1). Your greatest vulnerability is the highest-rated criterion in which you are rated as weak. Develop a game plan, and try to get back in the door.

The best way to avoid a backward movement in the buying process is to prevent it from occurring in the first place. That means doing a better job with each role the first time through the buying process. Find bigger problems and more serious needs. Apply more creativity when designing unique solutions. Put more effort into your competitive strategy. As a Doctor would say, "An ounce of prevention is worth a pound of cure."

All salespeople sell change. You want your prospects to become customers; as customers, they will need to do certain things differently in the future than they have done them in the past. All change involves risk. The greater the risk perceived by your prospect, the greater the probability that fear will be a factor.

By assuming the role of a Therapist, you help your prospects to resolve their fears, move past indecision, and arrive at the point of commitment. Now, the negotiations begin.

8

Sales Role #6: THE NEGOTIATOR

Discuss to Reach Mutual Commitment

Let us never negotiate out of fear, but let us never fear to negotiate.

John F. Kennedy

Even when you do a fantastic job selling innovative solutions that your customers believe provide great value, the issue of price never seems to disappear. At some point in any sale, you're likely to hear: "I'd like to buy from you, but your price is too high!"

These words can strike fear into the heart of even the most experienced sales pro. If you quickly concede by chopping price, you may win the order, but you lose valuable profit and set a dangerous precedent. If you stand firm on price, you instantly create a contest in which one party will win and the other will lose.

There is a way to avoid haggling over prices. It's called **win–win negotiating.** To achieve a win for you and a win for your prospect, you must change some old ways of doing things. When your buyer expresses concern over price, you must avoid a knee-jerk reaction—either quickly conceding or digging in and fighting over price. Instead, draw your counterpart closer to you by acknowledging and welcoming the expression of concern. Then disarm your counterpart before disagreement escalates into a price war and harms your relationship.

Throughout the Customer-Focused Selling process, you have worked hard to build a relationship built on mutual trust and understanding. You have walked on your buyers' path. So far, you have carefully studied their business *or* personal life, diagnosed their needs, designed solutions, showed them why you are their best choice, and helped them resolve their last-minute fears.

Now, as negotiations begin, your prospects should not fear you or think of you as an adversary. Rather, they should see you as a catalyst for growth, someone who is committed to helping them achieve their vision of the future. If they see you in this light, your negotiations can be conducted in a win–win atmosphere where the goal is a mutually satisfactory agreement.

Ours is not a perfect world, however. Negotiations are stressful, and different people respond to stress in different ways. Split personalities may appear as decision-day arrives. We have all sold to an amiable Dr. Jekyll, then watched in shock as Mr. Hyde emerged for negotiations.

As was mentioned earlier, many corporations have pushed decision making down the organizational chart in an effort to make their businesses more responsive and competitive. These new, lower-level decision makers may want to appear successful to their superiors by striking a "great" deal. It is possible to negotiate successfully with buyers hell-bent on prevailing at your expense—so-called "win–lose" prospects—but, to do so, you will need persuasive skills and diplomacy.

SALES ROLE #6: THE NEGOTIATOR

 For this step in the buy-*learning* process, you adopt the role of **Negotiator.** Negotiation is a discussion designed to reach an agreement between parties who share some interests but are at odds on others. Suppose you want to go out to dinner and to a movie, while your date wants to stay home for dinner and rent a video. Both of you are interested in dinner and a movie, but you differ on where and in what form. The only way you will reach a mutually satisfactory agreement is through negotiation.

To be a successful negotiator, you must first know what you want, then listen carefully to learn what the other person wants. Next, you must determine areas of agreement and, with an attitude of joint problem solving, create win–win solutions to resolve any differences.

Your goal in selling is always to achieve agreements that meet the present and future needs of your prospect, your company, and yourself. Successful agreements must stand the test of time. They must strengthen, not weaken, the buyer–seller relationship, if you are to keep the customer you have created. According to Roger Dawson, author of the video *Guide to Business Negotiating*, you will know you have achieved a win–win agreement when:

1. Each party felt the other party cared about his or her interests.
2. Each party felt the other party won as well.
3. The self-respect of each party is intact.
4. Each party feels the other will abide by the agreement.

Your commitment to a win–win agreement requires that, regardless of whether you negotiate with Dr. Jekyll or Mr. Hyde, your approach is always win–win. You can't control others, but you can control yourself. You need a single set of skills that is effective with both win–win and win–lose buyers. That set of skills is described in this chapter.

HOW TO APPROACH YOUR NEGOTIATIONS

Mike, a personal friend, is the President of Advanced Digital Systems (ADS), a supplier of computer products, based in Cerritos, California. During the spring and summer of 1994, Mike was attempting to sell his company's TV Tuner board to Compaq Computer Corporation for installation in Compaq's new line of multimedia PCs. Compaq is one of the world's leading manufacturers of personal computers. ADS's TV Tuner board would allow a computer user to work on a computer program—a word processing program, for example—and watch TV on the monitor at the same time.

After several months were spent trying to get in the door at Compaq, Mike finally located a product manager who expressed interest. After exchanging information during several phone calls, Mike was invited to Compaq's Houston headquarters to meet with several people. During the meeting, the Compaq representatives were very attentive, but did not show great interest. Mike got the feeling that the group had their "poker faces" on: they were very interested but didn't want him to know it. After all, Mike reasoned, there wouldn't be six people here in the room if they weren't interested.

During this meeting, Mike was asked what his best price was for a large quantity of units. Mike responded with a broad price range, and indicated that the exact quantity purchased per month and the length of the purchase agreement would have a significant impact on the final price per unit. At the conclusion of the meeting, Mike received an "action commitment" from Compaq representatives to test several TV Tuner boards for purposes of evaluation.

During the following six-month evaluation, Mike and fellow ADS representatives made nine more trips to Houston, meeting with a variety of Compaq representatives, including product managers, representatives from manufacturing, and members of Compaq's user focus group—the people who were testing Mike's product. The most important person Mike met with, however, was Compaq's Project Engineering Manager (PEM). The PEM was the key focal point for the sale, the kind of person I refer to as a Power Broker. Besides coordinating and interpreting all the information gathered by the various people mentioned above, the PEM signed off on the final product specifications *and* had the ear of Compaq senior management. (We will take a closer look at the Power Broker role in Chapter 11.)

Throughout these meetings, the ADS team did a good job of emphasizing certain strengths of their offering, including its ease of use and proven track record for reliability. During these meetings, Mike learned that Compaq representatives were also evaluating similar products from other manufacturers. Compaq representatives had clearly bought Mike's concept of a TV Tuner board. The question was: Would they also buy Mike's product?

At one point in the middle of the Step 4 (Comparison) process, Mike and the other vendors were asked about the possibility of adding certain features. Mike carefully considered Compaq's request, and responded that each change in capability would have a corresponding change in the price of his product. Some of Mike's competitors, anxious to appear responsive and flexible to a large prospective client, responded differently; they said that the change would *not* affect their price.

As Compaq representatives continued their learning process, they identified several more desired changes. It got to a point where Mike was placing a price figure on each proposed change—an audio jack would cost an additional $0.50 per unit, but to remove the ability to record motion video would save Compaq $1.25 per unit. As negotiations with the Purchasing Department neared, Mike's competitors who had not taken the position of affixing a cost to each change found themselves with a quoted price that was *below* what their actual production cost would be. To avoid losing money, two of Mike's competitors were forced to remove themselves from consideration.

Finally, Mike was asked to meet with Purchasing. During the first meeting, Mike resisted the temptation to cut price and "go for the close." Instead, he felt confident of his position. He knew he was not the lowest price, and, during the sales process, he had built strong alliances with Compaq product managers, including the key person, the PEM. Mike also knew that a few key members of Compaq's focus group considered his TV Tuner the easiest to use.

Negotiations began when the purchasing agent requested a shorter delivery time. Mike agreed, provided that Compaq would commit to issuing purchase orders sooner than scheduled. Next, the purchasing agent requested a lower price on a flexible range of unit quantities to be delivered over a five-month period. Mike grudgingly agreed to the lower price, provided Compaq agreed to a higher quantity of units, guaranteed each month, over a seven-month period of time.

Finally, Mike and the purchasing agent reached an agreement that served everyone's needs. Mike made a large sale and a decent profit. Compaq purchased a state-of-the-art multimedia peripheral that was installed on over one-third of all Compaq Presario PCs sold in 1995. And thousands of Compaq customers received a new multi-media capability that was very easy to use.

Mike's approach provides an excellent example of certain do's and don'ts of sales negotiations. Let's look at them one by one.

Negotiate Late in the Sales Process, Not Early.   The simple rule is: There's no reason to talk price until buying desire has been aroused. Often, inexperienced salespeople negotiate too soon. Never cut your price before the buyers recognize what they need and why they need it. A salesperson may mistakenly assume that by lowering price, a product or service suddenly becomes more attractive to the buyer. The reality is that it doesn't matter whether a product costs $50 or $50,000. If your customer doesn't need it, any price is "too high."

When Mike delivered his first presentation, he was asked about his "best price." Mike knew this was an "interest signal," not a "buying signal." Compaq's request for price was a typical question from customers who are in Step 2 (Discontent) and want to mentally compare the cost of buying with a vision of value—what they expect to gain by purchasing. If the value exceeds the cost, the prospect will usually recognize a need to buy. In responding to his prospects' request, Mike made the right choice by not committing to a specific figure. Instead, he responded with a wide price range, so his prospects had a general understanding of costs, but Mike still kept his profit margin intact.

Some buyers attempt to draw you into negotiations in the early stages of a sale. They may want to test the waters, or perhaps engage in "nibbling," a buying tactic aimed at gaining concessions at every opportunity. It's in your best interest, however, to postpone these types of discussions. You will have more negotiating power *after* your prospects know that they want to buy. Also, giving concessions too early will limit the concessions you can offer later, when you might really need them. Finally, quickly granting concessions creates an expectation of more concessions, which is not to your benefit. To postpone these types of price discussions, simply say, "Mr. Prospect, is now the right time for you to buy?"

Carefully Consider the Consequences of Any Concession You Make. Mike was careful to avoid making a concession on Compaq's change requests. He understood that any concession he made early in the process would become an expectation later on. Some of Mike's competitors were not so careful. They quickly "caved in" and were later forced to withdraw themselves from consideration.

Some salespeople confuse service with sales. The "satisfy the customer at all costs" attitude, which works well for salespeople in the postsale Satisfaction step, need not spill over into the sales process. Salespeople who attempt to meet *all* their customers' needs will end up abdicating their own. Yes, your goal is always to satisfy your customers, but you also have a responsibility to yourself and your company. Without profit, there is no purpose.

Make sure that you can live with whatever concession you make. Negotiate diligently, because whatever agreements you negotiate with your prospects will affect their expectations about future purchases. For instance, granting a 10 percent discount on the first order usually creates an expectation for a 10 percent discount on the second order. Don't give away the store! If you cut price now, you may be giving away future profit from repeat sales as well.

Don't Propose a Solution with an Already Discounted Price. Some salespeople cut price to make their initial proposal appear more attractive. Those who do so may actually be doing a disservice to purchasing agents who are judged by how much money they can save.

When Mike arrived for his first meeting with Purchasing, he still had a significant amount of gross profit built into his proposal. This margin gave Mike the flexibility to maneuver for a win–win result. The purchasing agent won some important concessions and Mike won a profitable sale. If you discount in advance, you limit your price flexibility, which may make the purchasing agent look ineffective.

The only exception to this rule applies when your first involvement in a sale comes late in the buy-*learning* process. This usually occurs when a buyer who is shopping during Step 4 (Comparison) calls you for information. In this case, you are at a distinct disadvantage because you and the buyer have no reciprocal knowledge of each other (you haven't had a chance to establish your credibility), and the buyer has other options. If you are the last salesperson in the door, your first goal should be to meet with the buyer personally to identify needs, buying criteria, and so on. Failing that goal, it may be prudent for you to lead with a price that is somewhat discounted because you may get only one shot at the sale.

When you receive a phone call that you know is coming late in the buyer's sales process, ask: "How did you hear about us?" If the buyer says he or she found you in the Yellow Pages, you know this sale will be a dogfight. On the other hand, the buyer may tell you, "My good friend George said you are the best." Now you know you are in a stronger position because the buyer was referred to you by someone who is known and trusted. (Evaluating the strength of your negotiating position will be discussed later in this chapter.)

Be Patient.   Often, salespeople feel pressured to get the contract signed, as if the prospect has all the power. This is an invalid assumption. The prospect wouldn't be negotiating with you if there was no desire to buy. The more you talk with your prospect, the more time both of you have invested in reaching an agreement. Relax and slow down!

Never Give a Concession Without Getting One in Return.   Negotiation is not capitulation; it's a discussion by two parties seeking to reach an agreement. If you give a little, you should expect to get something in return. Compaq's purchasing agent requested a lower price. Mike agreed to the lower price provided Compaq agreed to higher quantities and a longer contract period.

To a prospect who is requesting a lower price, you might say, "I would be able to offer an additional 5 percent discount, provided you increase the size of your order by 200 units. Is that acceptable to you?" Your prospect "wins" by getting a lower price, and you "win" by increasing the size of the sale.

YOUR CUSTOMERS' SIXTH STEP: COMMITMENT

 Throughout the first five steps of the buy-*learning* process, your prospects' focus has been on achieving value. They have examined their problems, determined the problems' seriousness, and examined the alternatives. They have a well-defined expectation of value because their attention has been on the benefits they will enjoy by purchasing. Now, in Step 6, Commitment, the focus changes from the *value* of your solution to its *cost*. No longer does a prospect wonder: "Why should I buy? Who is best? What happens if I buy?" Instead, the focus becomes: "How much?"

If your negotiation is occurring at the proper time, after the two of you have completed the first five steps of the buy-*learning* process, then there is good news: your prospect wants to buy from you! You and the prospect have a shared interest, and the prospect wants what you're selling. Congratulations—almost.

Negotiations between you and your buyer occur because your buyer wants a better deal than the one you initially offered. On one hand, the buyer wants to buy your product or service. On the other hand, the buyer's interests—a lower price, easier payment terms, faster delivery, more training, and so on—differ from the terms you proposed. The actual negotiation process begins when your prospect presents you with a purchasing request, demand, or condition.

WHY BUYERS NEGOTIATE WITH SELLERS

You may have the best product, with the lowest price and the best terms, and *still* your customers may maneuver for a better deal. Why? The most common reason is because it works. Customers have learned that when they ask for a better deal, they usually get it. In addition, buyers frequently challenge sales offers for reasons unrelated to the details of the transaction. It is difficult for you to strike a deal that will accommodate your customers' needs when these needs have little to do with your offering. Let's take a look at some of the trickier reasons buyers feel the need to negotiate.

Your Customers Will Negotiate Hard When Their Jobs Are on the Line

An individual's job description includes certain expectations that determine how his or her performance is measured. In the Student chapter, we discussed the three levels of a business: Support, Core, and CEO.

Your customers' job responsibilities will affect the type of climate in which you will negotiate—either win–win or win–lose. At the Support level, purchasing agents' effectiveness is judged by how much money they can save their employers. As was mentioned in Chapter 3, sales at this level are transactional. A transactional sale is a straightforward transaction in which price is the only (or at least the most important) consideration. Core- and CEO-level prospects are judged on other factors, such as efficiency of operations and return on investment. Sales at this level are of the consulting type. A consulting sale involves consultation and problem solving, and discussions are typically conducted about things other than price.

Jim is the Senior Vice President of Sales and Marketing for a leading freight and package carrier. Most of his 300+ salespeople are currently involved in transactional sales, calling on "freight managers." Sales made to freight managers are typically transactional sales because most corporations judge freight managers primarily on their ability to manage freight costs.

Jim's company's position in the freight industry is that of a value-added supplier. The company provides faster transit time and more dependable delivery than its competitors, but the services the company provides are not at the lowest price. The problem that Jim faces is that, because his company's value-added strengths (called his "value proposition") are not primary concerns of traffic managers, sales suffer.

Jim's goal is to refocus his salespeople on prospects who place more value on his company's services. In the freight industry, these prospects include manufacturing executives and warehouse managers. The manufacturing executive is judged on production levels, and if a package fails to arrive on time, the production line may have to be shut down. The warehouse manager would also benefit from Jim's value proposition, because the warehouse manager's responsibility is to supply raw material to manufacturing while keeping inventories at the lowest possible level. Dependability is important to a warehouse manager. Confidence that packages will arrive "just in time" allows effective operation with smaller inventories. These two managers are what I call "core managers," people who have their fingers on the pulse of the business and the organizational influence to act.

Transactional sales made to support-level prospects are usually negotiated in a competitive, win–lose climate. When you sell to a purchasing agent, you are selling to someone whose primary motivation is to save money. For a purchasing agent, achieving deep discounts is a job well done. As a seller, it is in your best interest to start your sales process at the higher Core or CEO level, so that you end up negotiating with a customer who is interested in a mutually satisfactory agreement. You will be more likely to make bigger sales and to negotiate more profitable agreements.

Consulting sales made to either the Core or the CEO level will usually be negotiated in a cooperative win–win climate because "lowest price" is not these prospects' primary motivation. Although price is still an important consideration, it's not the number-one priority. These buyers are less interested in nickel-and-dime solutions because they are judged by other factors besides price. Typically, they are judged by operational efficiency and productivity, so they're more interested in solving problems and achieving a return on their investment. They usually don't mind if you make a reasonable profit, as long as your solution solves a business problem and produces the results you promised. Additionally, Core- and CEO-level time is the most valuable time in the organization. Buyers at a higher level have less time to spend shopping other alternatives.

Selling to a Core- or CEO-level prospect improves, but does not guarantee, your chances for achieving a profitable win–win relationship. Your negotiations may suddenly involve other players who are very cost-conscious. The Purchasing Department often becomes involved during Step 6 (Commitment). In a trucking company, the freight manager almost always becomes involved. Some companies encourage all employees at all levels to seek discounts at every opportunity. For these companies, hard-line negotiating is expected of every employee. To meet every situation, you must be skilled in both win–win and win–lose negotiating situations.

Your Customers Will Negotiate Hard If They Want Admiration

Some prospects will haggle with you just to earn the admiration of others. Has a friend or family member ever boasted to you about what a great deal he or she negotiated on a new car? Once, in an elevator, I overheard an executive bragging to another about the great deal he had extracted from a salesperson selling office furniture. When you make concessions, buyers gain a story to be shared with others—a story in which the buyers are the winners and you are the loser.

Your Customers Will Negotiate Hard If They Enjoy Being Tough

Some prospects will seek major concessions just for the sport of it. They may enjoy testing you, and sharpening their own negotiating skills in the process. Strong-armed tactics are nothing new to these "organizational gamespeople." They see everything as a struggle, so why not make you part of it?

For two years, I sold dictation equipment to the legal market. For most lawyers, a day does not go by without some involvement in intense negotiations. Criminal lawyers negotiate plea bargains, personal injury lawyers negotiate insurance settlements, and family lawyers negotiate divorce settlements. Most successful lawyers are battle-tested negotiators, so when I negotiated multiple-machine contracts with them, I usually faced a hard-nosed counterpart.

BAD IDEAS

To negotiate effectively, you must be prepared for both win–win and win–lose negotiating climates. Even if you're sure you'll be negotiating with Dr. Jekyll, prepare as if you'll encounter Mr. Hyde. Always strive to achieve a win–win sale, even when your prospect is thinking win–lose.

Many books for both sellers and buyers have been written on the subject of negotiation. Several of them suggest "tricks" to help win–lose buyers win the negotiating game. These tricks lose much of their effectiveness if you can recognize the bluff. Here are a few of the most common "tricks" used by buyers in negotiations, and guidelines on how to recognize whether they are legitimate concerns or negotiating ploys. Usually, where there's a bluff, certain things don't add up.

Budget Limitation.   "We've only got $10,000. You're going to have to come in under that figure to earn our business."

In your Doctor sales role, you saw that in Step 2 (Discontent) the buyer often asks you, "How much will a solution cost?" The "ballpark" figure you quote allows the buyer to balance the seriousness of the problem against the cost of the solution. So the buyer has had some idea of purchase price since Step 2. Budget limitations that suddenly appear now, in Step 6 (Commitment), don't make sense. Budget limitations should have become an issue earlier, in Step 2 (Discontent) or Step 3 (Research) and certainly by Step 4 (Comparison) when you made your proposal or presentation. At this point, a budget limitation is most likely a negotiation trick designed to win major concessions. If you hold firm on price, the buyer will find the money.

Other Options.   "I've received a quote from your competitor for much less. If you don't lower your price, I'll have no choice but to buy from them."

If you come up against "other options," refresh your buyer's memory. If you did a good job in the Architect and Coach sales roles, your buyer has already recognized your unique capabilities because they are embedded in the "must-haves" and "nice-to-haves" you have already discussed. "Other options" is then a bluff. To win your customer's business without chopping price, justify why you are worth it. Revisit your unique strengths and why you are the best choice. (More about how to do this is covered later in this chapter.)

Foggy Recall.   "I remember that you said installation was included in the purchase price. That's what I told the committee. There is no way I'll get any more money now."

The foggy recall technique pits your memory against your customer's, and you *don't* want to get into an argument. The best way to handle foggy recall is to prevent it in advance by putting everything in writing, in your proposal. Don't trust memory, either yours or your customer's, on important terms and conditions!

MORE NEGOTIATING TRICKS

Some tricks taught in negotiation books and seminars apply to both buyers and sellers. With regard to salespeople using tricks in negotiations, my feeling is that although these tactics may obtain short-term results, they can backfire in the long term. They do not promote mutual respect between buyer and seller. On page 178 there are some maneuvers for both sellers and buyers that are based on psychological manipulation—methods to control the mind.

These tricks, when used by salespeople, are not effective with today's buyers. Your goal is to open a relationship by reaching an agreement, not to close a sale and move on. Also, today's buyers are too smart for these tricks. They are making more buying decisions and they're getting better at it, so they may be wise to these slippery tactics. You cannot control your buyers, but you can control yourself. Always strive for a win–win agreement, and refrain from using negotiating tricks, regardless of whether you are negotiating with a win–win or win–lose buyer.

THE NEGOTIATOR

When you negotiate agreements, be a NO TRICKS negotiator and refrain from all control-oriented negotiating techniques. To achieve the greatest possible success:

1. Analyze negotiating power (yours and theirs) using NO TRICKS.
2. Prepare to negotiate.
3. Reach agreement through discussion.

1. Analyze Negotiating Power (Yours and Theirs) Using NO TRICKS

In every type of negotiation, whether it's a labor negotiation, political negotiation, or buy–sell negotiation, negotiating power plays a major role. For each party in a negotiation, power is each side's perception of its strength or weakness in comparison to the other's. This perception of power affects the ability of each party to achieve its own goals. The more negotiating power you have in comparison to that of your buyer, the fewer concessions you will have to make.

Negotiating Tricks Used by Slippery Negotiators

Seller	Buyer
Good guy/bad guy	
The salesperson tells the customer everything that can be done, making a truly great deal seem enticingly close at hand. Then the customer meets with the salesperson's manager, who explains everything that *can't* be done. The whipsaw effect, a play on the emotions of the buyer, is designed to weaken the buyer and make the buyer more submissive to the seller's demands.	One buyer tells the seller that the sale is a "sure thing," then another buyer gets involved and says there's no way the deal will get approved on the existing terms. The whipsaw effect is a play on the seller's emotions, and makes the seller more submissive to the buyer's demands.
Wince	
If a customer makes an unrealistic price demand, the salesperson winces as if from pain. Although nothing is actually said, the salesperson powerfully conveys displeasure with the customer's request.	When the salesperson quotes a price, the buyer winces or, worse, gets angry. This visible display of emotion is often followed by a period of complete silence as the buyer waits to see how the salesperson responds.
Bait and switch	
The advertised price is very low, which draws new customers in the door. Then, when a customer asks for the advertised model, the last one has already been sold. The salesperson then tries to move the customer up to a more expensive model. This technique can be applied to all kinds of products and services.	The buyer requests a price on a large quantity of items—say, 100 units. At the last minute, the buyer decides to buy 25 units per year for the next four years. The buyer still expects the 100-unit price, as if all the units had been bought at once.
Nibbling	
After the deal has been set, small additional requests are made. The buyer agrees to buy a car from a car dealer. Then the buyer meets with the dealer's finance manager who tells the buyer that credit, life, and disability insurance premiums must be paid for along with the monthly payments.	The buyer makes small additional requests, either before or after a deal is done, such as: "By the way, if you could give us an extra 5 percent off, it would really help my boss out, and give you an advantage on our next purchase. What do you say?"

Many salespeople underestimate their strength in a negotiation. They feel anxious to make the sale and are afraid the buyer may buy from someone else. This perception of weakness often causes salespeople to grant overly generous concessions that bleed profits from the sale and result in agreements where the salesperson, and the salesperson's employer, lose.

By carefully analyzing your sources of negotiating power, you gain a more accurate perception of your negotiating strength. If your negotiating power is strong, and you recognize this, you are better able to negotiate more profitable agreements.

Through my research and sales experience, I have determined that negotiating power is derived from eight sources. Your job is to assess and develop your strength in each area. The stronger your position in each of these eight areas, the stronger your negotiating power. If you have successfully applied the Customer-Focused Selling skills throughout a sales process, you should find yourself in a strong negotiating position once you and your prospect arrive at Step 6 (Commitment).

The sources of negotiating power are:

Need
  Options

    Time
      Relationships
      Investment
       Credibility
        Knowledge
         Skill

Let's take a close look at each of these sources of negotiating power, how they apply to both the buyer and the seller in an actual sales example, and how the Customer-Focused Selling approach strengthens your position in each area. First, let's set the stage.

Chuck is a salesperson for American Sterilizer Corporation (AMSCO), a $500 million medical equipment supplier. AMSCO features a broad line of hospital equipment, including instrument sterilizers, washing equipment, surgical lights, surgical tables, and ancillary equipment for operating room settings. One of Chuck's largest accounts was in the process of constructing a new ambulatory surgery center that needed all-new equipment. Chuck's proposal to supply all the hospital's needs amounted to $820,000.

Two of AMSCO's products, surgical tables and gas sterilizers (devices that decontaminate equipment prior to usage), were highly technical and, thanks to Chuck's excellent selling skills and the quality of the products, certain influential doctors perceived them as being unique and desirable. During Step 4 (Comparison), the hospital evaluated surgical tables. During this time, Chuck and his fellow account team member—a "surgical specialist"—spent many hours listening to physicians' needs and influencing buying criteria. They were even allowed to join the physicians in the operating room, in case of questions. AMSCO's surgical tables were unique in that they had greater weight capacities (500 lbs./patient vs. 300 lbs.) and offered battery backup. The gas sterilizers were more durable than those of the competition because they were made of a material that better withstood corrosion. Also, the sterilizers had advanced controls that provided more adjustments and were easier to operate.

As the customer approached the end of the Comparison step, it became apparent to Chuck that he had the upper hand on the surgical tables and sterilizers. The hospital's project architect was incorporating AMSCO designs into the building plans. Chuck and his technical assistant spent many hours with architects and designers ensuring that the new facility would accommodate their equipment. Chuck provided information on structural support, seismic, and gas delivery codes. An AMSCO in-house architect was given a set of plans and asked to draw in AMSCO's gas sterilizers and surgical tables.

In all, Chuck and his account team invested over 150 hours of consultation, primarily regarding surgical tables and gas sterilizers. These two products, however, amounted to less than half the total sales opportunity, about $375,000, and Chuck wanted *all* the business.

The other products in Chuck's line, such as scrub sinks and gas columns (boom arms that deliver gas and electricity to the operating table), were much less technical, and were perceived by the customer as being the same as those offered by other suppliers. Chuck had one additional advantage—AMSCO was the only vendor that could supply *all* the hospital's needs.

When the time had come for negotiations, the customer was considering one of two options. Option A was to buy everything from Chuck for $820,000. Option B was to buy Chuck's tables and sterilizers for $375,000, and buy other products from a variety of suppliers, in a combined package totaling $710,000. As Chuck prepared to meet with Purchasing, here was his NO TRICKS negotiating power.

Need

The essential question here is: Who needs this sale more, the buyer or the seller?

The seller's negotiating strength comes from the magnitude of the buyer's need. The buyer buys to fulfill a need. How significant is that need? Will this purchase have a lasting or otherwise significant impact on results? If so, the prospect will *need* to buy, and the seller will have negotiating strength in this area.

When a buyer negotiates with a seller, the buyer has mentally accepted the seller's offering. Usually, the buyer negotiates with a seller because the buyer feels the seller's offering is best. The buyer may not want the seller to think that's the case, but the fact that the buyer is negotiating at all indicates a need for what the seller is offering and a mental acceptance of it. Many salespeople underestimate the simple fact that negotiations would not be taking place if the buyer didn't *need* what the seller has. Most people don't get involved in negotiations unless they are serious. Who has time to waste on half-hearted discussions?

The seller's negotiating strength is partly determined by the buyer's need and partly determined by the seller's need to sell. All salespeople want to make a sale, so buyers always have some power in this area. Sometimes, when the seller feels pressured to close a particular sale, the buyer's need power becomes much greater. Have you ever needed a sale at the "eleventh hour" to achieve quota? If so, you needed the sale badly, and were anxious to close it. Chances are that you granted extra concessions to make the sale quickly.

Chuck's Need Power in Action. The hospital's need to buy was unquestionable. From the moment the hospital's board authorized construction of the new facility, a need had existed.

Chuck felt a strong need to make the sale, because the size of the deal would surely qualify him for a large annual bonus. He also felt pressure because he needed the sale to win AMSCO's President's Club award, which had been his goal all year.

Customer-Focused Selling Strategies That Strengthen Your Need Power. In the Student role, you study a customer's business and search for opportunities where you can add value. In the Doctor role, you ask questions that increase a prospect's perception of need. When you help your prospect to recognize a BIG need, you intensify the desire to buy, thereby enhancing your need power. Also, you strengthen your need power by delaying the discussion of price until after buying desire has been aroused.

Options

The essential question here is: What are the options if an agreement is not reached?

First, the seller evaluates the buyer's alternatives. The fewer options that the buyer has, the greater the salesperson's strength in this area. A buyer who believes that a product or service is unique has no other options. A buyer who believes an offering is identical to those of competing sellers, however, has other viable options.

Next, the seller assesses the available options. How many other sales opportunities are waiting in the wings? If this sale is all the seller has, there is more pressure to close it. Conversely, if the seller can accept in advance the worst possible outcome—that is, the seller will simply move on if an agreement is not reached—the seller has negotiating strength in this area.

Chuck's Options Power in Action.   With regard to surgical tables and sterilizers, the hospital was committed to purchasing from AMSCO. The hospital did, however, have options with regard to less technical products. These options gave the hospital power in the negotiations.

Chuck, on the other hand, had no other sales opportunities large enough for him to make the number he needed. So, Chuck was weak in options power (although the buyers didn't know it).

Customer-Focused Selling Strategies That Strengthen Your Options Power.   In the Architect and Coach roles, you design unique solutions that lock out your competition. If your solution is the only one that's acceptable, or is at least somewhat unique in the customer's eyes, you have enhanced your negotiating strength.

You can also improve your options power by constantly developing new business opportunities. Effective prospecting activity will keep a fresh supply of new sales possibilities coming down the pipe, thereby increasing your options.

Time

The essential question here is: Are there any impending events that place a deadline on either the buyer or the seller?

If the buyer is under time pressure, this usually gives the salesperson negotiating strength (unless, of course, the salesperson cannot meet the delivery date). In commercial real estate, for example, the expiration of a lease may put time pressure on the tenant to find new office space. The time factor also affects many other purchases related to the move, such as hiring a contractor, selecting office furnishings and business equipment, and so on. A deadline creates time pressure and limits the buyer's opportunity to shop around.

If the seller is under time pressure, perhaps to close a sale by the end of a quota period, the buyer will have time power. Several years ago, I had the opportunity to win my company's annual incentive vacation—one week in Bermuda. On the last day of the year, I needed a $2,000 sale to achieve my annual quota of $3 million. Needless to say, I felt time pressure! I made some hefty concessions that day, but I won the trip.

Chuck's Time Power in Action. The hospital's goal was to open the new facility on January 1, and negotiations were taking place in August. For some of the equipment, especially those products that needed to be installed and then tested, a four-month lead time was required. Portable equipment required less lead time. The hospital knew that if the facility was going to open on time, a purchase order had to be issued by September 1. The buyers were feeling time pressure.

Chuck was feeling some time pressure, too, though not as much as the hospital. He knew that, in a pinch, his company could likely deliver with somewhat less than four months' lead time. Not wanting to push his luck, however, he felt it was in the customer's best interest to believe that a purchase decision had to be made by September 1.

Customer-Focused Selling Strategies That Strengthen Your Time Power. Be patient. Continually develop new sales opportunities so you don't find yourself pleading for an eleventh-hour sale.

Relationships

The essential questions here are: How strong is the seller's relationship with the prospect? And, how much importance does the prospect place on relationships?

Sellers develop negotiating strength in this area by nurturing a high *quantity* of high-*quality* relationships within each prospective account. Sellers also strengthen their position by establishing a close relationship with an actual buyer. If the buyer is the kind of person who values relationships, so much the better.

For the buyer, relationship power is similarly derived from a high quantity of high-quality relationships, inside both the buyer's and the seller's businesses. If, for instance, the buyer has his or her CEO's ear, the buyer has strong relationship power. If the buyer has the seller's CEO's ear (or a relationship with the seller's boss), the buyer may go over the seller's head to meet certain needs. If the buyer has relationships with people who work for competitors, the buyer has instant negotiating power in this area because of these alternate sources of information.

Chuck's Relationship Power in Action.   The hospital had been doing business with AMSCO for many years and appreciated AMSCO's quality products and knowledgeable technical support. The hospital's relationship with AMSCO was important, because hospital personnel lacked technical expertise in certain areas where AMSCO's representatives were able to help.

Chuck had strong relationship power because he was positioned *high*, with senior hospital officials, and *wide*, with department managers and users. He had been working the account for two years and, during that time, had met with hospital administrators, influential members of the medical staff, various department heads, and, of course, the Purchasing Department. In Chuck, these hospital officials saw a salesperson who was knowledgeable, enthusiastic, empathic, and caring. Chuck always followed up when he said he would, which made hospital officials feel that Chuck was a salesperson who truly valued their business. In addition, Chuck had an excellent working relationship with the Operating Room Director, with whom he and the architect had worked on the technical design specifications.

Customer-Focused Selling Strategies That Strengthen Your Relationship Power.   This entire book is about strengthening your relationship power, about becoming more significant in your buyers' eyes. Get into your customer's head and sell the way that customer wants to be sold to. Eliminate any selling techniques that may be perceived as manipulative. Be patient and don't push.

We all know that people like to do business with people they like. But in today's marketplace you need more than likability to sustain a relationship. You need knowledge. By studying your prospect carefully, and creating high-value solutions for important problems, you become more significant to your customer. Expert knowledge of your product and its applications, blended with knowledge of your customer's business and industry, is the recipe that produces the result you desire. You become a priority relationship in your customer's eyes.

In your Doctor sales role, you saw the importance of developing a sponsor, someone who sells for you in a prospective account. When you have a sponsor, you have relationship power, because someone else is selling your solution besides yourself. Study your prospect carefully and develop as many sponsors within the prospect's company as possible.

Today, many salespeople are losing relationship power. Layoffs and downsizing have placed a strain on buyer–seller relationships. Buyers have less time to socialize, and they can't necessarily buy from their favorite sources because they are expected to do more with less. For salespeople, the solution is to work harder at developing high-quality relationships with a variety of prospects.

Investment

The essential question here is: How much time and energy has been invested in the buying process?

The more effort someone invests in a project, the more committed he or she will be to reaching an agreement. The seller's negotiating strength in this area is enhanced when the buyer puts a lot of energy into a buying decision. If any action taken by the buyer involves time or energy, the seller's investment power increases.

Conversely, the buyer's power of investment is enhanced when the seller puts a lot of time and energy into a prospective sale. If the seller spends twenty hours preparing a proposal, that seller will have a hard time walking away from the deal.

Chuck's Investment Power in Action.   The hospital was heavily invested in the purchase of AMSCO's sterilizers and surgical beds, but that was not the key issue in the negotiation. The key issue was whether the hospital would buy everything from AMSCO. Because the hospital had little time and energy invested in simple products, there was little or no commitment toward any single supplier.

Chuck had invested a tremendous amount of time and energy in the sale. He had provided free consulting services to the hospital and its architect, and had sold other decision makers on AMSCO's high-quality product line. Chuck was heavily invested in the sale.

Customer-Focused Selling Strategies That Strengthen Your Invest-ment Power.   In the Doctor sales role, you make sure that each sales call concludes with something your prospect should do, an action step he or she should take. When you achieve these "action commitments" from your prospect, you strengthen your investment power because your prospect has expended time and energy in the buying process. Appointments, executive briefings, a visit to one of your installations, or an agreement to conduct a survey all represent time and energy your buyer invests in your sales solution.

Credibility

There are two essential questions here, reflecting individual credibil-ity and marketplace credibility. How much credibility does the seller have with this customer? And, would the seller gain significant cred-ibility with other customers by successfully selling to this customer?

A salesperson's credibility is his or her believability. Credibility reduces buyers' fear. Sellers have negotiating strength in this area if they have already had successful sales experiences with particular buyers. Those buyers know the sellers are dependable and credible.

On the other hand, buyers have credibility, too. Buyers' negoti-ating strength in this area is derived from their status in the buying community. If a seller wants badly to sell to a particular buyer in order to have that account to the seller's credit, then the buyer has an advantage. My first sales job was selling dictating machines for Lanier Business Products. Another salesperson in our Washington (DC) office sold a portable dictating machine directly to President Carter in the Oval Office. Subsequent photographs of the President showed his Lanier dictating machine on his desk. Lanier's credibil-ity was enhanced by having the President as a customer. If Mr. Carter had chosen to use his credibility power, he could have earned major concessions on price. Presumably, he was occupied elsewhere, negotiating the Middle East peace agreement.

Chuck's Credibility Power in Action.   As far as AMSCO and Chuck's credibility with hospital decision makers were concerned, credibility was strong. AMSCO representatives had always done what they said they were going to do. They had proven themselves to be reliable and trustworthy. A few of AMSCO's competitors, on the other hand, were perceived by some hospital officials as having a credibility gap. At one time or another, there had been an apparent disparity between what hospital officials were told and what actually happened.

In addition, the hospital had a medical school, which meant that many doctors-to-be were being taught there. If Chuck was successful in selling the hospital his entire product line, AMSCO's credibility with doctors in other local hospitals would be enhanced.

Customer-Focused Selling Strategies That Strengthen Your Credibility Power. To enhance your credibility throughout the sales process, you can:

- Dress professionally.
- Be prepared on every sales call.
- Use top-quality sales materials.
- Use customer lists, testimonials, and references.
- Demonstrate fast, professional follow-up.
- Honor your promises.

In the final chapter, on the Farmer sales role, we will address other credibility-enhancing tools to add to your customer satisfaction tool kit.

Knowledge

Again, there are two essential questions here: Who knows more about all aspects of this sale? And, which party believes it has the upper hand in negotiating strength?

Knowledge *is* power. Sellers have knowledge power when they thoroughly understand their customers' problems and needs and can foresee how the products or services offered will help them.

Conversely, if customers know as much as the sellers do, or perhaps more, about the application of a seller's solution, the customers have knowledge power. In addition, the more customers know about the seller's situation, including how much the seller needs the sale, the more knowledge power the customers have.

The other knowledge sellers need is self-knowledge. Sellers' awareness of their negotiating strength also gives the sellers knowledge power. By carefully examining each NO TRICKS area, sellers become more knowledgeable about the relative strength—or weakness—of their position. This knowledge helps sellers see the negotiation process in a different perspective—that of an observer. When sellers can step back from the situation and objectively assess their negotiating power, they are able to negotiate from a strong position, and avoid making emotional concessions they will later regret.

The more sellers know about each of the eight NO TRICKS areas of negotiating strength, the more strength sellers have. Power is a *perception*, a mental awareness or comprehension. The NO TRICKS model will help sellers remember and focus on what they should be thinking about.

Conversely, the more knowledge buyers have about their negotiating strength, the less receptive they will be. Suppose a salesperson is unaware that a buyer is also negotiating with a competitor. The buyer knows something very significant of which the seller is unaware. This means the salesperson is weak in both types of knowledge power.

To keep their knowledge power at a high level, sellers should develop several relationships, at different levels of buyers' organizations. If a seller has only one source of information about a particular sale, even if that source is an "insider" or a "top person," the seller's perception of what's going on can be easily manipulated. A seller who has at least three good sources of information regarding every sale will get a much more accurate sense of the true negotiating stance of the buyers and won't be led into any dead-end preliminaries.

Chuck's Knowledge Power in Action.   Hospital officials knew little about Chuck's two highly technical products. They needed technical knowledge and support during the buying process to ensure their needs would be met. They also needed excellent support *after* the sale because physicians and surgeons, many of whom depend on instant response from support units, would need to adapt to the new equipment. Hospitals officials knew a lot about the more basic products, because these products were less technical. Decision makers knew that, with regard to less technical products, AMSCO was not "the only game in town." Other companies offered products as good as, and in some cases perhaps a bit better than, AMSCO.

Chuck's knowledge power was high. He knew the doctors wanted his sterilizers and surgical tables, but he didn't limit his sales efforts to that one favorable group. He consulted with the hospital's project architect, hospital administrators, the purchasing unit, and the operating room director. He spent far more time with the prospect than his competitors had, because he had been involved in the design process and had made that involvement a learning experience. He knew that hospital officials saw value in standardizing with one company that could meet all their needs, but he wasn't sure whether they would be willing to pay an extra $110,000 for the package. Chuck also had taken a few minutes to think through his negotiating power. On the morning he arrived for negotiations with Purchasing, he fully understood the strength of his position.

Customer-Focused Selling Strategies That Strengthen Your Knowledge Power.   Become an expert in your field as well as your customer's. When you study each customer carefully throughout the sales process, you will arrive at Step 6 (Commitment) with knowledge power.

Keep your eyes and ears open throughout the sales process, as Chuck did. Chuck learned, early in the selling process, that key doctors wanted his surgical tables and sterilizers.

Remember the NO TRICKS model before your next negotiation, and run through each area in your mind to get an accurate perception of your negotiating strength. Then prepare your negotiating session as described later in this chapter.

Skill

The essential question here is: Who are the more skillful negotiators?

Buyers are making more buying decisions today, and they're getting better at it. Many buyers have attended negotiating seminars to improve their negotiating skills, which means they are gaining more skill power. Sellers must improve their skills just to keep up with today's buyers.

As sellers progress through their careers, they will likely become involved in larger negotiations that are of greater personal importance. The sooner sellers sharpen their negotiating skills, the greater their future advantage.

Chuck's Skill Power in Action.   Negotiations began with the Director of Purchasing presenting Chuck with a spreadsheet that indicated AMSCO's proposal of $820,000 was $110,000 more than the other alternative the hospital was considering. The Director pointed out that the construction of the new ambulatory care center was already 20 percent over budget, and hospital administrators were pressuring Purchasing to cut costs wherever possible. "Chuck," the Director said, "if you want all our business, you'll have to sharpen your pencil."

Chuck thanked the Director for telling him about the price differential, and then he drew on his preparation and negotiating skill to state his case. Chuck had anticipated that he would need to justify his higher price. He had prepared an accounting of the 150+ hours of free consulting time he and fellow AMSCO representatives had already invested in the project. Chuck also pointed out that much more time would need to be invested *after* the sale, to properly integrate the surgical tables with the lights, the lights with the gas columns, and so on. He reminded the Director that his competitors did not have a "surgical specialist" position; they offered technical support only via the phone. Chuck also emphasized the importance of standardization. If the hospital purchased everything from AMSCO, there would be no confusion in servicing, no finger-pointing if problems in integration were to occur. For these reasons, Chuck explained, his solution was worth more. On the other hand, because Chuck sensed that he needed to flex a little bit to help the Director save face, he grudgingly agreed to reduce his proposal to $800,000.

Chuck knew that, regardless of what happened during the appointment, the chances of his "closing" the sale at the end of the appointment were not good. He resisted his temptation to close, maintained his patience, and left the appointment optimistic of his chances at winning the entire order. The following day, his optimism was confirmed with a call from the Director of Purchasing. Chuck had won the order by negotiating thoughtfully and reducing but not slashing the original price.

Customer-Focused Selling Strategies That Strengthen Your Skill Power.   How skillful are you at negotiating? Do you ever enter a sales negotiation without preparing thoroughly in advance? Do you sometimes grant overly generous concessions that you later regret? Do you ever feel panic as an important deal seemingly crumbles before your very eyes?

Study this chapter carefully, and make any necessary adjustments in your negotiating approach. Then, become your own sales manager. Learn from *each* negotiating situation by observing yourself. After each sales negotiation, ask yourself: What did I do right?

What could I have done differently? What will I do differently the next time?

The NO TRICKS Analysis Worksheet.   Figure 8.1 is a worksheet designed to help you analyze your negotiating power using NO

Figure 8.1   NO TRICKS Analysis Worksheet

Seller		Buyer
	Who <u>N</u>eeds this sale more?	
	What are the <u>O</u>ptions if an agreement is not reached?	
	Are any impending events creating a <u>T</u>ime deadline?	
	How strong is my <u>R</u>elationship with the buyer(s)? How important is the relationship to him or her?	
	How much energy has been <u>I</u>nvested?	
	How much <u>C</u>redibility do I have? Is the buyer's <u>C</u>redibility crucial to me?	
	Who has more <u>K</u>nowledge about this solution? Which of us believes he or she has the upper hand?	
	Who is the more <u>S</u>killful negotiator?	

TRICKS. As you read it over, think about a deal you are working on now.

2. Prepare to Negotiate

After you have analyzed your negotiating strength, it is time to prepare for your discussions.

The first step in preparation is to figure out what you want. Many salespeople overlook this step. What does your "best case" agreement look like? What's the least you could live with? List your goals on a piece of paper.

Establish a range of flexibility. Your "minimum" position is the least amount you are willing to accept. Your "best case" position is your most favorable list price scenario. Your "target" position is what you hope to achieve at the conclusion of negotiations. For instance, as a district manager for Lanier back in the mid-1980s, one of my responsibilities was to hire and train a team of salespeople to sell small business telephone systems. Our systems were priced fairly competitively, but practically all buyers wanted a discount off the list price, which adversely affected the salespersons' commission. Lanier responded by raising prices by 10 percent, then changing the salespersons' compensation plan to allow a 10 percent discount without affecting commissions. In effect, Lanier raised its best case by 10 percent in hopes of achieving a higher target price—the price that previously had been the best case.

The minimum, target, and best case positions for a small business telephone system might include:

Item	Minimum	Target	Best Case
Price	$10,000	$11,250	$12,500
Payment terms	Three monthly installments, no interest charges	25% down, balance due in 30 days	50% down, balance due upon installation
Service contract	One year for free	One year for $500	Two years for $1,000
Installation charges	$1,000	$1,500	$2,000
System's feature package	Basic	Standard	Premium
Electronic key telephone features	10-button non-speakerphone	10-button full speakerphone	20-button speakerphone w/LCD display

After you identify minimum, target, and best case, begin negotiating at your best-case level. If you must give ground on price, then try not to accept the minimum payment terms. In fact, a concession in one column should ideally be balanced by an advantage in another.

Prepare Justifications for Each Item

When you are negotiating, you must be able to clarify and justify the reasonableness of your offer, so you should prepare a justification for each best-case item. Why is your product worth $12,500? (Remember to run through any value-added services that are included with the product, and state their dollar value.) What unique capabilities do you offer and how will those capabilities help your customer? Why are your terms of 50 percent down, full payment upon installation reasonable? Why is your two-year service contract worth $1,000?

Many consultants and professional service providers encounter "sticker shock" when they quote their hourly or daily fees. If you were a buyer of professional services and were quoted a fee of $1,000/day, you might feel sticker shock, too.

If you are a self-employed consultant, you know that you can bill no more than 70 percent of your work time, because of downtime for personal development, training, travel, marketing, and administrative duties. Also, expenses including rent, office supplies, office equipment, travel, and so on, must be deducted from your income. Social Security taxes for a self-employed individual are double what an employee pays, because the self-employed person has no employer who matches funds.

Consultants must justify their fees by explaining to the client each factor mentioned above and proving that their fee is "in the ballpark" compared to other consultants with *similar credentials*. Regardless of what you sell, you must justify your price in your own mind first, so you can justify it to others convincingly. Why are you *worth* it?

Generate a List of High-Value Concessions

In a negotiation, many buyers tend to focus on one issue: price. However, many factors other than price come into play during negotiations. Examples of other items include delivery terms and conditions, packaging, postsale support, disposal of unused goods, and order entry processing. It is in your best interest to generate a list of possible concessions other than price reductions. How else might you sweeten the deal for your buyer? Look back to your buyer's "must-haves" and "nice-to-haves" criteria. Focus on criteria other than price that the buyer considered most important. For instance, suppose you sell laser printers and an important criterion for your customer is reliability. You may offer a concession such as a surge protector—a device that protects the printer's components from sudden fluctuations in electricity. Other examples of concessions are added services, additional options, training, customization of your product or service, future considerations in ordering, payment schedule adjustments, and so on.

When you make your list of possible concessions, place a dollar value next to each one:

Important Buying Criterion	High-Value, Low-Cost Concessions	Dollar Value of Concessions
Reliability	Surge protector	$350

In this way, should your prospect ask for a concession in price, you can counteroffer with a concession that is of high value to your prospect but low cost to you.

Step Inside Your Customer's Mind

Next, imagine you are your customer. Go back to the first step in preparing to negotiate, and review the sale from the customer's perspective. This helps you better understand the customer's needs and what he or she hopes to accomplish by negotiating. It also helps you anticipate the customer's demands.

3. Reach Agreement Through Discussion

Negotiations begin when your buyer presents a demand. The first demand is often an extreme one. At precisely this moment, many salespeople make a big mistake: they immediately react. As human beings, when someone pushes us, our knee-jerk response is to push back. When we push back, we react emotionally in some way. We either confront and "fight it out," or we concede immediately in order to end the conflict.

Salespeople need to change their attitude about a buyer's initial demand. Don't confront it, welcome it. Tom Crum, the author of *The Magic of Conflict*, says we need to change how we respond to confrontation. Crum uses the martial art of Aikido as a metaphor for handling conflict. The purpose of Aikido is to render an attack harmless without harming the attacker. This is the result you want from your sales negotiations.

In Aikido, you handle an attack by moving *toward* the source of the attack, not away from it. Think about it. A punch is relatively harmless if your face is two inches away from your attacker. Another example might be how you regain control of your car in a skid. You turn your wheels *toward* the skid, not away from it. You go with the energy, not against it.

When presented with an unrealistic demand in a sales negotiation, don't dig in, hold your ground, and fight. Instead, use indirect action, the opposite of what your buyer thinks you'll do (and what you feel like doing). Welcome your prospect's demand, acknowledge it, draw it toward you, and destabilize your attacker without harming your relationship. Here's how:

1. Move toward the attack by paraphrasing the demand. Reword your prospect's demand to show you listened. For instance, "Jim, what I hear you saying is that you are requesting a 25 percent discount. Is that correct?"

2. Next, destabilize the attack by asking, "How did you arrive at that figure?" This gets your buyer to present tangible reasons for making the request. If unable to justify the request, the buyer may drop it, or at least modify it to a less extreme position.

Remember, many buyers challenge your offers for reasons unrelated to the transaction—job responsibilities, the need for admiration, a desire to win. If your buyers can't justify a request, they are probably seeking a better deal just for the sake of winning. You now know you are in a fairly strong position.

If your buyers are able to justify a demand, you gain valuable insight into the motivation that lies beneath it. Roger Fisher and William Ury, authors of *Getting to Yes*, say, "Don't attack their position, look behind it. When the other side sets forth their position, neither reject it or accept it. Treat it as one possible option. Look for the interests behind it, seek out the principles which it reflects, and think about ways to improve it." Once you discover these underlying motivations, you may have concessions other than price discounts that you can offer to serve these interests.

Fisher and Ury make the crucial point that there is a difference between a *position* and an *interest*. A position is typically a tangible request, such as a "25 percent discount." The interest behind that position is what causes the buyer to make the demand in the first place. So, the interest behind a request for a 25 percent discount may be to "improve value," to "reduce cash expenditures," or to "match all our other vendors' 25 percent discount." You can discover the interests that lie behind your prospects' positions by simply asking, "Why?" or "How did you arrive at that figure?" or "What's your justification for that?"

Some buyers challenge your price because they lack understanding of the transaction's value. When one of Chuck's prospects said, "Chuck, your price is too high," he responded, "Thank you for mentioning that. May I ask you, how much of a difference are we talking about?" The prospect said, "You are 15 percent higher than Company A." Chuck said, "I can certainly understand your concern. I'm wondering, however, how did you arrive at that 15 percent figure?" The prospect then said, "Company A's model 2020 bed is $5,250 and yours is $6,000." Chuck instantly recognized that the customer was not "comparing apples with apples." The competitor's surgical bed did not include a built-in scale or an integrated air surface, a feature that reduces pressure on the patient. Once Chuck pointed out these differences to the prospect, the prospect recognized why Chuck's bed was more expensive. Chuck went on to say, "Our model that's comparable to Company A's model 2020 is $5,350. Is that more along the lines of what you had in mind?" In the end, Chuck sold the more expensive beds at $5,900 each.

3. Next, you want to get all additional demands out in the open before you make any concessions. This will prevent "nibbling"—a buyer tactic of whittling away on one issue, then moving on to whittle another. To get all additional demands on the table, simply say, "Are there any other issues besides price that we need to address?"

4. Once you understand your prospect's interests, seek win–win solutions that serve your buyer's interests as well as yours. The key question to ask yourself is, "What would satisfy my interests and at the same time satisfy the buyer?" Your interest is to protect profitability.

Creativity is the key to generating win–win solutions. Revert back to your Architect sales role for ways to improve your creativity.

Because of the preparation you made earlier, you already know which variables are negotiable and how flexible you are willing to be. When you start your negotiations, begin with your smallest concessions. For example, if price is a major issue for you but delivery is a minor issue, you may offer priority overnight shipping. By gaining agreement on smaller issues first, you set a positive tone for the negotiations, which is important as you move toward the major issues.

Never give a concession without getting one in return. Give concessions one at a time, and give them in decreasing amounts. For example, your first concession might be for $100, your second for $50, and your third for $20. This signals to your buyer that you are approaching the bottom, and that additional requests will be responded to with less and less value.

5. Never make an important decision on the spot. How do you know what an important decision is? You can feel it in your gut; you get tight, or you start to sweat. There is no reason why you should feel pressured to decide immediately.

How can you buy time? One way is to ask an open-ended question that gets your prospect talking—so you can think. Another way is to ask a question about a different issue in the negotiation. By shifting your buyer's attention to a different issue, you gain time. Many salespeople find it helpful to keep a "higher authority required" limitation so that they don't make concessions they later regret. For instance, a salesperson may inform the buyer that any discounts above 15 percent require managerial approval. By excusing yourself for a few minutes to call your boss, you gain time to think. Regardless of how you handle an important decision, the key is to assume an attitude of detachment. If you imagine you are an observer of the negotiation, not an active participant in it, you may see the dynamics of the situation more clearly.

Questioning and Listening: Your Most Important Skills

Throughout Step 6 (Negotiation) you should be asking questions. The more you know about your prospect's needs and motivations, the better your ability to create options that resolve your differences. Open-ended questions—questions that can't be answered with a simple "Yes" or "No"—are usually more effective because you learn more about your prospect, you gain time to think, and your buyer's time to think is reduced. Examples of open-ended questions in a negotiation would be:

1. To gather new information about the negotiations:
   "Can you tell me more about that?"
   "Is there anything else I should know?"

2. To identify underlying interests:
   "Why is that important to you?"
   "What's the reason for that?"

Closed-ended questions, questions that can be answered with a "Yes" or "No," are also useful. For instance:

3. To test for a buyer's receptiveness and gain a commitment:
   "Can you see why that's important to us?"
   "Would 7 percent off be acceptable to you?"

Stephen Covey, author of *Seven Habits of Highly Effective People*, says most people are either speaking or preparing to speak. To negotiate effectively, you must take the opposite approach. You must be either listening or preparing to listen. When you are listening, you will be alert to nonverbal cues, such as crossed arms or a scowl that indicates displeasure. You will discover the underlying motivations of your prospect, and you will be more creative at discovering win–win solutions to difficult negotiating problems. Simply put, the best negotiators are the best listeners.

Get It in Writing

Once you have reached an agreement, confirm it in writing immediately. This prevents foggy recall, which occurs later on when one or both parties have become confused about the details of the agreement. Written confirmation clarifies the terms and prevents misunderstandings that can harm both your agreement and your new relationship.

ASKING FOR COMMITMENT

If you have successfully applied Customer-Focused Selling concepts, up to and including the negotiation of terms, getting a buyer's commitment should come naturally. You have earned your customer's trust, helped with recognition of needs, and proved that your solution is best.

For many salespeople, traditional "closing" situations are occurring less frequently, so closing skills are becoming less important for them. If you are selling to a customer who is not authorized to give you final approval, such as a lower-level decision maker within a business, closing techniques are relatively ineffective. This person lacks the power necessary to make a commitment. Salespeople who sell in this way often learn they have won the sale when their key contact, a person whom I refer to as the salespersons' "sponsor," calls them with the good news. The sponsor is any person who has credibility and influence with key decision makers and who exercises that influence by selling to other decision makers on your behalf. Usually, sponsors work for your prospective client, but sometimes they can be influential nonemployees, such as consultants or lawyers. We will take a close look at sponsors in Chapter 11.

As mentioned earlier, your goal is to open the relationship, not to close the sale. In the Customer-Focused Selling process, I refer to the abilities needed to ask for the agreed-on order as "commitment skills," not "closing skills." Closing skills attempt to get the buyer to commit. Commitment skills are different because, in the Customer-Focused Selling process, there is *mutual commitment* at the point of sale. The customer commits to you, and you commit to the customer. The commitment I suggest you make is described in the next two chapters, which describe the Teacher and Farmer sales roles.

Prospects who are knowledgeable about selling *expect* you to ask for their business. If you fail to do so, they may mistakenly assume you are weak or indecisive.

Here are a few nonmanipulative ways to ask for commitment:

1. Ask, "What should be our next step?" This question is typically most appropriate for a buyer who has a clear vision of how events should unfold. In the chapter describing your role as Coach, I referred to this type of prospect as the "expert." This is a simple, honest question that asks your buyer to suggest a commitment to you.

2. Describe in detail what happens between now and installation, delivery, or commencement of service. If you have an implementation plan, now is the time to share it. Then, simply ask, "Does that sound acceptable to you?"

3. Ask, "Would you like to give us a try?" This commitment question is soft, yet direct, because it asks for a "Yes" or "No" answer.

By this point, you and your prospect have come a long way together. Although these commitment techniques are usually successful, some prospects may be reluctant to buy. In this case, you must deal with the salesperson's old nemesis—objections.

WHAT ABOUT OBJECTIONS?

The premise of this book is that many salespeople are not getting inside the buyers' mind. They focus on their sales process, without carefully considering how people buy. This focus causes them to sell too fast. Salespeople who sell too fast will encounter a stream of objections because they arrive at the "close" long before their prospect does. I believe that many objections are actually *caused* by salespeople. If you change how you sell to match how people buy, you should see a reduction in the quantity of objections you encounter.

As was mentioned earlier, over 80 percent of the directly stated objections that salespeople face are price/value objections: "It costs too much," "I can't afford it." In your Doctor sales role, you learned that these objections are symptoms of a greater problem—low perception of value. If a price objection arises early in your sales process, ask history, symptom, cause, complication, and cure questions to help your prospect recognize the seriousness of the ongoing problems and, therefore, the increased value of your solution. By adopting the role of a Doctor, you *prevent* price objections, thereby avoiding the necessity to overcome them.

If price objections occur late in the sales process, find out what underlying interest is causing the concern. Two typical causes trigger a concern over price late in the sales cycle: (1) fear and (2) the desire to get a better deal.

Once you know the underlying reason for the price objection, you have two choices:

1. If the underlying concern is fear, adopt the role of a Therapist and draw the fear out into the open. Remember, traditional objection-handling techniques are not effective with fear. They move too quickly to a logical conclusion and don't get to the heart of the problem. Fear is emotional, not logical.

2. If your prospect's price objection is caused by the desire to get a better deal, adopt the role of a Negotiator and create a win–win agreement, as described in this chapter.

A final option for price objections, or for any other type of objection, is to use the "verify/feel/felt/found" technique.

When I was a sales manager selling business telephone systems, we offered three product choices for small businesses. These "hybrid key telephone systems" had capacities of 6 lines/16 phones, 12 lines/32 phones, and 21 lines/56 phones. Our salespeople faced a common objection of "expansion capability"—concern that our system could not grow enough to meet the prospects' future needs.

Here's how I would handle this objection using the "feel/felt/found" method. I avoided saying "feel/felt/found" verbatim because the technique has been around for many years, and customers may have heard it before.

Suppose my prospect expressed a concern, such as, "No, I'm not in a position to go ahead with it."

1. I found out more by asking, "May I ask why?"

Assume the prospect responded, "I need 8 incoming lines and 22 phones now. But a few years from now, my business will certainly have grown. I'm not sure your system meets my future needs."

With my prospect's objection now out in the open, I needed to *verify* that system capacity was, in fact, the real concern.

2. I verified the objection by saying, "If you felt comfortable about our system's ability to fulfill your growth requirements, would you then feel confident that our offering is the best choice?"

If the prospect responded, "No, I would not," that meant the true objection was something other than system capacity, and I'd return to question 1. If, on the other hand, the prospect verified that "system capacity" *was* the objection, I would then proceed to feel/felt/found.

3. "Mr. Prospect, I understand your concern [feel]. Mary Thompson, owner of Thompson Graphics down the street, expressed the same concern to me just last week [felt]. Once she learned more about just how flexible our system is, however, she decided to go ahead. Here's what helped her . . . [found]." Then, I'd show the prospect how the 12-line/32-phone key service unit (KSU) was packed with exactly the same component cards as our 21-line/56-phone system. Should the customer purchase our 12-line system today for $12,000, upgrading at a later date would simply involve purchasing a larger box for $950, after trade-in.

If you respond to an objection in this way, be sure to have materials that substantiate your claim. Third-party testimonials—letters that describe a similar situation experienced by another one of your clients—are worth their weight in gold at this crucial point of the sale. How to obtain these letters will be addressed in Chapter 10.

YOU DID IT!

Now you have a plan for reaching win–win agreements with buyers who negotiate from either a win–win or win–lose perspective:

- You analyze negotiating power using NO TRICKS.
- You prepare to negotiate by determining what you want from the agreement (using a high, medium, and low range) and by generating a list of high-value concessions, other than price, to use as bargaining chips if needed.
- You reach agreement with your customer by clearly identifying your customer's interests, determining areas of agreement, and creating win–win solutions to resolve differences.
- You ask for commitment in a nonmanipulative way.

The result is a signed contract. Congratulations!

9

Sales Role #7: THE TEACHER

Teach Your Customer How to Achieve Maximum Value

All things are difficult before they are easy.

John Norley

In the previous chapter, we examined the buying process right up to the point where your customer signed on the dotted line and your agreement was complete. Is your sale a done deal? Nope. You've got a deal, but your work is not done.

Early in my sales career, I sold dictation equipment to business and professional people. For executives who generate a lot of letters and memos, dictation equipment saves time, because people can speak much faster than they can write or type. I sold two types of dictation systems, desktop and remote. A desktop system consists of a tape recorder on the executive's desk and a transcriber on the secretary's desk. Recorded tapes are passed from the executive to the secretary, enabling the secretary to listen and act on the executive's instructions. The remote system consists of a simple microphone in the executive's office wired directly to a recorder/transcriber on the secretary's desk. Because the executive's voice is recorded on the secretary's desk unit, there is no passage of tapes, and this speeds the flow of information.

One of the prospects in my territory was Alan, a successful trial attorney. When I first met with Alan, he owned an antiquated, overburdened desktop system that was repeatedly breaking down.

Alan was intrigued by the remote system, the likes of which he had not seen before, and I sold one to him.

The day we installed Alan's new system, I met with him briefly and explained a few of the capabilities of his new system. Alan was busy preparing for an important hearing in court the following morning, so he didn't have much time to talk. He did express enthusiasm for the remote capability, which he tried out by dictating a few short instructions to his secretary. Late the following afternoon, I called Alan's secretary to followup and, once again, received a positive report. I hung up the phone, mistakenly thinking I had created another satisfied customer.

The next day, an urgent message from my office notified me that Alan had called. Alan had told our switchboard operator that if I did not arrive at his office within the hour, he would "throw his new equipment out the window." Uh-oh.

When I arrived at Alan's office thirty minutes later, I was immediately ushered in to see him. He was furious. His face was bright red and he was cussing at his new equipment. I listened with empathy, saying only, "I see," "Then what happened?" and "Tell me more." I knew he needed to blow off steam before a rational solution could be reached.

Alan was frustrated because he had been unable to rewind the tape to listen to previously recorded dictation. As it turned out, he often revised his letters and memoranda after dictating them. With his old system, if he wanted to add an afterthought to a letter or memo, he would simply put that particular tape back in his unit, rewind it and listen to where he left off, and then record his additional comments. With the remote system, when the microphone was put back in its cradle, an electronic "roadblock" was automatically recorded on the tape. To rewind past this roadblock, Alan needed to push the rewind button *twice*. This special rewinding capability was explained in the instruction book, but Alan had not bothered to read it and, not knowing the manner in which he worked, I had not emphasized it in my initial instructions.

After Alan had cooled down, I asked him, "Would you like to know how to do what you need done?" Finally, I had his full attention. I then showed him how to push the rewind button twice, which solved his problem. Next, I gave him a refresher course on other capabilities of his new remote system. At last, Alan was content, and when I called him the following day, he was in love with his new machine! Alan was a satisfied customer, but I had come dangerously close to losing his business.

Alan's anger was caused by the difficulty of change that is required when a new product or service is implemented. For customers to achieve their expectations of value, they must first pass through a learning process, and learning can be annoying, frustrating, and time-consuming.

Have you ever noticed that the customers who are the most enthusiastic and pleased on day 1 are the most likely to suddenly be dissatisfied on day 2? What causes this customer dissatisfaction?

The root cause of most customer dissatisfaction is a difference in perception between buyers and sellers. For most salespeople, the sales process comes to an *end* when the customer says "yes." For most buyers, the sales process is just *beginning* when they say "yes." To keep customers for life, you must change your frame of reference, get into your customer's head, and see things from the customer's perspective. You must start seeing the "close" of a deal as the beginning of a new sales process, not the end of an old one. Staying supportive of your customer after your solution has been delivered is the single most important thing you can do to maintain a good relationship and generate repeat business.

To increase profitability, companies today are placing a much greater emphasis on *keeping* customers, because the cost of acquiring customers is five to six times the cost of retaining existing customers. In addition, an eighteen-year study, the Profit Impact of Market Strategy (PIMS), proved conclusively the bottom-line benefit enjoyed by companies rated by their customers as superior in service quality. The PIMS study, conducted by the Strategic Planning Institute in Cambridge, Massachusetts, in cooperation with the Harvard Business School, analyzed 3,000 business units in 450 firms. The study found that service leaders charge 9 to 10 percent more for their products and services, yet grow twice as fast as their low-service competition. Market share growth of top-service providers averaged 6 percent per annum, while low-service providers saw their market share erode by 2 percent per year. Creating and keeping satisfied customers clearly pays.

Many companies are recognizing the crucial role salespeople play in satisfying and retaining customers. Watson Wyatt Data Services, the U.S. survey arm of the international compensation and benefits consulting firm, recently conducted a study of training needs that 350 companies of all shapes and sizes consider most important for high-performance sales. Their findings were published in the November, 1994 issue of *Inc.* magazine. The two most important needs on their "sales training hit list" were "customer relations" (cited by 92.5 percent of respondents as *very important*) and "retention of customer base" (cited by 87.2 percent of respondents as *very important*). Postsale selling skills are becoming much more important. Salespeople skilled at achieving customer satisfaction and retention can expect customer loyalty, a precious asset beyond value.

YOUR CUSTOMERS' SEVENTH STEP: EXPECTATIONS OF VALUE

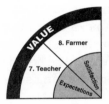 Welcome to the last stage of the buy-*learning* process. Having completed the Need, Learn, and Buy stages, your customers now enter the Value stage, which consists of Step 7, Expectations of Value, and Step 8, Satisfaction. Step 7 begins when your customers approve a sale and ends when they have successfully implemented your solution.

The Five Phases of Learning to Use a New Product or Service

Buying requires change. Implementing a new product or service almost always demands a modification of behavior, a change in how things are done. To successfully integrate your product or service into their way of life, customers must move through a learning process. To achieve improved customer satisfaction, you must understand this process, realize what your customers are experiencing, and recognize your responsibility in facilitating their learning.

Robert Pike is a speaker, author, and consultant in the field of training and development. In his book, *Creative Training Techniques Handbook*, he identifies the five phases of a learning process. These five phases, which help us understand how we learn, can be applied to any learning situation. When we apply these five phases to the buy-*learning* process, we gain a better understanding of what customers go through during Step 7 (Expectations of Value).

- **Phase 1: Unconscious Incompetence.** *Your customers don't know that they don't know.* During this phase, your customers feel enthusiasm. Throughout the buying process, they have focused on the results and benefits they expect to achieve once a purchase is made. In focusing on results, however, your customers often ignore what must be done to get those results. The expectations of value are high, and the difficulty of learning is underestimated.

Take, for instance, the impact of the sale and installation of a new business telephone system. Suppose you sell a telephone system to a corporation. Just prior to and following the installation of your system, representatives from your company train your customer's employees on the operation of their new system. During this training, the employees learn about the system's capabilities, many of which are new and different. They can see how these new features will be of benefit, so they feel enthusiastic about their new system.

However, at this early stage, your employee–customers have not yet had an opportunity to use all the capabilities of the new system. They aren't even aware of certain advantages because they haven't tested all the bells and whistles. The truth is that your customers are not yet competent at using the new system—and, so far, they don't realize what they're missing.

- **Phase 2: Conscious Incompetence.** *Your customers know that they don't know.* During this phase, your customers feel frustration as the difficulty of change sets in. Habitual ways of doing things, tasks done unconsciously in the past, must now be altered. Productivity plummets as new procedures are created, often through trial and error. Customers may feel that your solution has made things worse, not better.

  Suppose a week after the installation of the new phone system, the CEO asks her executive assistant to arrange a conference call (one phone call in which three or more people participate). Accomplishing this task requires pushing several buttons in proper sequence, and the assistant quickly discovers that the new system's operating commands are different from those of the old system. Tempers may flare as the executive assistant, the CEO, and others are inconvenienced by the unfamiliar operations of the new phone system. Your customers can't get the system to do what needs to be done—and they know it.

- **Phase 3: Conscious Competence.** *Your customers work hard at what they don't know.* During Phase 3, your customers renew their determination. New procedures are in place and your customers are becoming more proficient at operating the new product or using the new service. Results improve, providing positive reinforcement that encourages your customers. Your product or service begins to make a real contribution to your customers' business.

In our phone system example, the CEO's executive assistant finally determines how to set up a conference call. She makes a list of the specific buttons to push and the sequence in which they should be pushed, as a quick reference guide for future use. When she refers to this guide, she can do what needs to be done.

- **Phase 4: Unconscious Competence.** *Your customers don't have to think about knowing what to do.* During this phase, your customers feel a sense of accomplishment. Results are being realized. Your new customers have successfully integrated your product or service into their way of life.

    A phone system typically takes a few weeks to master. After a month, your customers are no longer disconnecting people by accident, and they can operate the system quickly and effortlessly. They no longer have to think about the steps involved.

- **Phase 5: Conscious Unconscious Competence.** *Your customers can easily explain to others how to do what they can now do.* By now, the CEO's executive assistant is so proficient at arranging conference calls that she can teach coworkers how to do it. As new employees join the firm, the executive assistant may be sought out as an "in-house expert." Many of your customers are capable of reaching Phase 4, but it's much more difficult to reach Phase 5. Enabling certain customers to transfer what they know to their coworkers will ensure that your solution achieves value for months and years to come.

The more complex your product or service, the more time is required to progress through the five phases of learning. Learning a new computer program can be complex, while learning how to operate a new fax machine can be fairly simple. The longer the learning process, the greater the feeling of frustration in Phase 2.

The sophistication of your customers also plays a role. Inexperienced customers tend to underestimate the difficulties of change, so they expect immediate results. The more unrealistic your customers' expectations of immediate value, the deeper their plunge into frustration will be.

Sometimes, the people who make the decision to buy your product are not the ones who will use it. In this case, those who are expected to use the product may feel threatened. They may see the product or service as making their work more difficult, or as threatening their job security. Some products and services are designed to replace people. Many salespeople have successfully pitched their sales to senior executives, only to have the ensuing implementation of their solution sabotaged by resistant users. For your solution to be a success, you need to take into consideration not only the learning curve of your buyers, but also the experiences of whoever will be using your product or service. You must show those who use your product or service how it benefits their self-interest. This means more effort for you, but it is the only way to ensure buyer satisfaction.

Expectations of Value

During the earlier stages (Need, Learn, and Buy), buyers formulate expectations of value, a mental picture of the results once they make a purchase.

For most buyers, especially inexperienced ones, the expectations of value that emerge from the buying process are intangible, vague, and undefined. Take, for instance, a business buyer's expectation of an "improved competitive position." This expectation is unclear because it can't be measured or tracked. The danger here is that the buyer is unable to determine whether the expectation has been achieved. For your buyers, intangible expectations lead to an uncertain perception of the value of your product or service. If a buyer has not become convinced that your solution is valuable, you may never make it to Step 8 of the buy-*learning* process, Customer Satisfaction. In a later section, we'll take a closer look at the issue of tangible versus intangible customer expectations.

Expectations of You

Adding to this dilemma of intangible and unachievable expectations of *your product's* value, customers have high expectations of *you*. In Step 7, your new customer is watching you like a hawk. For a moment, you try playing the customer. Suppose you decide to sell your home and move into a larger home. You interview several realtors, and select one to be your listing agent—to provide you, the customer, with the service of marketing and selling your home. If you sign the listing papers on a Wednesday night, are you going to expect to see sales activities occurring by the weekend? You bet you are. You want to see an ad in the weekend paper. You want an open house on Sunday. You want to see prospective buyers walking through your home. You are looking for visible indications of effort being expended on your behalf. Your customers look to you for the same level of activity.

Most buyers have felt the frustration that occurs when salespeople who made them feel important during the sales process dump them once the sale has been made. Throughout the sales process, sellers tell prospects about their commitment to customer satisfaction. Customers watch closely to see whether the sellers "walk the talk." The customers' question is: "Does this salesperson (and his or her company) *really* care about me?" Well, do you?

Step 7 (Expectations of Value) comprises several challenges for salespeople, because the customer may:

- Be ignorant of the learning process that change requires.
- Lack familiarity with the changes that must be made to implement the solution.
- Have undefined and unrealistic expectations of the value of the product or service.
- Have lofty expectations of the seller's involvement in postsale activities.

You can overcome all of these obstacles and create a customer for life by assuming the role of a Teacher.

SALES ROLE #7: THE TEACHER

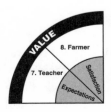

In the role of **Teacher,** your activities consist of three steps:

1. Set realistic objectives and expectations.
2. Show, then help to do.
3. Test to measure progress.

Use these steps to benefit both you and your customers.

I. Set Realistic Objectives and Expectations

If you were a school teacher preparing a lesson plan, you would begin by identifying what your students should be able to do at the *end* of the session. Your objectives would be clearly stated so that your students' expectations about the course can be realistic and specific. Your students deserve to know at the beginning of a course how they will benefit from it at the end.

In your sales role as Teacher in the Customer-Focused Selling process, you must see that realistic objectives and expectations are set. The objectives agreed on by you and your customers should be achievable and measurable. Once these objectives are set, it's up to you to *teach* your customers how to attain them.

The Forum Corporation conducted a five-year research project to study both the expectations of today's customers and the behavior of people in companies that consistently manage to give customers what they want. Richard Whiteley, cofounder of Forum, wrote about these findings in his book, *The Customer-Driven Company*. Forum's research determined that the companies that deliver what their customers want "provide high quality not according to definitions they've developed on their own, but rather as the customer defines it." As a salesperson, you influence the essence of these definitions and you are present when they are conceived. That places a major portion of the responsibility for customer satisfaction squarely on your shoulders. With this responsibility, however, comes opportunity. When you manage your buyers' expectations effectively, you greatly enhance your chance of creating satisfied customers.

Needs Versus Expectations: Why Many Customers Are Disappointed

An unsatisfied customer is one whose expectations are not met. Unhappy customers have excellent memories. They won't buy from you again, and they tell others of their unhappiness. It's not a pleasant scenario.

Some dissatisfied customers are just cranky and impossible to please, but many are otherwise reasonable people. What causes a customer to turn on you? Feelings of being unappreciated, let down, or even betrayed. Unhappy customers are often created by salespeople who are unaware of their customers' expectations.

A major cause of postsale customer dissatisfaction is a lack of understanding, by both buyers and sellers, regarding the difference between a *need* and an *expectation*. Webster's New World Dictionary defines these terms as follows:

need: an urgent requirement of something essential.

expectation: to look for as likely to occur or appear.

Thus, a *need* is something people *require;* an *expectation* is something people *anticipate seeing.* The difficulty is that you can fulfill your buyers' needs without satisfying their expectations.

Suppose you sell cash registers. Your prospect is the owner of a small deli on a busy street. Business is good, but the owner desires more repeat business. His current cash registers are cumbersome and frequently malfunction, which slows down transaction time and forces customers to wait in long lines, especially at lunchtime. Your prospect is interested in buying your new cash registers, believing that this simple step will guarantee a high level of repeat business and therefore greater revenues. Because he has an unrealistic expectation of what your cash registers will accomplish, he will be a dissatisfied customer, unless you point out to him that his level of repeat business is affected by a multitude of factors besides the length of time customers spend waiting in line. You can clarify for him exactly what your cash registers will do to help his bottom line. In concrete terms, better cash registers will enable him to serve more customers more quickly. Cash registers will not affect the quality of the food, the speed with which it is prepared, the deli's location, the cost of supplies, and so on.

The objective, for both you and your customers, is to eliminate surprises and disappointment. By helping your customers to identify what they expect to *see* after a purchase, you help them identify more realistic expectations.

Why Customers Are Becoming More Demanding

Many companies and salespeople are frustrated by the fact that customers are becoming more demanding. Or, put another way, customers have become less accepting. Today's consumers want proof, justification, and documentation. Patients get a second opinion; shoppers want to see product ratings before buying; everybody wants a guaranteed positive outcome for any money or effort expended. One reason customers' demands are continually rising is that customers have never been sure how to measure the value salespeople deliver to them in the first place. If customers don't know what to look for, they won't know when they find it. So, naturally, they will expect and look for more. It is sellers' responsibility to help new customers identify the *observable* effects of a product or service that indicate value is being achieved. Don't expect your buyers to recognize these effects without your help as Teacher.

How to Set Realistic Customer Objectives and Expectations

One way to keep your customers' expectations realistic is to define them clearly at the time the sales order is signed. By identifying in specific terms what your customers can expect immediately after purchase, you give them a benchmark, a point of reference against which to measure and judge your success. Also, you "freeze" your customers' expectations and prevent them from rising. Finally, you give yourself a specific goal to shoot for.

In all my years of selling, sales management, and sales consulting experience, I have found that fewer than one in fifty salespeople place any real emphasis on specifying what customers' expectations and objectives should be after the sale. Many salespeople ignore this gap; others simply assume their buyers already know what to expect. Yet, when salespeople make a point of discussing the postsale value of their offering, they are often surprised to learn that their customers' expectations are much different than they had thought. If you want to know what your customers expect, you must *ask*.

If the implementation of your product or service achieves an immediate result (such as a reduction in costs), your customers' expectations will be tangible (for example, a specific dollar figure). In the telecommunications industry, many customers are able to buy newer technologies that improve service and immediately cut costs, because new technologies are less costly to manufacture, deliver, and support. If your product or service has an immediate impact on costs, your customers' expectations of value should be easy to measure.

For many salespeople, however, measuring value is not that simple. Intangible products and services, such as advertising, financial services, insurance, and many business services, often have primarily intangible value. Even if you sell tangible products, you can still experience difficulty in accurately measuring value, because all tangible products have some intangible benefits.

You can solve this problem by asking your customers a few "measurement questions"—have them tell you how your value can be measured. Two of my favorite measurement questions are:

"Six months from today, how will you know this purchase was a success?"

"What things will be happening when the value you expect is being achieved?"

Your goal in asking these questions is to get your new customers to tell you how they will *notice* that your product or service is a success. If you sell copy machines, your customer may tell you: "I won't have a line of people waiting at the copier." If you sell securities and financial services, your client may respond: "The value of my account should increase equal to or better than the S&P 500 index." In each of these examples, the customer's expectations of value have been clarified, and observable indications that value is being achieved have been identified.

The purpose of setting realistic objectives and expectations is to focus attention. For your customers, it means focusing on what value they expect to achieve and how they will know when they get it. For you, it means focusing your teaching efforts in a way that allows your customers' expectations to be exceeded. Once a realistic objective is set, the power to accomplish it will begin to flow.

Why Unrealistic Expectations Can Be Damaging

Suppose you sell advertising. Everything is going along fine with your sales presentation until you ask what the customer hopes to accomplish and are told: "My goal is to increase sales by 20 percent." The problem is that this expectation is unrealistic: sales figures alone do not measure the effectiveness of advertising. Among the many other factors that affect sales are:

- Economic conditions.
- Competition.
- New products.
- Pricing.
- Management decisions and practices.
- Government regulation.
- Personnel changes.
- Product quality.
- Sales training.

Most of these factors are changing daily. All of these factors are totally out of your control. Even if a client's sales go up 20 percent while your schedule of ads is running, how can the client know that the advertising is responsible? The answer is that the client can't know. Too many other factors are involved. That's why companies serious about measuring the value of their advertising investment measure other things besides sales figures. Some measure direct response by simply asking customers, "How did you hear about us?" and then documenting the answer. Advertisements that include telephone numbers for respondents to call may list a different phone number in each ad. In this way, advertisers can measure the response generated by each ad. Companies with a presence on the World Wide Web include their Web address in their print advertisements. The number of people who then "stop by" their Web site can be measured.

The value of most products and services cannot be determined by obvious indicators such as profit and loss statements. Yet, if you don't clarify your customers' expectations, these types of measurements will be used to judge you. Suppose a customer's sales *dropped* by 20 percent while your ads were running. Who would get blamed? You would! Customers usually recognize when you screw up, but they seldom realize when you perform well.

To protect against this scuttling of your profitable relationships, you must help your customers identify realistic and observable indicators of your value. If you fail to do so, you are linking your personal success with dozens of factors that are totally out of your control.

Measuring Brand Awareness

Most advertising salespeople are constantly trying to get new customers to change their expectation of value from immediate sales increases to something more measurable, such as increased brand awareness. Brand awareness is defined as the total sum of what people think of you, your product, and your company. Why is brand awareness so important? Chuck Pettis, author of *Techno-Brands* says, "Brands stand as comfort anchors in the sea of confusion, fear, and doubt. Once customers have made a decision about a brand and its associations, they can be exceptionally loyal to that brand, continuing to buy it in the future, recommending it to friends, and choosing the product over others, even those with better feature sets or lower prices."

Brand awareness takes time to develop. You can't run one ad and expect buyers to know who you are. Savvy marketers know, however, that a consistent message delivered with high frequency can pay huge dividends for years. Do you remember which computer company ran the computer ads featuring the Charlie Chaplin look-alike? Sure you do, it was IBM. Since 1991, Intel Corporation, with its "Intel Inside" ad campaign, has patiently strengthened its brand image. The message is that having an Intel processor inside a PC means cutting-edge technology and greater performance. Corporate leaders such as Intel and IBM know that the primary value of advertising is its ability to build brand awareness.

How do advertising salespeople persuade their prospects to discard their goal of immediate sales increases in favor of long-term brand awareness? The most effective way is to study the buying process of their prospects' customers.

Steve Vito is the Associate Publisher of *Federal Computer Week*, whose readership consists of people who buy information technology for the federal government. *Federal Computer Week* is owned by International Data Group (IDG), a large computer publishing and research company. IDG has compiled an extensive body of research on the importance of brand awareness. One survey of computer buyers, conducted for IDG by IntelliQuest, found that the most important factor driving the selection of a notebook PC was brand awareness and not, as one might expect, price. This survey also found that, despite myriad notebook PC choices, purchasers considered, on average, just 2.7 notebook PC brands prior to their last purchase. Steve points out to prospective advertisers—that is, companies that are considering placing ads in his magazine—that their goal should be to generate awareness in a buyer's mind *before* the buyer starts shopping, so that the advertiser's product is one of the few considered during the buying process.

Brand awareness can be measured. Some publications (or their advertisers) measure the value of advertising by conducting a "benchmark awareness study." For instance, 500 new customers may be called before an ad campaign to measure brand awareness. Then, following the ad campaign, another 500 new customers are called. In this way, brand awareness is compared before and after the ad, to measure improvement.

If your customers' expectations are realistic and measurable, they are achievable. If they are unrealistic, the customers' perception of your value will soon be diminished. To prevent this misfortune, you must first help your customers recognize an unrealistic expectation, then set realistic objectives. If you don't, your customers will see you as another salesperson who overpromised and underdelivered.

2. Show, Then Help to Do

Customers who are ignorant of the learning process required when a new product or service is implemented usually expect immediate value. With these customers, you must walk a tightrope. On the one hand, you don't want to say something that will frighten them and perhaps cost you your sale. On the other hand, you must be honest about what typically happens (good and bad) once your product or service is installed. This is an instance where postsale selling techniques are important. Immediately after the sale, you must show your buyers how to make the most of your offering so that their experience will be as good as it can possibly be.

Teachers know that learning has not occurred until behavior has changed. Success is measured not so much by how much students learn as by what students *do* with what they learn. That's why teachers provide information and techniques first (show), then give students the opportunity to practice them on their own (help to do). These practice sessions should be positive, successful experiences for students; otherwise, they will lose confidence.

Good teaching requires much more than simple knowledge of the subject matter. Most people at some point have encountered an expert who was unable to effectively communicate his or her knowledge. (I had a chemistry teacher who was undeniably brilliant but whose lectures were incomprehensible.) A good teacher must understand how people learn and be able to teach in a way that allows students to learn. Telling everything you know is not teaching. As a salesperson, it is not enough for you to lecture and leave.

Most products and services have many different capabilities. If you try to teach your customers too much all at once, all may be forgotten. That's where clearly defined objectives come in: they reveal what your customers must do with your product or service right away. Which capabilities are most important? Define the "need-to-know" information versus the "nice-to-know." Ask yourself, "What will my customer need to *know and do* to utilize my product in this way?" Then ask, "What does my customer already know?" The gap between what is needed and what is already known defines what you must teach.

When customers don't know how to operate your product, provide direction. Show them each operating step, then gradually "let go of the reins." If you sell alarm systems, show your customers how to arm the system. Then stand back, and have the customers *show you*.

To avoid being a dull teacher, vary your style of interacting. Discuss key points and ask questions to make sure your customers understand. Divide the entire instruction into distinct tasks, and teach one task at a time. In our alarm system scenario, one task would be how to arm the system, another would be how to disarm the system. Mix your activities in such a way that your customers alternate between passive (listening, observing) and active (talking, doing) involvement. Keep pace with your student(s). Don't overload them with details.

Create a "cheat sheet" for your customers. Most instruction booklets provide far too much information for the average user. Make a short list of a few key tasks that your customers will need to remember after you leave.

When customers experience frustration, you must provide support and encouragement. Resist the temptation to jump in and perform the task for them. Adults learn by doing, which requires practice by your customers and patience by you. Let your buyers know that a little frustration in the initial stages is normal. If a user of your product or service is not the decision maker who bought it, make sure the user knows why your product or service is important. Show how it will benefit the user personally.

When today's salespeople were in elementary school, much teaching consisted of rote memorization. Today, many teachers have progressed to a more analytical approach that uses real-life situations. The goal is to help students acquire the knowledge and attitudes they need to lead a useful, rewarding life. Your goal is to enable your customers to incorporate your offering into a useful, rewarding life.

When You Are Most Vulnerable

A student who drops out of a course does so at the beginning of the course, not at the end. In the beginning, everything is new, but a student's initial enthusiasm (Phase 1: Unconscious Incompetence) can give way to discomfort (Phase 2: Conscious Incompetence). Similarly, your customers may be initially delighted with your offering because they are as yet unaware that there is a great deal they still have to learn. Phase 1 can give inexperienced salespeople a false sense of security; they may mistake the initial enthusiasm as customer satisfaction. Fooled into thinking the sale is complete, they then move on to a new prospect.

Salespeople who are aware of their customers' learning process will recognize initial enthusiasm for what it is: the new customer is not yet proficient at operating a new product.

How to Handle the Postsale Frustration Slump

In Phase 2 (Conscious Incompetence), your customers' excitement about your solution suddenly declines. For some customers, this decline is dramatic; for others, it is less pronounced. Stay close to the situation to provide direction and support. If you aren't in touch with your customers at this point, your relationship with them may collapse. Here are some things you can do, soon after a sale is made, to prevent your buyers' inevitable learning curve experience from ruining your new relationship:

- *Reassure your customers.* Remind them that learning can be hard work and that it is normal to feel frustration. Reassure them that after they practice and learn, they will be exceeding their expectations of value. Be supportive.

- *Be very visible immediately after the sale is finalized.* As mentioned earlier in this chapter, once your customers buy, they begin to watch you like a hawk. Make sure they can *see* you. In Chapter 6, we addressed the components of a proposal, one of which was an implementation plan. It's important for you to perform several *visible* activities soon after the purchase decision. Examples of activities that I perform soon after receiving a sales training design contract include "field ride observations of salespeople" and "interviews with sales managers." These activities allow me to build credibility with key members of my client's organization, and "the Hawk" is certain to receive positive reports on me. Remember, a closed sale is the start of a new sales process, not the end of an old one. Put extra time in, early.

- *Don't assume all responsibility for implementing your solution after the sale is made.* If you don't involve your customers— that is, if you tell them exactly what to do—they will blame you the first time a problem comes up. Instead, collaborate with your customers when planning an installation. The customers will then take ownership of that plan and will be more inclined to solve subsequent problems on their own.

The goal of teaching is to help others learn. Students should be taught to apply what has been learned, to improve their life. Without teachers, people would have to learn everything by themselves. Don't require your customers to learn everything on their own. They will not derive maximum benefit from your product or service until you help them learn to use it well.

3. Test to Measure Progress

The third step in the teaching process is to check your students' progress to find out whether the objectives set at the beginning of the session have been achieved. For students, testing provides feedback on their progress. For teachers, testing provides feedback on their own effectiveness. From test results, both teachers and students can determine what should happen next. If the objectives set at the beginning of the session have been met, the student is encouraged to move forward. If not, action is taken to improve the situation. Teachers know that students must master basic information and skills before they move on to advanced topics.

How you test for your value depends on the complexity of your sales process. For salespeople selling smaller-ticket items, testing for value may be a simple follow-up phone call two months after delivery. For salespeople selling multimillion-dollar equipment, testing for value may involve months of tracking, analysis, and reporting. Regardless of what you sell, it is in your best interest (as well as your customers') to gain some understanding of the value of your offering.

Why Should Salespeople Bother to Test for Value?

Your value in the marketplace is determined by your customers' ability to recognize that they have benefited from your offering. If you can't measure your contribution, your customers can't recognize it. You can't sell something you don't have. If you can't sell your value, you have no choice but to sell by offering the lowest price.

Imagine how you would benefit if you could show a prospect *proof* of your value. I'm talking about proven results, quantified and measured, of the value you have provided to your customers. You would spend less time having to differentiate your product from others; your results would speak for themselves. Because your competitors haven't measured their value, you would stand alone. Mack Hanan and Peter Karp, coauthors of *Competing on Value,* say that, from your customers' perspective, adding to their value is your sole reason for being in business.

Hanan and Karp go on to suggest that salespeople should think of a new customer as a bank. The bank (your customer) lends you a lump sum of cash (usually in the form of a purchase order) with the assurance that you will repay the loan over time, plus interest. The interest the bank receives, the return on investment, is your *value*. In deciding whether to lend you money, a bank asks three questions:

1. How quickly will I get my money back?
2. How much interest will I get?
3. How can I be sure that this borrower will make the payment?

The only way you'll be able to answer any of these questions is by finding a concrete way to measure your value.

Try thinking of your prospects as lenders. What changes would you make in your sales approach if your customers' payments to you were loans?

Here are several more reasons why you should measure your value:

- *You'll find new sales opportunities.* When you measure the impact of your product or service, you may uncover new needs to be met. These needs can lead to further sales. "Add-on" purchases require less time for customers' deliberation, because you have already proven yourself.

- *You insulate yourself against lost relationships.* As mentioned in Chapter 1, your prospects are vulnerable to layoffs, downsizing, and reorganization. Have you ever lost an important sale because your key contact lost his or her job? I have. When you measure your value, you have tangible evidence that can prove your worth to the company in the event that your contact person exits the picture.

- *You'll discover "best practices."* When you measure your value, you find out how your product or service is being used. You will be amazed at the extent to which some buyers get more value out of it than others! Once you identify "best practices," you can share them with others. Your customers' usage— and, therefore, their return on investment—will increase.

- *You'll be able to bridge the communication gap between the executive buyers who approved the purchase and the users who actually operate what was bought.* Your product or service can provide great value, but if that value is not recognized by everyone involved in the purchasing decision, you have not achieved customer satisfaction. Executive decision makers often move on to other projects after a decision is made. If they don't hear any complaints and they don't hear from you, they will quickly focus their attention elsewhere. Don't mistake customer complacency for customer satisfaction. You can solidify your position by taking the time to show your buyers in concrete terms what you have done for them. By measuring and then communicating to all decision makers the results achieved, you create positive and lasting perceptions of satisfaction in the minds of people who are, as you know, very results-oriented.

- *You may find new ways to improve your product or service.* When you measure your value, you are in close touch with your customers while your product or service is in use, and listening carefully to your customers will pay off. A study performed by M.I.T. found that 80 percent of the ideas for all technological innovations come from customers.

- *The quality of service you provide will improve.* Since I began measuring the value of my services, I have noticed a dramatic improvement in both the quality of service I provide and my customers' satisfaction with me. When I know before I start that I will be measured after I am finished, my entire approach changes. I become much more focused. I quickly discard the "trivial many" things I could talk about, and set my sights on the "vital few" issues that will offer the greatest impact for my audience.

- *Don't just measure value for your customers; measure value for yourself.* Salespeople are motivated by many different factors; one of the most important factors is the need for achievement. When you measure your value, you are measuring the magnitude of *your* accomplishment—what *you* accomplished for another.

Why Most Salespeople Don't Measure Value

There are lots of reasons why salespeople don't measure value. Are any of these reasons yours?

- Never thought of it.
- Don't know how.
- Don't have the time.
- My value can't be measured.
- I'm afraid I won't find any.

My key question to you is: Do you have difficulty justifying your price? If you truly don't have difficulty, perhaps you won't benefit by testing for value. If you are having difficulty justifying your price, what are you going to do about it? You can't just ignore this problem. To change the results in your life, you must first change the activities. You can't continue to do the same activities and expect different results. As the saying goes, "If you always do what you've always done, you'll only get what you've already got." Testing for value is an alternative. Why don't you give it a try with one of your key accounts?

Where Does Value Come From?

Your product or service is a means to an end, not an end in itself. Your product is like a hammer or a saw: when it is used properly, it will yield results. Your customers must climb three steps before they will LUV your product or service. These three steps are represented in Figure 9.1

First, your customers must learn about your product. They must know how to operate it and must recognize how they personally benefit by doing so. Next, they must use it. If they don't use it as much as they should, they won't achieve the greatest possible value. Finally, by using it, its value to them becomes clear.

Figure 9.1   How Customers Learn About the Value Gained from a Purchase

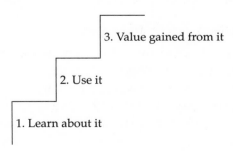

3. Value gained from it

2. Use it

1. Learn about it

For your customers to reach the value step, they must master using your product. You've taught them how, but what can you do to help them gain the utmost advantage from it? You have less control over usage than you do over learning, because usage occurs when you're not there. To increase usage, focus on it. Gain support from influential people. Brainstorm additional ways your service can be utilized. Your goal is to increase usage. Follow up with your customers to find out how much they are using your product.

Try a Questionnaire

One way to measure your value is to create a quick-answer questionnaire. Prepare a cover memo for an executive contact's signature, so users will take the time to respond. The questions you ask should be directly related to the expectations you set with the customer at the beginning of the teaching process.

Some of the questions you ask should be closed-ended (sometimes referred to as "forced choice" questions). If you sell printing services, you may ask, "The new printing service [is/is not] an improvement over our previous supplier. (Please circle one.)" This question might enable you to determine that "94 percent of your branch offices reported that the new printing service is an improvement."

Open-ended questions ask for a more extensive response. For instance, "Can you provide an example of a way in which the new printing service has helped you?" Open-ended questions generate higher-quality responses, but the answers take more time to evaluate and tabulate. Answers to these questions often provide specific examples of value achieved. When you receive the completed questionnaires, summarize your findings in a report to your customer.

Figures 9.2 through 9.5 are examples of the tools I utilize to measure the effectiveness of my service, sales training. I have adapted actual correspondence to illustrate how to test for value. Also included are specific findings from one questionnaire and the presentation that communicated those results to my customer.

Persuade Your Company to Perform a Case Study

A case study is a careful examination of a customer during the period before, during, and after your product or service arrives. The purpose of a case study is to measure your value. To perform your own case study, you may want to follow the example of Steelcase, a leading manufacturer of office furniture. Steelcase sees the value it has added for customers as increased productivity, not furniture,

Figure 9.2   Cover Memo, from Customer Executive, Requesting Employees' Input on the Value of a Purchase

XYZ CORPORATION
Internal Memorandum

TO: National Account Salespeople

FROM: John Doe, Senior Vice President of Sales

SUBJECT: Sales Training Impact Questionnaire

DATE: November 1, 199X

Thank you for your hard work both during and after our sales training session six months ago.

Now, we would like to measure the effectiveness of our training investment. What IMPROVEMENTS in your SKILLS have you noticed since the training? What RESULTS have you enjoyed by applying those skills?

Please take a few minutes to complete the enclosed questionnaire and return it to Sally Jones, here at headquarters. The deadline for your response is December 1, one month from today.

These forms are anonymous and your response is strictly confidential. That's why there is no space on the form to write your name.

If you have any questions, please call The Kevin Davis Group at (510) 831-0922, or e-mail them at kdavissell@aol.com.

Figure 9.3   Questionnaire Distributed for Employees' Input

Sales Training Impact Questionnaire

1. What ideas from the training have you applied so far?

   a.

   b.

   c.

2. Have you noticed specific RESULTS from these ideas? (i.e., made a sale you might not have without the new skills, won a sale that you otherwise would have lost to the competition, etc.?)

   YES   NO

   Example:

3. As a result of the *Customer-Focused Selling* class, delivered by representatives of The Kevin Davis Group, do you now have a better understanding of your customer?

   YES   NO

   How has this changed or improved your interactions with your customers?

4. Are you setting action commitment "Go Forward" call objectives? (Call objectives that focus on what specific action you want your prospect to take?)

   YES   NO

5. Has the "Doctor" method of questioning improved your ability to develop needs and/or create value for our services?

   YES   NO

   Example:

Figure 9.3   Continued

6. Did the training help you to improve your effectiveness in competitive selling situations?

   YES   NO

   Example:

7. The April sales training session WAS / WAS NOT a valuable use of my time. (circle one)

8. Please complete the following sentences.

   a. The single most important skill I learned in the training was:

   b. The one topic from the training that I feel I need a "refresher" on is:

9. How have your skills improved as a result of the training?

Please complete by December 1st, and return to Sally Jones.

Figure 9.4   Cover Letter for Questionnaire Analysis

4115 Blackhawk Plaza Circle, Suite 100 • Danville, California 94506
(510) 831-0922 • Fax: (510) 831-8677 • E-Mail: kdavissell@aol.com

December 2, 199X

Mr. John Doe, Senior Vice President
XYZ Corporation
123 Main Street
Los Angeles, CA 90210

Re: Measure Results from Sales Training

Dear Mr. Doe:

Thanks very much for taking time to meet with me in Atlanta in September. I enjoyed our time together and I look forward to seeing you again in Florida next month.

As you know, my company was selected to collaborate with the ABC Division to increase sales effectiveness. Our solution has been to focus on an ongoing *process*, not a one-time event.

As part of our process, my company delivered a customized sales training program last April. Your managers and our training consultants went into the workshop with specific behavioral objectives—our goal was to teach certain new skills that salespeople would utilize in the field. Following the training, your managers coached these new skills, because research has found that 87 percent of sales training is lost within 30 days without follow-up coaching.

Six months after the training, we sent a questionnaire to all participants. The purposes of the questionnaire were to measure our effectiveness at achieving our behavioral objectives, and to gather information on specific results that the new behavior/skills have achieved.

Mr. Doe, I am very pleased with the results of the survey! The questionnaires indicate that:

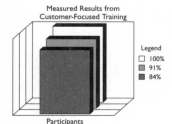

- 100% of program participants report they use one or more skills learned in the training program.
- 91% report they now have a better understanding of their customers.
- 84% report specific results from the sales training.

Speaking/Consulting/Training • *Sales & Sales Management*

Figure 9.4   Continued

Mr. John Doe   Page Two   December 2, 199X

For example, one participant wrote: *"The Customer-Focused Selling class made me reevaluate my customers/prospects to identify what stage of the decision-making process they are in and the most productive fashion to proceed in a 'Go Forward' fashion to secure a sale. I have also become more active in formulating strategies for new and existing accounts to discover problems and ultimately fulfill them through the use of XYZ products. When dealing with current customers, I try to maintain a high level of enthusiasm for XYZ, by making sure the client's needs and expectations are fulfilled."*

Another example: *"With the emphasis toward the customer buying versus the salesman selling, my approach and questioning skills put me in a better position from the start with an account that I had not been able to get anywhere with. The end result was an identified level of dissatisfaction and a sale of $36,000."*

Another participant reported: *"The Customer-Focused Selling system has made me put myself in the place of the customer. I am better prepared and much more professional in my approach to selling XYZ products and services now that I understand the customer's decision-making process and can recognize the 'Complex Buying Team.' I feel more confident."*

A detailed analysis of the questionnaires is enclosed. Also enclosed are all responses to two question: *(1) Have you noticed specific results from training? (YES or NO) Example? and; (2) How have your skills improved as a result of the training?*

Mr. Doe, I believe that by increasing sales effectiveness, XYZ Corporation can gain a sustainable competitive advantage. I am proud of the progress that together we have made, and I look forward to continuing our performance improvement process in 199X.

Sincerely,

Kevin Davis
President

KD/vbs

Figure 9.5   Sample Page of Report on Questionnaire Responses

Sales Training Impact Follow-Up Analysis

Description: On April 20–22, 199X, XYZ Corporation salespeople and managers attended a sales training program in Miami, Florida. The program was designed and delivered by The Kevin Davis Group.

On November 1, a questionnaire was sent to all participants to gather information about the IMPACT of this training. This report is an analysis of the responses we received.

1. Responses received: 115 Total

2. All respondents (100%) have implemented one or more behaviors learned in the training.

    a. 77 report implementing *three* or more new skills

        28 report implementing *two* new skills

        10 report implementing *one* new skill

    b. 88 report implementing the "Doctor" selling role

        70 report implementing "Action Commitment" call objectives

        45 report implementing competitive selling skills

3. 84% of your salespeople report specific results from these new behaviors. (See attached for specific examples of results.)

4. 91% report that the training gave them a better understanding of their customer.

5. 98% report they now set results-oriented "Action Commitment" call objectives.

6. 84% report the "Doctor" selling role has improved their ability to develop needs and/or created value for XYZ Company's services.

7. 98% report that the training has helped them to improve their effectiveness in competitive selling situations.

8. 98% report the April sales training was a valuable use of their time.

and the company's case studies confirm that view. These case studies describe in detail the buying process from the customer's perspective, and conclude by documenting the results that were recognized one year after purchase.

New office furnishings can contribute to many long-term goals. In one Steelcase case study, the customer's needs, expectations, and results measured were:

Need	Expectation	Results After One Year
Cultural change	Create an environment that helps "eliminate issues related to status" and makes *all* employees feel important.	The customer reports the "us versus them" attitude has disappeared.
Cut costs	Reduce space requirements and real estate costs.	$4 million saved.
Increase productivity	Improve the work environment and create an environment that would "facilitate communication."	Managers report productivity is up. Employees report "their workstations and offices are more efficient and functional than before." They report they are more comfortable.

Steelcase then uses these case studies as marketing tools with customers and prospects alike, to prove the company is committed to providing value-added solutions for their customers. You can do the same.

Some salespeople are afraid to test for value. Let's face it, testing for value is a risk. What happens if you don't find any? Remember, though, your customers took a risk in buying from you. Shouldn't *you* take a risk to prove they made the right decision?

Successful companies and salespeople have a common focus: CUSTOMERS. They recognize that if they don't satisfy their customers, someone else will. As a Teacher of selling, you help your customers to pursue their own goals.

When you commit yourself to exceeding your customers' expectations, not only in words but also in deeds, you place service above self. Throughout all of human history, great people have become great because they gave of themselves in the service of others. Shouldn't we all aspire to do the same?

10

Sales Role #8: THE FARMER

Nourish Satisfaction and Grow the Account

You must give to get. You must sow the seed before you reap the harvest.

Scott Reed

Today, companies striving to be the best have made customer satisfaction and retention their cornerstone business strategy. On this foundation, they add product innovation, product quality, and a productive and responsive workforce to achieve business success.

Emphasis on customer relations is required in order to keep up with today's tough customers, who have higher expectations and more buying power than ever before. Customers have more options to choose from, so companies must fight harder to retain their existing customer base. For many companies, this challenge is compounded by technological improvements, which have made it more difficult for buyers to distinguish between alternatives. As products become more and more alike, postsale services are becoming increasingly important criteria in the buying process.

During the past few years, tens of thousands of salespeople have experienced a radical change in their pay structure. A growing number of companies are measuring customer satisfaction and linking the results to how much a salesperson is paid. *Sales &*

Marketing Management magazine recently published the findings from a study conducted by Management Compensation Services (MCS), a division of Hewitt Associates, a sales compensation consulting firm. MCS collected data on 18,000 salespeople representing 217 sales organizations and found that 26 percent of the companies surveyed explicitly rewarded customer satisfaction in sales compensation programs in 1994. This figure compares to only 6 percent in 1992.

This significant change is occurring as employers conclude that they can no longer afford to compensate salespeople on the basis of sales volume alone. Sales executives are recognizing that the key to sustainable sales growth is not so much *closing sales* as it is *opening* and then nurturing *relationships*. IBM, Ameritech, Motorola, Sears, and BellSouth are just a few of the companies that are measuring customer satisfaction and compensating their salespeople accordingly.

National Fuel Gas Distribution Corporation, a billion-dollar company based in Buffalo, New York, is an example of a company that has altered its sales compensation to include customer assessments. Profiled recently in *Selling Magazine,* in a cover article titled "Look Who's in on Your Performance Review," National Fuel Gas asks its 165 largest clients to rate its salespeople on everything from frequency of contact to product knowledge and problem-solving ability. This customer feedback, primarily obtained through telephone surveys, counts for 15 percent of each salesperson's annual performance review. Grades given to salespeople by their clients have a direct impact on the size of their pay increases.

The role that salespeople play in achieving customer satisfaction is growing. The days of "hit-and-run selling"—closing the sale and quickly moving on—are over. Acting now as account managers who are in charge of their company's relationship with its clients, salespeople are being judged and compensated on their ability to perform these new duties.

The message for salespeople is clear. To survive and thrive, you must get closer to your customers, not just *during* the sales process, but *after* it, too. By applying the seven selling roles prescribed so far in this book, you are well on your way to satisfying and retaining your customers. By applying the last role, that of a Farmer, you can solidify your customer relationships for years to come. Having happy customers means not only that you'll make more money, but also that you'll make a long-term, positive impact on the success of your company.

THE NUMBER-ONE KILLER OF
CUSTOMER SATISFACTION

Unhappy customers are usually produced by a seller who has become complacent and has started taking customers for granted. Complacency is a *feeling of satisfaction in the mind of the seller, and not necessarily in the mind of the buyer.* If you think customers are happy because they haven't complained, think again. According to research performed by the White House Office of Consumer Affairs, 96 percent of customers who are dissatisfied with service don't complain, at least not to the people who provided the service. Apparently, today's customer would rather switch than fight.

When I was a rookie salesperson with Lanier, I observed firsthand the cost of salesperson complacency. Our company's largest west coast system installation was located at Stanford University Medical Center. The system consisted of 150 doctor dictate stations (microphones that doctors spoke into) located throughout the Center. The stations were wired to a huge bank of recorders housed in the Medical Records Department. Representatives from our district office had sold the system to Stanford five years before, and we were proud of the excellent service our people had provided. Our employees bent over backward responding to Stanford's needs, and their medical records personnel, who had high expectations, were pleased with our service quality. Frank, our salesperson handling the account, paid quarterly visits to the Medical Records Department, just to make sure of continued satisfaction with our service support.

During one of these visits, Frank learned that hospital administrators and the Director of Medical Records had decided to investigate purchasing a new central system. Frank returned to our office excited about his new sales opportunity. A short time later, hospital decision makers began talking to our competitors, one of which was our arch enemy, Dictaphone Corporation. Frank began to see the "wheels coming off" his sales opportunity.

About two years before, unbeknownst to Frank, an aggressive Dictaphone salesperson had started making sales calls on other departments within the Center. These departments utilized dictation equipment too, albeit in smaller quantities than the Medical Records Department. Locked out of the large medical records system, where our equipment was in operation, our wily competitor had sought to sell smaller, stand-alone desktop units elsewhere. He was incredibly successful at selling 5 and 10 units at a time, for a total of well over 200 machines. Apparently, Pediatrics had started it off by purchasing 5 new units. Then Neurology added 10, and Cardiology purchased 20. Radiology first purchased 10 units, then gradually added more, until 75 new machines were in operation there. Other departments, including Orthopedics, Pathology, and Oncology, had followed along.

When one of the administrators mentioned to Frank that many departments had recently purchased from Dictaphone, Frank was astonished. To Frank, it seemed as if the entire hospital had changed over to his competitor's desktop units. How could it be?

Frank had become complacent. He had felt satisfied with the large account in Medical Records, while ignoring the smaller needs of other departments right next door. Frank had not stayed close to his largest customer.

The Dictaphone salesperson, cunning as a fox, wasn't content with the success he had achieved so far. All along, his eyes had been fixed on our prize possession, the large central dictation system. Now, as hospital decision makers evaluated a new system, the Lanier system in Medical Records was surrounded by departments using Dictaphone desktop machines.

For the Dictaphone sales representative, the time had come to spring his trap. Remember the 150 doctor dictate stations wired to the central system? He pointed out that the operating commands for Dictaphone's dictate station were significantly different from Lanier's, but *identical* to the operating commands of the 200+ stand-alone desktop units he had sold to the various departments. If the hospital purchased a Dictaphone central system, our competitor reasoned, doctors would have continuity between their desktops and the central system. Why, he asked, would the hospital want two systems of operating commands when it could have just one? Hospital administrators agreed, and we lost our largest customer to our top competitor.

To avoid becoming complacent with your customers, stop thinking "account maintenance" and start thinking "account development." Don't just hold your ground, move forward. The best way to keep the business is to grow the business.

The requirements for a long-lasting and profitable relationship are mutual trust, understanding, and value achieved. If you put extra effort into achieving customer satisfaction by becoming proactive with your customer after making a sale, you will be generously rewarded. The result will be a relationship that adds value for everyone involved. Your customer's level of satisfaction with you will go up. You'll make more repeat sales, and you'll receive more referrals. As you learn more about each customer, you will discover new ways to help each one grow. When you apply this knowledge, you gain more competitive advantage, because knowledge is power.

YOUR CUSTOMERS' EIGHTH STEP: SATISFACTION

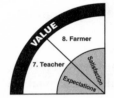

In this, the final step of the buy-*learning* process, your customers form a perception of *satisfaction* based on four factors:

1. Value achieved.
2. Product quality.
3. Service quality.
4. Price.

The questions in your customers' minds are linked to those factors. Your customers wonder:

1. Am I achieving the results I expected?
2. Is the product performing as expected?
3. Does the way I am treated by the seller's support services people make me feel important?
4. Did I pay a fair price?

If the customer feels confident that the answer to each question is "yes," you have achieved customer satisfaction, at least for now.

The challenge for salespeople is that, although the answer to these questions may be "yes" today, one or more of these answers may change to "no" tomorrow. Customers become more demanding, not less. As your customers become aware of new product developments, they may become less satisfied with what they already own. For example, most people are initially satisfied with a new car, but become less satisfied over time as new, more stylish alternatives enter the market. The same is true for any of the four criteria listed above.

Be warned that customers quickly get used to fine service. It's human nature to develop a taste for things we enjoy. Nordstrom has built a reputation for providing fine customer service. A frequent Nordstrom shopper may be perceived as a very demanding customer to another, less service-oriented department store. Because your customers' expectations are always increasing, you and your company must be committed to continuous value improvement, just to keep what you've already got. If you relax and stand still, you'll quickly fall behind.

The Satisfaction Spectrum

A salesperson's customers can be placed across a spectrum from least to most satisfied:

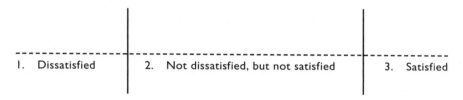

| 1. Dissatisfied | 2. Not dissatisfied, but not satisfied | 3. Satisfied |

"In most cases, the factors contributing to dissatisfaction are quite different from the factors that contribute to customer satisfaction," says Earl Naumann, author of *Creating Customer Value*. Naumann says that the attributes of your product tend to be associated with dissatisfaction, while the attributes of your support services are associated with satisfaction. If your product performs to customer expectations, you have avoided a dissatisfied customer but you have not necessarily achieved customer satisfaction.

Several years ago, as a district manager for Lanier, I worked closely with our healthcare market account executive on two large sales opportunities. During the same month, we sold the same central dictation system to two different hospitals. At "Hospital A" the installation went flawlessly, and the system was up and running in no time. At "Hospital B," we went through hell. Immediately after the installation, doctors' usage of the system skyrocketed. The backlog of work in process grew rapidly, placing severe stress on our system's capabilities. A bug in our system's software was exposed by the heavy usage. The results were lost patient records, frustrated doctors, and angry hospital administrators.

As the district manager, it was my responsibility to see to it that the problems were resolved, and I threw at the problem every resource I had. Our technicians pulled a few all-nighters. I negotiated with my company's home office for the loan of a second system to the customer, and obtained approval to install a backup. Also, my account executive and I camped out in the customer's office, serving as "lightning rods" to take the heat and to keep our technicians from being interrupted. I had frequent conversations with our R&D department, whose software engineers were working feverishly to isolate and correct the glitches. Finally, our teamwork paid off, and Hospital B's problems were corrected.

A few years later, Hospital A (the "satisfied customer") informed us that they had just purchased a new system from our competitor. Hospital A hadn't even bothered to look at our latest offering! (The account executive and I had not been diligent in staying close to Hospital A.) On the other hand, Hospital B (the "dissatisfied customer") remains, to this day, a loyal Lanier customer who wouldn't think of doing business with anyone else. The difficult times we had shared with Hospital B had bonded us together; those buyers saw firsthand how much we cared. Has anything like this ever happened to you?

The key to customer satisfaction, then, is not just *what* you deliver, but *how* you deliver, service, and support it in your sales role as Farmer. Meeting your customers' expectations is not enough. Customers want personal acknowledgment from you after the sale. They want to know you care. Customers want you to make them feel important. Are you doing everything you can to make your customers feel important?

SALES ROLE #8: THE FARMER

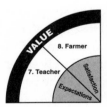

The Customer-Focused Selling role for Step 8, Satisfaction, is **Farmer.** Farmers have a "salt of the earth" image. They are well known for being strong, no-nonsense people. Farmers work hard to make a valuable contribution—the provision of food that sustains life. Every day, they deal with unpredictability—torrential rains, sudden freezes, or infestations of bugs. Using their wits, and their wisdom from years of experience, they constantly adapt their strategies to meet each crop's changing demands.

In your Farmer sales role, you have an important contribution to make. You help improve the lives of others. You must have a strong character and deliver what you promise. You must work hard in the field, and follow through quickly on all customer requests.

You must pay attention to your customers, the way a farmer pays attention to the land, the crops, and the weather. Furthermore, all farmers are aware of this simple truth: *You must sow before you reap.*

In the Customer-Focused Selling process, the role of a Farmer is to:

1. Nourish a productive relationship with your buyer.
2. Sow new applications for your product or service.
3. Cultivate the account.
4. Reap the fruits of your labor.
5. Plan your next season.

Let's see how you can use these five steps to enhance your contribution to your customers.

1. Nourish a Productive Relationship with Your Buyer

The soil is the farmer's "customer." All crops depend on fertile soil. The farmer knows that if he takes care of the land today, the land will reward him tomorrow. That's why he nourishes the soil by fertilizing it with substances necessary for growth. The Farmer plows back into the ground a certain amount from each harvest. The farmer wants the soil to produce for him, not just this year, but for many years to come.

As a salesperson, you want your customers to yield future results for you, so you must nourish your customers today. You must give before you get. Plow a portion of your profits from each sale back into your customers by investing more time and energy to ensure their satisfaction. The more profit you earn from a sale, the more time you should put back in. Look for opportunities to exceed your customers' expectations. Take a long-term view of each customer, and accept responsibility for his or her satisfaction.

Conduct Regular Account Reviews

Farmers regularly run tests on their soil to identify harmful viruses or fungi before it's too late to combat and correct them. Salespeople should conduct account reviews to test their customers' perception of value and spot early indications of dissatisfaction. Problems that are either undetected or ignored can destroy a profitable relationship. Because customers' expectations are always increasing, one follow-up account review is not enough. Do reviews at regular intervals—

quarterly, semiannually, or at least annually. Account reviews help you stay close to your customers. Here are some things to keep in mind when you conduct an account review.

Identify Your Customers' Perceptions of What Constitutes Good (and Bad) Service.   Ask customers to share examples of when they received great service from a supplier. Their examples will reveal to you their most important "satisfiers," things you can do that they value the most. For instance, a major purchase may have demanded a difficult delivery schedule. The supplier met the delivery schedule on all the items, except one that was manufactured incorrectly. The supplier then bought a replacement item from a competing supplier in order to meet the delivery date. Now you know how important on-time delivery is to this customer.

Ask for examples of terrible service. The answers will reveal those things you must avoid doing. For instance, you may hear of a salesperson who misrepresented a product, and how it cost your customer tens of thousands of dollars to purchase additional equipment in order to achieve the anticipated result. Now you know: don't overpromise!

Ask Open-Ended Questions.   Encourage open discussion by asking:

- What do you like best about our products and services?
- What, specifically, would you like to see changed or improved?
- What are your expectations?
- How have your goals changed since the last time we met?
- What more can we do to help you achieve those goals?
- Why did you buy from me? (you might be surprised by the answer you hear!)

Seek Specific Answers to Your Questions.   Vague answers or non-responses are early warning signs. Remember, many unsatisfied customers would rather flee than fight. Complaining takes time, and complaints are often ignored anyway. So customers think, why bother?

Customers often hide their unhappiness by responding to a salesperson's questions in a nonspecific way. You've probably done the same thing in other circumstances. Suppose you dine out at an expensive restaurant, but receive poor service. After your meal, your waiter or waitress asks you, "How was everything?" If you choose to avoid the hassle of complaining, you will respond in a nonspecific way, "Fine." Only by asking more questions and seeking specific answers might he or she learn the real story: the salads arrived too late, the vegetables were overcooked, and the meat was too tough. To discover what your customer *truly* thinks of your product or service, seek *specific* answers to your questions.

Look at Problems as Opportunities in Work Clothes.   Sometimes, during an account review, problems may surface. When you discover a problem in one of your accounts, see it as a chance to show your customer you care. If you throw your energy into solving the problem, you might find new sales opportunities!

Get References from Satisfied Customers.   Ask your customers why they chose you and how your product or service has fulfilled their needs. After interviewing them, ask your customers if you might obtain a letter, on the company letterhead, expressing satisfaction. Barry Farber and Joyce Wycoff, authors of *Breakthrough Selling*, suggest salespeople produce tape-recorded testimonials. Farber recommends taking your top three or four customers, those who know and value you the most, and interviewing them about their positive experience with your product and your company. You can create an effective tape by:

- Introducing yourself.
- Stating the name, title, and company of your customer.
- Mentioning the types of products or services the customer has in use.
- Asking the customer why he or she chose you and what the results have been.
- Encouraging the customer to be specific in order to enhance the impact of the recorded statement.

When you have a satisfied customer, advertise your success. Let others know the value you have to offer. If you sell to businesses, let other decision makers within your customer's business know of your success.

Besides a testimonial audiocassette, a testimonial letter is a powerful tool for persuading a reluctant prospect to become your customer. Don't do what everybody else does, by getting a few generic "atta-boy" or "atta-girl" letters. These letters are generally supportive of what you do, but they lack the specifics necessary to convince doubtful prospects. Instead, seek letters that serve a definite purpose. When I began my sales training business in 1989, I purchased the marketing/delivery rights to a popular basic selling skills training program. As I began selling this program in my local area, I encountered several objections. I kept a list of these objections in my Day-Timer. Every time I encountered a new objection, I added it to my list.

One of the most common objections I heard from my prospects with regard to my old program was, "It's too basic." One of these objections came from the vice president of advertising sales for a national business publication. I addressed this prospect's concern by saying that, in my opinion, many experienced salespeople engage in selling activities as if on "autopilot," often forgetting the basics, and not thinking in much depth about what they are doing. My response was successful in resolving my prospect's concern. When I subsequently delivered the training program to her sales team, I received excellent reviews.

Following the program, after I had verified my client's satisfaction with the results, I asked her for a testimonial letter, and she agreed to provide one. In an effort to acquire a letter that would serve a specific purpose, I then reminded her about her initial concern that the program was "too basic." We then discussed what I had said that helped her to overcome it. Finally, I asked her about specific results she was getting from her investment. One week later, I received the testimonial letter shown on page 243.

Thereafter, whenever I heard the objection, "This program seems too basic," I was ready! My client's name carries a lot of credibility, and the letter was very effective in convincing other prospects who had a similar concern. Notice that this testimonial letter:

1. Restates the objection the prospect had (second paragraph).
2. Recounts what helped the prospect overcome the concern during the sales process (third and fourth paragraphs).
3. Describes in specific detail the results being enjoyed now (fourth paragraph).

Follow a similar format to acquire testimonial letters that overcome the most common objections you hear about your product or

National Business Publication
(Name withheld upon request)

August 3, 1990

Dear Kevin,

Thank you for leading a great sales seminar.

      Going in to your (name of my old program) several weeks ago, I had the feeling that a sales motivational program that covers all the fundamentals may be too basic for our salespeople, many of whom have been selling for 10+ years. After having gone through the program, I can tell you that it was not at all too basic. Each of our salespeople got something out of each and every module!

      I agree with you, that many experienced salespeople sell "helter-skelter." They do what they do without thinking a lot about it. They forget that "by failing to plan each sales call they are planning to fail."

      What was most helpful was to review the basics, and at the end put them all together in a systematic way. We now have a system for approaching, questioning, presenting, handling objections and closing that we didn't have before. It gives us a feeling of control during each step of the sales process.

      I highly recommend your services to any sales executive interested in increasing the productivity of experienced salespeople.

Sincerely,

---

service. Your goal should be to get specific testimonial letters that serve a definite purpose.

Obtain Referrals.   For many salespeople, attempting to obtain referrals can be a frustrating, unproductive activity. Customers often provide either poor referrals or none at all. Many salespeople underestimate the risk that buyers feel when they are asked to supply referrals. When you ask for a referral, you are asking your customers to put their personal credibility on the line. A referral represents a new type of risk, one that is different from the risk of buying.

    Another difficulty is that your buyers may not know which of their associates may need what you have. Customers have a hard enough time recognizing their own needs, let alone guessing about someone else's. This confusion may prevent your buyers from giving you names.

With just a few minor adjustments, however, you can get many more, high-quality referrals. Here's how:

- *Ask at the right time.* Traditional sales training techniques teach salespeople to ask for referrals at the close of sales, but that's too soon. Your new customers haven't yet achieved value, and you are, in effect, asking them to send you off in another direction at the precise time when they need you the most! At best, your request for a referral will be ignored. At worst, the trust you have worked so hard to build may be damaged or ruined. Don't ask for a referral too soon! The key is to ask for a referral after value has been achieved. Help your customers through Step 7 (Expectations of Value) and make sure your customers are satisfied *before* asking for referrals.

- *Ask in the right way.* You must be subtle and simple in your approach. According to David Garfinkel, author of the audiocassette program *Referral Magic,* one way to ask for referrals is to say: "Mr. Jones, you know more people in your field than I do. Whom should I talk to next?" This method is simple and unthreatening. Another method Garfinkel recommends is to prepare in advance a list of prospects to whom you want to be referred. Show your customers the list and ask whether they know anyone on it. In this way, you save your customers the hassle of remembering names and speculating over who has needs similar to their own. This method also ensures that the referrals will be of consistently high quality.

2. Sow New Applications for Your Product or Service

In the mid 1800s, the "great potato famine" killed about 750,000 people in Ireland. Hundreds of thousands more were forced to leave their homeland; many of them emigrated to the United States. The potato famine occurred because all Irish farmers had planted a single variety of potato, the "white" potato, which was susceptible to a certain type of virus. When that virus infected the potato crop, the staple of Ireland's diet was quickly wiped out. Today, farmers know that each variety of crop has different types of resistance to disease. If Irish farmers had planted different types of potatoes, the famine would have been averted.

As a salesperson, you are susceptible to viruses in your accounts. A virus is often created by change: changing jobs, people, needs, technologies, and so on. Change alters how your product or service is utilized and, therefore, the value it provides. Have you ever lost an important account because your customer lost his or her job? Have you ever lost an account because your customer's needs changed? It has happened to all of us.

That's why it's important to diversify your risk. Search for new ways for your customers to benefit from your product or service. Stockbrokers know, for example, that a client who has a single account consisting of common stocks is more likely to switch brokers than a client who has several accounts, including fixed income securities, retirement funds, and a variety of investments. From the client's perspective, multiple accounts is an indication of value that the client perceives is being provided by the broker.

Diversify your risk by selling add-ons—additional products and services that increase the usage and value of your product. When you provide several products and services to an account, not only do you increase your sales revenues, but you also raise that account's "switching costs." The more services a customer buys from you, the more difficult it is to change suppliers. Banks, for instance, strive to sell you a variety of services—checking, savings, credit cards, mutual funds, computer access, and so on—partly because the more services you buy, the greater the hassle if you change banks.

In your sales role as Farmer, you must stay in close touch with your customers. Anticipate changes within your accounts and sow new applications for your products or services before it's too late. In this way, should a problem arise with one of the services you provide, your entire relationship is not wiped out.

Share Best Practices

If your product or service is operated by many different people, some will get more out of it than others. In Chapter 9, we addressed the importance of measuring value and determining "best practices." When you share best practices with your customers, you increase both your customers' return on investment and their level of satisfaction with you. One buyer's "best practice" is another buyer's new application.

For example, Wayne is a sales representative for F. W. Dodge/McGraw-Hill. Dodge researches construction projects and provides information on building products requirements to building products manufacturers. Essentially, Dodge sells sales leads to building products salespeople.

Wayne regularly measures the value he provides to key accounts, to ensure they continue purchasing Dodge information. Wayne sends surveys to his users, his customers' salespeople. His surveys always uncover ways in which some salespeople are utilizing the information to gain even more value. For instance, one company was buying his service to learn of, and participate in, more bids. Wayne's questionnaire discovered that some of his customer's salespeople were using this information to get in the door during the time construction plans are written—long before a construction project's bid phase. This enabled salespeople to influence the bid specifications in their favor.

When Wayne's key contact, the Vice President of Sales, learned of Wayne's discovery, he was excited. He was convinced his salespeople needed to enter the buying process at an earlier stage, but he wasn't sure how to tell them to do it. Wayne's discovery gave him the answer he was searching for, so he invited Wayne to address his entire sales force at the next national sales meeting. Wayne's efforts had enhanced the customer's perception of Dodge's value and dramatically increased the usage of Dodge's services. Wayne has a strong relationship and, perhaps, a customer for life, all because he took the time to find out how people were *really* using his service.

3. Cultivate the Account

After a farmer plants his fields, he cultivates them. He irrigates the crop and controls weeds and pests. The farmer puts in extra effort to improve the quality of his harvest because he knows that consumers will pay more for higher-quality foods.

The weeds and pests you must battle are your hungry competitors. You'll find them buzzing around your key accounts, because that's where the food is. If they are successful at infesting one of your key accounts, they will savor a double victory, a big win for themselves and a big loss for you.

You can control these pests, and retain your key accounts, by staying close to your customers over the long haul. This is not easy to do, because your customers are getting busier. They are being forced to do more with less, so it's easy for them to drift away. To retain a priority relationship and keep your buyers interested in talking to you, you must continue to generate new ideas to help them grow. Look for new information about their competitors, news about trends that may affect their company's future, or "best practice" applications for your product or service. The secret is to continue to provide, on an ongoing basis, something of value that your customers don't get or can't do by themselves.

Become the One-Call, First-Call Information Resource

If your customers see you as an expert, they will use you as an information resource, which means you will be the first salesperson to learn of new sales opportunities. Being the first on the scene gives you a major competitive advantage: you can uncover needs and influence buying criteria before your competitors become involved. Responsiveness and expertise will pay dividends for you.

Bill is a top sales consultant for Blanchard Training & Development, a provider of corporate consulting and organizational development services. Bill works hard at being an expert in his field. He reads industry periodicals, studies his company's services, and compares Blanchard's services to those of his competitors. He subscribes to an on-line clipping service, and mails articles of interest to his clients, along with a personalized note. He makes frequent visits to key customers, questioning and listening instead of talking, and he keeps in touch with his customers' emerging issues. If one of Bill's customers has a question about organizational development or training, the customer calls Bill first. Through these attentive activities, Bill grew an account from $10,000 in billings in 1991 to over $800,000 in just three years. Bill credits the lion's share of his success to his one-call, first-call strategy.

All top salespeople have a burning desire to grow their key accounts. They know the "80/20 rule,": 80 percent of their sales will be produced by 20 percent of their customers. They are constantly learning about their products, services, selling skills, customers, and customers' industries, because the more knowledge they have, the higher the value of service they provide.

4. Reap the Fruits of Your Labors

For farmers, harvest is the time when hard work and patience are finally rewarded. In your sales role as Farmer, it's now time for you to reap the fruits of your labors. Your extra efforts—those you made postsale in order to further cultivate the account—can yield these results:

- *New, larger sales.* By proving yourself of value on a first-time sale, you place yourself in the running for other, often larger sales opportunities. Every chance you get, demonstrate your ability to add value. Remember, the more you give, the more you get.

- *Faster, more profitable repeat sales.* Customers who have profited from your solutions in the past will pay more for your solutions in the future. And they'll take less time to decide.

- *Quicker sales on new products and services.* Established customers are great prospects when you offer new products and services. They know your value and they trust your ability to deliver it, so they feel they are less at risk in buying from you.

  Never damage this trust by selling new, unproven products to your key accounts. Bugs often must be worked out. The opening of Denver International Airport, originally scheduled for October 1993, had to be delayed until February 1995—a delay that cost taxpayers an estimated $1 million *per day*. The primary reason for the delay was a high-tech baggage handling system that didn't work. Only after much of the system was removed, and replaced with more traditional equipment, was the airport able to open. Make sure what you sell to your accounts has been thoroughly tested!

- *More competitive advantage.* Some things you do, such as introducing a new product or raising prices, are easy for competitors to observe. Improvements in your service quality, however, cannot be easily detected. If you continue to improve over time, you can strengthen this important advantage.

A successful, mutually profitable sale is a satisfying accomplishment that no one can take away from you. As Farmer, you get the most you possibly can out of each sale by maximizing its importance to your customer. At this point, you and your buyer should be pleased with each other and with what you accomplished together. However, as every farmer knows, the quiet days after a harvest are best put to use in planning the next crop.

5. Plan Your Next Season

Throughout the first seven steps of the Customer-Focused Selling process, you learned a great deal about each account. In Step 8, Satisfaction, which includes the months and years after a customer's purchase, your knowledge of the customer gradually becomes outdated. If you don't continually grow your knowledge of the customer's personal and business needs, you will miss opportunities to profit from change.

To learn more about a customer, return to the Student role. Study your customer's changing industry, problems, applications, and so on. In this way, you can anticipate your customer's needs and continue to fulfill them. Just as the customer ultimately returns to the first phase of the buy-*learning* process on the buying wheel, so will you, the salesperson, ultimately return to Step 1 of the Customer-Focused Selling cycle. When you do so, you will enjoy an endless supply of new sales opportunities that can make an important difference in the lives of other people.

YOUR FINAL ROLE: CHIEF SATISFACTION OFFICER

A tremendous amount of time and energy is invested in creating new customers. You invest personal time and energy. If you have an employer, your employer invests in you. With so much invested to *create* customers, you must do everything in your power to *keep* your customers. That's why the first principle of growing a business is to keep what you've already got.

You are your company's "Chief Satisfaction Officer." You are responsible for creating high-value recommendations, and then delivering on your promises. If other people in your company drop the ball, you must pick it up.

Your customers have changed, so you must change, grow, and improve yourself to meet their new needs. The future will demand more from you than the past. Anyone interested in persuading others to invest in a product or service must be more knowledgeable, creative, innovative, flexible, and responsive than ever before. And above all, that person must always see selling through the buyers' eyes.

For years, those who buy have known more about selling than most salespeople have known about buying. That's not right. To truly understand selling, you must understand buying. Now that you have taken this step, the path to reach your goals should be revealed.

11

WINNING THE COMPLEX SALE

The Politics of Selling to Multiple Decision Makers

> If a man will begin with certainties, he shall end in
> doubts; but if he will be content to begin with doubts, he
> shall end in certainties.
>
> Francis Bacon

When I was a sales manager, one of the salespeople in my office, John, sold dictation equipment to lawyers. John had approached a fourteen-attorney firm and had been successful in scheduling an appointment with the senior partner who was, in essence, the CEO of the law firm. The prospective sale amounted to $10,000, a sum that would provide a new machine for each of the fourteen lawyers. John met several times with the senior partner. He was effective at building trust and developing the senior partner's awareness that the firm needed new equipment. After their fifth meeting, the senior partner told John that the unique features of his newest machine were extremely beneficial. John had no information that indicated the senior partner was looking at any competitor's products, so he felt certain the sale would be his.

When John arrived for his final appointment with the senior partner, he was told that the firm had, only minutes before, signed a contract with John's competitor. John was shocked! He thought he had done everything right.

John, now older and wiser about the dynamics of complex sales, had *not* done everything right. He had not contacted and sold to all of the people involved in this buying decision. John had assumed, incorrectly, that the senior partner would make the buying decision on his own. However, behind the scenes, as John later discovered, other lawyers in the firm feared the senior partner's inclination to "buy the newest gadget." One of these lawyers, after investigating other options, had convinced the senior partner that another choice was best. John had been successful in developing a good rapport with the senior partner and a need for new dictation equipment, but he had lost the sale. Sometimes, selling the top executive is not enough.

THE COMPLEX BUYING TEAM

If your product or service is typically purchased by a group of individuals or a committee, then your sale can be termed *complex*. In a complex selling situation, several people in the buying organization participate in the purchase decision, either because they are directly affected by it or because they have information that can help improve the quality of the buying decision. I refer to this cluster of decision makers as the *Complex Buying Team*.

SHOULD YOU WORRY ABOUT COMPLEX SALES?

A simple, straightforward sale is one you make to an individual buyer. Simple sales are rarer than you might think. Although many sales appear simple on the surface, there may actually be, behind the scenes, several important players who have the power to affect the buying decision. In situations such as these, it is up to you, the seller, to figure out what's going on. This chapter will show you how.

Technology Is Making Buying Decisions More Complex

Changing technology in today's marketplace is forcing buyers to use a collaborative decision-making process. Many salespeople who sell technological solutions to businesses today are finding their sales becoming more complex because products and services are becoming more integrated. For example, office computers are networked together, not only within a department but across divisions. Telephone systems don't simply transmit voice communications; they transmit data as well. As technological progress allows greater integration of products and services, the number of people affected by each advance increases. In general, the greater the number of people affected, the more complex the sale.

Buying Decisions Are Being Pushed Down to Lower Levels

Many complex buying decisions are no longer being made in the CEO's office. Instead, they are being pushed down to lower-level decision makers. There are two reasons for this transfer. First, downsizing has flattened the organizational hierarchy, forcing CEOs and senior executives to delegate more decision-making authority. Top-level executives simply don't have the time to study the intricate details of every purchase.

Second, many senior executives are technologically illiterate and must rely on the recommendations of others who are more astute. A recent *USA Today* cover story, titled "Underlings' Skill Can Give Them an Edge," stated that "Despite the presence of 34 million computers in U.S. workplaces, technology is the Achilles' heel of many managers." Many of today's managers, schooled in the 1960s and '70s, missed the computer revolution. Even for technologically literate executives, technology is moving forward faster than their ability to keep up.

The *USA Today* article described how Nike CEO Phil Knight expressed his personal frustration in adapting to a new Macintosh computer, which he now claims he couldn't live without. "I am a Ticonderoga 2½ (pencil) in a Wordperfect world," Knight is quoted as saying. "I am suspicious of technology. I know it's important but I resist it emotionally." From Knight's comments, one might surmise that he needs some help when making expensive decisions about technological changes for his company.

For decision makers at any level of a corporation, there is more at risk today. Responsibility for buying is delegated to them; permission to fail is not. Mistakes can be costly, not only for their employer but also for themselves. This is another reason why buying decisions are made by committees: everybody shares the glory—or the blame.

Even Low-Tech Buying Decisions Can Be Complex

Your product or service need not be technical for your sale to be complex. Cliff sells roof tile for use on newly constructed residential homes. Roof tile is a low-tech product, but Cliff's sale is complex. In a typical sale, he sells to the builder/owner, general contractor, sub-contractor, roofing and waterproofing consultant, and an architectural firm. Each of these entities may have several individuals on the buying team. An architectural firm, for instance, may have a principal, project manager, project architect, and specifier, each with an interest in the purchase. What makes Cliff's sale complex is the multitude of people involved.

THE POSITIONS ON THE COMPLEX BUYING TEAM

On the Complex Buying Team there are six key decision-making positions (Figure 11.1): Gatekeeper, Integrator, Virtual Authority, User, Power Broker, and Sponsor (GIVUPS). There are two kinds of Sponsors: A Sponsor and an Antisponsor. A Sponsor is someone who wants you to succeed and an Antisponsor is someone who wants your competition to succeed. To win a complex sale, you must identify and influence the Power Broker, the person who has a "direct line" to the Virtual Authority. In most companies, the Power Broker is also a User, Integrator, or Gatekeeper. Sometimes, the Power Broker is also the Virtual Authority.

If you can find and develop a Sponsor who wants you to succeed, you will probably have gained someone who can influence the Power Broker on your behalf. Your best scenario is to identify the Power Broker early in a sales process and turn him or her into a Sponsor. Your sale is then almost assured.

Every member of the Complex Buying Team has a distinct role or combination of roles. Contact each one of them with equal attention. Sell each of them on the value of your product or solution. Do not ignore anyone or prejudge which member or members might be most valuable to you.

The number of people in the buying group does not affect the model shown in Figure 11.1. It is not uncommon for one individual

Figure 11.1   The Complex Buying Team

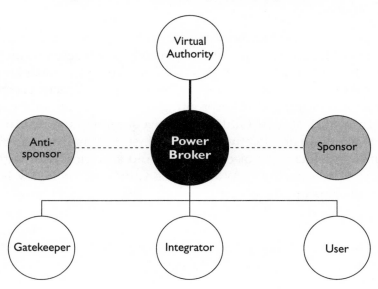

to play more than one key position, whatever the size of the buying team. In a smaller group, decision makers may play more than one position. Even in a large group, some people may be at more than one position. To make the sale, you must identify each member of the buying team, his or her respective role in the decision-making process, and the extent of each member's individual influence. First, we'll take a close look at each role, then we'll see an example of a buying team in action.

The Gatekeeper

The individual who controls the flow of information to members of the Complex Buying Team is called the Gatekeeper. A Gatekeeper can wield considerable power because information affects the buy-*learning* process. An example of a Gatekeeper would be a purchasing agent who gathers information from salespeople, effectively screening salespeople from other members of the Complex Buying Team. Other examples of typical Gatekeepers include office managers, executive assistants, and receptionists.

The Integrator

Anyone possessing expert information that buyers feel will improve the quality of their decision can be termed an Integrator. The Integrator looks at the "big picture" and helps evaluate how a particular solution will affect different aspects of how the company functions. An Integrator judges a solution based on its compatibility with the existing systems or procedures. Although Integrators don't have final authority, they can exclude you from the sales opportunity if you don't meet their minimum acceptable standards.

In high-tech sales, Integrators are technologically literate individuals whose expertise is sought out by others. Sometimes they are from outside the company—for example, a professional consultant or adviser. The purchase of a telecommunications system, for instance, may be significantly influenced by a "telecom consultant" hired by the buyer to provide advice during the buying process.

The Virtual Authority

This person issues the final OK. The Virtual Authority has the power to say "yes" and the power to say "no." Typically, the Virtual Authority is most interested in the bottom-line impact of a solution. The Virtual Authority wants a return on his or her investment—fast. The Virtual Authority's motto is: "The buck stops here."

Why do I refer to this person as the *Virtual* Authority? Because his or her importance in a buying decision today is often artificial: it exists in the salesperson's mind but not necessarily in the minds of the Complex Buying Team members. Salespeople frequently mistake the individual with the most senior title as being "the decision maker." As mentioned earlier, the power to decide is being pushed down to the frontlines to people who have firsthand knowledge of the problem. The Virtual Authority's role is frequently "hands-off," relying instead upon the recommendation of other members of the buying team. The Virtual Authority is still cast as an important member of the team, but don't be surprised if he or she turns out to be less dominant.

You may be thinking, "Didn't I read, in the Student chapter, that I should call on the CEO level? Now I'm being told that senior executives may not be as important to the Complex Buying Team as they once were. Which statement is true?"

Both are. Many salespeople, provided they can get in the door, find the CEO level a great place to start a relationship with a prospective client. There is no faster way to jump-start a sales opportunity than to persuade a CEO-level prospect that there is a need for change. Once this need has been recognized, however, much of the actual buying process will likely be delegated. For you to win the sale, you must convince these lower-level team members that your product or solution is the best choice.

The User

A User operates your product or service. A User's function on the Complex Buying Team is to assess the potential impact your product will have on job duties. Users usually have the power to say "no" to a particular vendor, but they don't have the power to say "yes." Rarely can they tell their Purchasing Department to prepare a purchase order. Often, several Users are involved in a complex buying decision.

The Power Broker

All members of the Complex Buying Team are not created equal. In every complex sales decision, at least one individual has the greatest personal interest in the buying decision and the political clout to sway other buyers. This Power Broker derives his or her influence from credibility with CEO-level executives. That's why, in the Complex Buying Team graphic, a straight line connects the Power Broker to the Virtual Authority. This person is the hinge on which the entire deal swings. When the Power Broker talks, the other buyers listen.

Sometimes, especially in technology sales, the Power Broker is also the Integrator, the recognized technical expert. To this computer master, a "good time" means a cruise on the information superhighway. Some Power Brokers are Users who recognize that great value would be achieved from buying. The Power Broker may also be the Virtual Authority, a senior executive who retains control of decision making. Any multilayered organizations that have resisted downsizing, such as government agencies, will tend to have senior-level managers who pull rank.

The Power Broker derives his or her power from credibility with the Virtual Authority, perhaps by being the recognized technical expert. Or, the Power Broker may be the Virtual Authority's trusted adviser, the so-called "right-hand person."

A winning sales strategy must first identify and then influence the Power Broker. It can be difficult to identify this trusted adviser: job titles are not reliable clues. Look for the *informal* leader of the Complex Buying Team. The Power Broker will be the person who:

- Has access to senior managers.
- Has the most to gain—politically—from a buying decision.
- Is involved in other key projects.
- Is self-confident.
- Desires authority.
- Understands company goals and objectives.
- Is listened to by others.

The Power Broker may exert influence only on the Virtual Authority, or may sway the opinions of the entire buying team.

The Sponsor

Any member of the Complex Buying Team who wants you and your product or service to win the sale is called a Sponsor. If you look back on every complex sale you have ever made, chances are there was at least one individual within the buying group who wanted you to succeed, someone who supported your selection and helped to persuade others. Your Sponsor is your supporter and your key information resource. Ideally, you will cultivate more than one Sponsor in a complex sale.

Your Sponsor must have credibility with other members of the buying team, especially the Virtual Authority and Power Broker. Without credibility with others, the sales effectiveness of your Sponsor is greatly diminished, and any access to inside information is limited. If you align yourself with a Sponsor who lacks credibility with higher-ups, your credibility with higher-ups will suffer, too. Your situation will be similar to "guilt by association." If your Sponsor is perceived as being weak, you will be seen as weak. If your Sponsor is perceived as ineffective, your solution will be seen as ineffective. You'll do better to align yourself with a rising star, someone whose perceived value is rising, so you too are seen as adding more value.

The Sponsor is different from the Virtual Authority, User, Gatekeeper, Integrator, and Power Broker in one vital way: the

Sponsor has to be *developed*. The other members of the buying team exist, whether you like it or not. Someone gives the final OK (Virtual Authority), someone screens information (the Gatekeeper), someone uses what you're selling (User), someone judges the technical compatibility of your offering (Integrator), and someone is a heavyweight (Power Broker). The key to winning a complex sale, however, is taking on each member of the Complex Buying Team, especially the Power Broker, and turning one (or more) of them into a Sponsor.

Because you need at least one Sponsor to win a major sale, it makes sense to develop one early in a sales process. If you can identify the Power Broker and turn him or her into a Sponsor, your sale is *almost* assured.

How do you find a good Sponsor, someone who will sell others for you? Simple. Find someone with the personal qualities shared by the very best salespeople—someone who is just like you. All top salespeople and Sponsors have:

- Above-average ambition.
- High levels of empathy.
- Intense goal orientation.
- Strong willpower.
- Impeccable honesty.
- Above-average intelligence.
- Willingness to accept responsibility.

Why would a buyer want to become your Sponsor? The answer lies in his or her personal agenda, what the Sponsor hopes to achieve, personally, as the result of buying. The best Sponsor is the person with the strongest *personal* benefit associated with your unique solution. Although business buyers have an interest in achieving their organization's goals, their motivation in the buying process is usually derived from both their personal and social goals. Each member of the Complex Buying Team has both business goals and personal goals. Figure 11.2 lists what these goals *may* be. Naturally, goals change, depending on the personal priorities of each individual team member.

The Antisponsor

While you are cultivating Sponsors for your cause, your competitors will be busy developing Sponsors for their counterattack. An

Figure 11.2   The Complex Buying Team's Goals

Complex Buying Team Role	Possible Business Goals	Possible Personal Goals
Gatekeeper	To save time for other team members	To have more influence in the workplace
Integrator	To integrate solution well with other internal systems	To appear knowledgeable and needed
Virtual Authority	To get a good return on investment	To achieve more personal success
User	To make his or her job more productive	To keep his or her job safe from layoff
Power Broker	To achieve business goals	To gain more authority
Sponsor/ Antisponsor	To achieve business goals	To gain recognition

Antisponsor is any member of the Complex Buying Team who wants your competition to cross the finish line first. The Antisponsor is your greatest threat to your winning a complex sale. The most successful strategy against this is to neutralize the Antisponsor by being proactive. Identify who is against you, assess that person's power and influence on the decision, and take action to diffuse the threat. Do not sit back and wait! (More advice on coping with Antisponsors appears later in this chapter.)

HOW TO IDENTIFY MEMBERS OF THE COMPLEX BUYING TEAM

Buying is a process, not a single event. As the process progresses, new players can become involved and others can fade away. This is true not only of the decision-making team, but also of sellers. If you are selling against the competition, competitive advantage often shifts to the salesperson who is closest to the inner dynamics of the Complex Buying Team.

You must identify and contact as many members of the team as possible. Many a sale has been lost because certain decision makers were not contacted and influenced. The more decision makers you have who support your solution, the greater the momentum will be in your favor.

Frequently, salespeople are unable to contact certain behind-the-scenes decision makers. This is another reason why it's so important to have a credible Sponsor, a Sponsor who can sell for you.

As much as 75 percent of a complex sale can take place when the salesperson isn't present. The sale is made by Sponsors who sell other decision makers on the need to buy. Usually, the Power Broker recognizes a need to buy and then sells the need to fellow buyers. In situations such as these, the salesperson is a catalyst for a chain of conversations between buyers that results in a favorable buying decision.

Because sales evolve over time, you must be an information gatherer throughout the buying process, not only at the beginning. As new information becomes available, you may need to alter your sales strategy. This need for inside information is one reason why a Sponsor is so important. Your Sponsor is a key information resource.

To identify members of the Complex Buying Team, ask your Sponsor general questions, then gradually get more specific. For instance:

- How will your organization go about making this decision?
- Who else will you need to speak with?
- How does our success help each of these people to "win"?
- Who will give the final OK?
- Which single individual will likely have the greatest interest in this decision?
- Is there any individual who may be opposed to my solution?

Your Sponsor may not be readily able to identify, say, the Power Broker, but he or she will have insights and information that will point you in the right direction.

Once you have team members identified, you must then determine how you will sell to them. Specifically, how will your solution benefit the self-interest of each member of the Complex Buying Team?

How do you discover what motivates each team member? One excellent way is to ask your Sponsor: How is that person measured? People do what they are paid to do, and what they are evaluated on. How a person is measured by the organization will tip you off to their personal motivators, the few specific goals each team member is striving to achieve. Prospects will rally in support of your cause if they perceive that your solution will be personally beneficial. Your job is to approach each member of the team and help each to understand how your solution will positively impact his or her personal goals. As you do so, however, be sensitive to where each contact is in the buying process.

IDENTIFYING WHERE EACH BUYER IS IN THE BUY-*LEARNING* PROCESS

It is possible, indeed probable, that various members of the Complex Buying Team will be at different steps in the buy-*learning* process. That means that you must sell to each member of the team in a different way. A buyer in Step 2 (Discontent) needs help in recognizing a problem and its seriousness (the Doctor role). A buyer in Step 3 (Research) needs help in designing a solution (the Architect role). A buyer in Step 4 (Comparison) needs proof that you're the best choice (the Coach role). A buyer in Step 5 (Fear) needs you to draw out some fears and help to resolve them (the Therapist role).

How you proceed depends on the position each player fills on the Complex Buying Team. For instance, in Step 4 (Comparison), the decision makers will all approach their comparisons from a different point of view. The User will want to know why your product is the easiest to use. The Virtual Authority will want to know whether the return on investment will be highest if the company buys from you. The Integrator will want to know that your solution will be the easiest to merge with other systems and procedures already in place. You must provide and solicit information for all the decision makers based on answers to these questions:

1. What role does each member of the Complex Buying Team have?
2. What is each buyer's interest (both professional and personal) in the purchase?
3. Which step of the buying process is each buyer on?

Each member of the Complex Buying Team influences the ultimate decision in some way. It's important for you to sell to the buyers as they want to be sold to. If you don't, you're bound to experience the consequences—a "sure-thing" sales opportunity for you that suddenly turns into a sale for your competitor.

How do you sell to a behind-the-scenes person whom you are unable to meet? Through your Sponsor. Work with your Sponsor to determine where each buyer is in the buy-*learning* process, and help your Sponsor sell to each person in the way he or she should be sold to. Suppose your Sponsor has just completed Step 4 (Comparison) and believes your offering is the best choice. Your Sponsor tells you, however, that the company's vice president (Virtual Authority) is not convinced of the need to buy. The vice president is at Step 2 (Discontent). The solution is to work with your Sponsor to develop a cost/benefit analysis that justifies your solution. Help your Sponsor to identify the personal goals of the vice president and to position your solution as helping the vice president achieve those goals.

THE COMPLEX BUYING TEAM IN ACTION

Several years ago, in the course of my search for potential clients who needed sales training services, I called the Vice President of Sales for a New York City-based company that operates, installs, and designs data management systems for financial institutions. This company employs about 200 salespeople. During my conversation with the Vice President of Sales, he told me that, in a recent sales managers' meeting, a decision had been made to provide a sales training program to the company's fifty major-account sales representatives. The timing of my call had been perfect, I had located a prospect who had just arrived at Step 3 (Research). He knew his sales organization needed sales training, but he wasn't sure what type and with whom. The Vice President of Sales directed me to call Patricia, his San Francisco-based Regional Sales Manager who, he told me, would be "doing the legwork," looking for the appropriate sales training solution.

    Near the end of my first meeting with Patricia, after I'd taken time to build her trust in me and help her clarify her needs, I asked, "Can you help me understand how this decision will be made?" She said that her mandate was to study her company's training needs, to research and evaluate three alternatives, judge each vendor based on compatibility with her company's sales process, and then to make a recommendation to the Vice President of Sales. Patricia told me that the Vice President of Sales would be the final decision maker, but that he placed a lot of importance on her recommendation. She also said she would be keeping the other Regional Sales Managers informed on her progress, and she expected the Vice President of Sales to discuss the decision with all his sales managers during a conference call before he awarded the contract.

Relying on this information, I knew the Complex Buying Team for this sale had the positions shown in Figure 11.3.

Patricia played several roles in this sale. As a User, she evaluated my solution as if she were a salesperson applying my sales approach in a typical selling situation. As a Gatekeeper, she checked my references and controlled the flow of information to both the Virtual Authority (Vice President of Sales) and the other Users (Regional Sales Managers). As an Integrator, she judged the compatibility of my sales approach with her company's buy–sell process. She was a heavy hitter in the decision-making process. For this sale, Patricia was also the Power Broker.

Over the next few weeks, I gathered more information directly from salespeople and met again with Patricia to share my findings with her. During this meeting, I helped her recognize and better define her needs, while at the same time designing a solution that both met her needs and locked out my two competitors (sales role 3: Architect). Throughout this time, my credibility was rising with Patricia, who gradually developed into my Sponsor.

Then Patricia moved to Step 4 (Comparison) and met with two of my competitors. When her evaluation of all three alternatives was

Figure 11.3   Locating Complex Buying Team Members

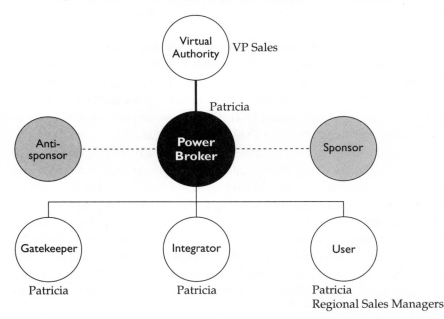

complete, she recommended to her boss that my company be hired, and told me that the Vice President of Sales wanted to meet with me.

Before the date set for the meeting, Patricia called to ask me to send information regarding my company and training program to Jim, her company's Vice President of Marketing. This was the first time I'd heard about Jim. Patricia said that Jim's "feathers were slightly ruffled" because training was part of Marketing's budget, and he had not been consulted on the decision to hire me. Uh-oh; a possible Antisponsor. I immediately sent the information, followed up with a couple of phone calls, but never got a response.

After the Vice President of Sales had studied my proposal and Patricia's recommendations carefully, he and I met. He questioned me closely about my solution and, shortly afterward, I was awarded the contract.

A few months later, my associates and I delivered our training program to a group of 50 major-account salespeople. The program received rave reviews. Jim, the Vice President of Marketing at Patricia's company, was one of the attendees, and I asked him to join me for lunch. During our time together, Jim was very positive about what he was seeing and hearing in the training sessions. Jim said the Vice President of Sales (the Virtual Authority) was extremely pleased with the results of the program and assured me that my firm would be hired to train the remainder of his company's sales force. Naturally, I felt confident about winning the next, much larger contract.

For reasons unknown to me, the Vice President of Sales was fired a few weeks later. Ouch! A search began for a replacement. In the meantime, Jim, the Vice President of Marketing, took control of the decision to train the larger group of 150 salespeople. Jim, I soon learned, was well-positioned with the company president (the executive who had fired the Vice President of Sales).

I knew my prospective sale was in jeopardy when, once again, Jim did not return my phone calls. Patricia, my Sponsor, told me that Jim perceived me as a threat because I had been hired without his stamp of approval. Jim was, indeed, an Antisponsor. Patricia also told me that Jim was upset with her for not having included him in the original decision to hire me. Not only was I on shaky ground with a key member of the Complex Buying Team, but my Sponsor's credibility with the Power Broker was also in question. Last but not least, Patricia told me that she had "heard through the grapevine" that Jim had been in contact with other sales training

Figure 11.4   The Revised Complex Buying Team

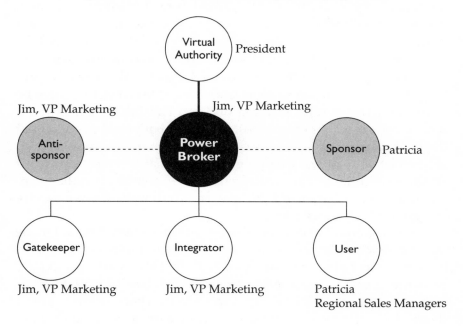

firms. My "sure-thing" sale was in big trouble. The Complex Buying Team for the larger sales training contract had now changed, as shown in Figure 11.4.

I needed another Sponsor—one with credibility in the home office. Pete, the company's midwest regional manager, came to mind. Pete had been very pleased with the first training session, and he had recently been appointed to the president's "Quality Action Team."

I called Pete to ask him how he had felt about the services my firm had provided. He repeated his enthusiastic support. Then I queried whether Pete felt our sales training program was the best choice for the remainder of his sales team. His reply was "Yes, I am convinced. Have we scheduled the dates with you yet?" I then reported that people in Pete's home office were looking at other options, and that I sensed my firm had already been ruled out. Pete's response was very surprised and disapproving. He promised to look into the situation.

A few weeks later, Jim met with three training companies. Despite our in-depth knowledge of his company's needs and our proven record of success, my firm was not one of those companies. Jim (the Power Broker, Antisponsor, Gatekeeper, and Integrator) had screened me out. In addition, Jim bypassed consulting the Users—the other sales managers—and ignored Pete. Although frustrated, Pete was unwilling to risk his status by going over Jim's head to the President.

How did it all turn out? Everybody lost. I lost the sale. The sales training program that Jim selected didn't make it past the initial pilot stage. It lacked support from the field sales managers, who were upset that a sales training decision had been made without their involvement. Jim lost credibility with both the president and the field sales managers, because time and money were wasted on an ineffective pilot training program. Eventually, he lost control of all sales training decisions. The salespeople lost because the training project was postponed for 18 months, until well after a new Vice President of Sales was hired.

What should I have done differently? From the moment I made initial contact with this account, my goal should have been to make the *second sale* rather than the first. With that attitude, I would have been much more sensitive to the first "red flag"—Jim's feathers being "slightly ruffled." When Jim didn't respond to my calls, I should have persisted in making contact with him. I should have flown to New York and involved him in the design and delivery of my services. Unfortunately, many of the lessons we learn in selling are expensive and nonreimbursable.

HOW TO SHARPEN YOUR
POLITICAL SKILLS

To win a complex sale, you must be a savvy strategist. First, neutralize your enemies. Identify those who may see your success as a threat, and try to help them see a sale to you as personally beneficial, or at least neutral. Your worst enemies will be the Antisponsors.

Identifying Antisponsors

Take a moment to reread Francis Bacon's words, quoted at the beginning of this chapter. The greatest barrier you face in winning a complex sale is *yourself*. Overconfidence about how a sale is progressing may lull you into a false sense of security. Do not make assumptions. Stay alert, or you'll face a nightmare. The more complex the sale, the more the members of the Complex Buying Team have invested in it, and the more inquisitive and suspicious you must be. Investigate all clues with the thoroughness of a detective. If something doesn't feel right, it probably isn't.

Some Antisponsors are difficult to recognize. They may prefer to operate surreptitiously, not wanting you to know they exist. During a meeting with you, stealthy Antisponsors may say wonderful things about you and your solution. As soon as the meeting ends, they begin pulling strings to make you lose. The key to identifying these secretive Antisponsors is to have multiple sources of information (at least three) on the buying team. Don't rely on a single Sponsor for information; the Antisponsor may know who your supporter is, and hiding from one person is comparatively easy.

Not all Antisponsors are hard to detect. For instance, a User who has had previous experience with a competitor's product or service will probably feel more comfortable with that known solution.

Neutralizing an Antisponsor's Threat

After you identify an Antisponsor, determine how much influence he or she will have on the Complex Buying Team's decision. The key question is: How much credibility does the Antisponsor have with the Power Broker? If your answer is "A lot," arrange to see the Antisponsor in person, one-on-one, and use direct probes: "How do you feel about my solution?" or "I get the feeling that you have a concern about what I'm offering." (Tips on detecting and resolving fear and on handling objections are in Chapters 7 and 8.) Dig deep to uncover the real concern and then resolve it.

You might try overwhelming an Antisponsor with superior numbers. If you can develop several Sponsors among the members of the Complex Buying Team, you can create enough momentum for your solution to overpower the Antisponsor's opposition.

Imagine that you are a salesperson selling computer outsourcing services. If a company signs up with you, your company will perform the client's data processing activities. This means, however, that your customer's data processing employees will lose their jobs. Naturally, the data processing manager sees you as a threat. To neutralize the manager's concern, you could explain that, although the employees' jobs would be lost, the manager's job would actually become more important because of the manager's crucial role in developing the customer–supplier relationship.

Savvy sales strategists are sensitive to late arrivals to a Complex Buying Team. They know that a heavyweight who becomes involved at the eleventh hour can change the entire sale. Even when your sale seems assured, don't become overconfident. Overconfidence can lead to complacency, and complacency can lead to disaster. Identify latecomers and don't underestimate their influence. If you adopt the Therapist role (as described in Chapter 7), you will remain close to your prospective customer late in the sales process and you will be sensitive to any changes.

Don't underestimate the importance of personal agendas. The best supplier with the best offering does not always win. Suppose you made a sale to Department A that was successfully implemented. Now you are trying to make a similar sale to Department B. If Department B's manager is at odds with the manager of Department A, you may lose the sale to B because you were successful with A. Remember, the salesperson who wins the sale is the one who helps the Power Broker advance his or her personal agenda.

After you have identified the members of the Complex Buying Team, formulate a strategy to win the sale. First, determine the factors that are in your favor, such as a Power Broker who is your Sponsor, or a Virtual Authority who wants to buy and thinks your solution is best. Next, identify the factors working against you, such as not knowing who the Power Broker is, or knowing that the Gatekeeper is an Antisponsor.

Finally, create a plan to overcome your weaknesses by capitalizing on your strengths. Suppose one of your strengths is a User who is your Sponsor, and your weakness is an Integrator who is in Step 3 (Research). You are weak with the Integrator because he or she has not yet identified the requirements necessary to best integrate with existing systems. If the Integrator identifies criteria that you can't meet, the sale will be lost. You may ask the User's help in scheduling a meeting between you and the Integrator, so you can adopt the Architect role and influence the Integrator's identification of compatibility criteria.

COMPLEX BUYING TEAM WORKSHEETS

Figure 11.5 offers you some worksheets designed to help you win complex sales. You should use these worksheets at the end of Step 2 (Discontent) and during Step 3 (Research). You should also use them whenever there is a change in decision makers. Keep a sharp eye on the credibility your Sponsor has with other buyers, and the credibility the Power Broker has with the Virtual Authority. A

Figure 11.5   Complex Buying Team Worksheets

1. The decision makers on the Complex Buying Team are as follows [enter the names alongside the positions]:

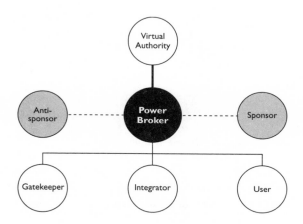

2. Each decision maker is at the following step in the buy-*learning* process [enter the names alongside the appropriate sections of the wheel]:

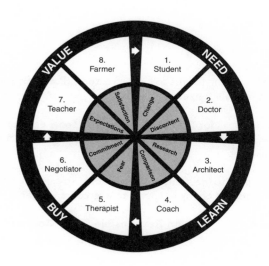

Figure 11.5   Continued

Buyer Role	On Which Step?	Matching Sales Role
Gatekeeper(s)		
Integrator(s)		
Virtual Authority		
User(s)		
Power Broker		
Sponsor(s)/Antisponsor(s)		

3. My solution will help each buyer as follows:

		Goals Met	
Buyer Role	Problem Solved or Opportunity Gained	Business Goals	Personal Goals
Gatekeeper(s)			
Integrator(s)			
Virtual Authority			
User(s)			
Power Broker			
Sponsor(s)/Antisponsor(s)			

4. My position is strong for the following reasons: (Power Broker is my Sponsor; User wants my solution, etc.)

5. My position is weak for the following reasons: (Some decision makers not identified; new decision makers introduced, Antisponsor has credibility with the Power Broker, etc.)

6. Here is my plan to neutralize Antisponsors, strengthen important relationships, and capitalize on my strengths to overcome weakness:

Action Item	Person Responsible	Completion Date

senior executive who becomes involved at the last minute assumes the role of Virtual Authority, which instantly changes the political structure of the Complex Buying Team. Use these forms to analyze your strengths and weaknesses as the landscape of the sale changes.

CONCLUSION

Winning a complex sale is difficult. Complex sales are bigger-ticket sales, and because your competition wants them as much as you do, success takes more than simple desire and a strong will. Winning also takes skill, the ability to separate yourself from the pack and make a difference for your customer.

My goal in writing this book has been to make a difference for you by helping you to race ahead of your competition. This is a lofty goal, and one that can be achieved only by *your* hard work, the extra effort you put forth to apply these skills in your professional life. As Herbert Spencer said, "The great aim of education is not knowledge, but action."

So, I pass this baton on to you, and trust you will run with it. Now is the time for you to act. Now it's *your turn* to make a difference.

APPENDIX

Sample Sales Proposal

To illustrate a Customer-Focused Selling proposal, we continue with the copier example used in Chapters 5 and 6. Suppose you sell copiers for CPC Corporation, a nationwide office equipment company. Your prospect is a medium-size public relations firm specializing in retail marketing plans. As a Student, you learned that your prospect wants to expand the business by serving larger clients. As a Doctor, you learned that to grow the business, and help her retail clients reach more people, your prospect's copier usage would increase to perhaps 9,000 copies per month. When you first arrived on the scene, your prospect was experiencing a problem with "misfeeds," caused by an antiquated document feeder that frequently jammed. By asking "complication" questions, you helped your prospect recognize that the amount of time being lost by misfeeds was significant. Continuing with the Doctor approach, you helped your prospect recognize additional problems she was experiencing with copy quality and copier service. Copy quality deteriorated on large jobs (the background became distorted), and portions of jobs had to be redone. Service support was slow, averaging a day-and-a-half response time. Complications triggered by downtime included overtime and higher photocopying costs (jobs were outsourced to meet deadlines). On one occasion, the quality of the job performed by an outside firm was unacceptable to the client, the job had to be rerun, and the client subsequently switched to another PR firm.

You ask your prospect a cure question, "If you were to invest in a new copier, how would that help your business?" Your prospect responds, "It would enhance my image with large prospective clients by allowing me to present more aggressive marketing plans." Next, you ask, "Is that something you need to do?" "Yes," she says.

"Tell me about your copiers." Aha! She has completed Stage One. She has recognized the need to buy.

As an Architect, you then design a solution that meets your customer's needs, and, as best you can, locks out your competition.

When it's time for you to present your solution to your buyer, follow this example of a customer-focused sales proposal and you'll be in a great position to win the sale.

CPC Corporation

April 30, 19XX

Ms. Elizabeth Adams
Partner
T. Day & Associates
123 Fourth Avenue
San Francisco, CA 94105

RE: Proposal to Provide a High-Performance Copier for
       T. Day & Associates

Dear Elizabeth,

Thank you for your interest in our copy machines designed to increase productivity. It has been a pleasure meeting with you and Sally and learning about the challenges and opportunities involved in expanding your business. Our high performance copier and rapid, professional support services will help you achieve your growth goals.

Enclosed is our proposal for CPC's Model 3500 copier, including:

I. Executive Summary

II. Why T. Day & Associates Needs a New Copier

III. T. Day & Associates' Goals and Objectives

IV. Requirements Necessary to Achieve Your Goals—and a Description of Our Solution

V. Why CPC?

VI. Financial Particulars and Profit Improvement Summary

VII. Delivery and Implementation Timeline

VIII. References and Related Materials

Elizabeth, I will call you on May 8th to answer any questions you may have. Thanks again. We look forward to helping your business grow with ours.

Sincerely,

I. EXECUTIVE SUMMARY

Your goal is to grow your business, to increase your value to your clients. But your current copier is holding you back. Frequent misfeeds and extended downtime hamper productivity and raise costs. Deteriorating copy quality is inconsistent with your high-profile corporate image. Combined, these problems are costing you $490 per month. (See Section II of this proposal.)

To attract larger clients now, you will soon begin a major new marketing plan, and that means a 25 percent increase in the number of copies made per month. To implement this plan effectively, you need a CPC Model 3500 copy machine. If you don't take action soon, the problems you are experiencing will become much worse. By investing in a model 3500 now, you will achieve:

- Improved document quality.
- Greater performance and speed.
- Reduced copier downtime.
- Ability to produce double-sided pamphlets and newsletters.
- Increased administrative productivity.
- Simplified billing procedures for both you and your clients.
- A $6,180 Annual Net Profit Improvement (see Section VI of this proposal).

The CPC Model 3500 will meet and exceed all your expectations, as the information below describes. Outstanding copy quality, high performance reliability, and fast double-sided copy speed are just a few of the 3500's unique strengths that will pay off for you.

CPC Corporation's support services are the finest in the industry. We provide fast, professional response, a twenty-four-hour help line, and a free loaner if you need it. Our "Total Satisfaction Guarantee" ensures that you WILL be satisfied. That's our commitment to you.

Invest in a CPC copier today, then watch what we can do for you!

II. WHY T. DAY & ASSOCIATES NEEDS A NEW COPIER

To attract more large clients, you will soon begin a major new marketing plan. This plan will require an estimated 25 percent increase in the number of copies made.

Your existing copier is not capable of handling the added workload, nor can it produce the high-quality documents you need to achieve your goals. There are three primary problems with your current machine: (1) misfeeds, (2) inconsistent copy quality, and (3) extended downtime. By taking a close look at each of these problems, Sally (your office manager) and I discovered:

1. *Misfeeds.* In the past thirty days, your copier's document feeder suffered *twelve* misfeeds. A misfeed occurs when paper jams as it's being fed into the machine, forcing the halt of operations. Because your machine is located in the copy room, sometimes employees are unaware of misfeeds when they occur. This results in:

   • Delays in job completion.

   • Mangling and/or destruction of original documents.

   • Reduced productivity.

2. *Inconsistent copy quality.* Your employees have noticed deteriorating copy quality, particularly on large jobs of 500 copies or more. Section VIII of this proposal (References and Related Materials) is an example of this deterioration. As you can see, the background of the 500th copy is distorted. The deteriorating quality of solid images, such as headers and footers, is also quite noticeable. Inconsistent copy quality leads to:

   • Complaints from your largest clients (two complaints in April).

   • Inconsistent image for you and your clients.

   In response to this problem, your receptionist now performs spot checks on copy quality. When she identifies unacceptable copies, she discards them and makes additional copies to replace them. This has improved the situation, but Sally remains concerned that unacceptable documents are slipping through.

3. *Extended downtime.* Your copier does not perform as well today as it did two years ago. It has broken down three times in

the past two months. Each of these breakdowns occurred in the middle of large jobs for key clients. In each situation, your copier was inoperable for between two and three days. This downtime forced:

- Outsourcing of jobs to meet deadlines.
- Additional administrative time and energy.

THE FINANCIAL IMPACT OF PROBLEMS AND SOLUTIONS

Sally and I carefully analyzed the financial impact of each problem described above. The specifics of our analysis are listed below. Purchasing a new copier would pay off in two ways. First, costly problems would be eliminated. Second, our solution would cut additional costs and provide an opportunity to increase revenues.

I. The Costs of Your Current Situation

Cost of Misfeeds. Sally estimates that misfeeds result in loss of five hours of administrative time each month, which, at an average of $20 per hour, means that misfeeds cost you $100 per month.

Cost of Inconsistent Copy Quality. The cost of client dissatisfaction is difficult to measure, and we haven't attempted to do so. However, your receptionist reports that she discarded over 1,000 poor-quality copies last month. At an average cost per copy of .02, that's $20 per month. Add to that an estimated two hours of extra administrative time ($40 cost), and your total measurable cost of inconsistent copy quality is $60 per month.

Cost of Extended Downtime. Outsourced jobs cost $.06 per copy, as compared to $.02 per copy in-house. In April, 1,500 copies were farmed out. Outsourcing in this way costs you $60 per month. Four additional hours of administrative time were expended to complete these jobs on time. Two of these hours were overtime @ $30 per hour, for a total labor cost of $100. The total *measurable* cost of extended downtime is $160 per month.

2. Financial Improvement Provided by Our Solution

There are additional ways our copier will help you save and make money. Certain capabilities of a new copier, missing on your current machine, will deliver bottom-line benefits. Here are two specific *cost improvements* provided by a new copier.

Reduced Paper and Postage Costs. The CPC Model 3500 features *automatic double-sided copy capability,* so you save money by using less paper and paying less postage. Sally estimates that making double-sided copies will save approximately $50 per month.

Fewer Hours Spent Handling Paperwork. Additional administrative cost savings will occur because of the Model 3500's *automatic stapler/sorter capability.* Sally estimates three hours will be saved per month, for a total of $60.

A new copier will enable you to expand your marketing efforts and attract new clients, thereby *increasing revenues.* Sally estimates, based on current advertising response and conversion rates, that a new copier would enable you to increase monthly revenues by $1,000. Sally further estimates that this $1,000 revenue figure translates into a net profit per month of $400.

Summary of Financial Improvements Provided by Our Solution

Item	Monthly Cost Savings	Monthly Revenue Increase
Misfeeds	$100	
Inconsistent copy quality	60	
Extended downtime	160	
Reduced paper/postage costs	50	
Automatic stapler savings	60	
Total cost reduction	$490	
Total revenue increase		$1,000

Important Note on Business Financials. Every dollar you save in costs represents a dollar increase in profitability.

Revenue increases, however, do not have the same dollar-for-dollar effect on profitability. Each dollar increase in revenue has costs associated with it, such as costs of goods sold, and selling, general, and administrative expenses. This is a major reason why companies today are so anxious to cut costs: the savings go directly to the bottom line.

Section VI of this proposal combines the above financial information with CPC Model 3500 copier purchase particulars, resulting in a complete profit improvement summary.

Additional Benefits of Buying

For every measurable cost, there is at least one *intangible* cost to be considered too. An intangible cost is difficult to measure, but that doesn't mean intangible costs should be ignored. Intangible costs, such as reduced morale, dissatisfied customers, and lost business, are usually much more damaging than tangible costs. The difficulty is that you can't easily *see* these costs, but they are there.

What About the Cost of Delay?

Soon, you will implement a major new marketing plan that will increase the number of copies by 25 percent, to 9,000 per month. Increasing the usage of your copier is sure to complicate the problems you are currently experiencing—misfeeds, poor quality copies, and downtime. Investing in a new copier today will pay immediate dividends, including improved client satisfaction and an enhanced corporate image for T. Day & Associates.

DON'T DELAY—ACT TODAY!

III. T. DAY & ASSOCIATES' GOALS AND OBJECTIVES

Based on our needs analysis, the following is a list of the goals and objectives you would expect to achieve with the purchase of a new copier:

1. Faster copier that produces more copies in less time.
2. Improved copy quality.
3. Reduction in copier downtime.
4. Production of double-sided pamphlets and newsletters.
5. Copier that requires less monitoring and supervision.
6. Simplified billing procedures by tracking copies made per client/job.

The result of achieving these goals and objectives will be the production of more documents of consistent high quality, thereby enhancing the corporate image of both T. Day and your clients.

IV. REQUIREMENTS NECESSARY TO ACHIEVE YOUR GOALS—AND A DESCRIPTION OF OUR SOLUTION

GOAL 1. Produce More Copies in Less Time

Your Requirements	The CPC Model 3500 Solution
Your current machine is a 25-CPM (copies per minute) unit that was designed to produce only 6,000 copies per month. To implement your new marketing plan, you must have a copier capable of GREATER CAPACITY and SPEED. A business such as yours, averaging 9,000 copies per month, would be best served by purchasing a 35-CPM copier.	The Model 3500 is capable of 10,000+ copies per month. The 3500 delivers 35 copies per minute, and its two-sided copy capability is among the fastest in the industry.
Your current sorter, the series of output bins that separates completed copies, has 10 bins that hold up to 30 sheets each. Although this has been adequate for most jobs, Sally reports that a LARGER SORTER, perhaps as much as 15 bins/40 sheets, may be necessary in the future.	The CPC Model 3500 large sorter features 20 bins, each of which can hold up to 50 sheets of paper.

GOAL 2. Improve Copy Quality

Your Requirements	The CPC Model 3500 Solution
You must have EXCELLENT COPY QUALITY.	The Model 3500 offers the finest copy quality of any 35-CPM copier, providing great solids and a clear background. Sample copies are provided for comparison (in Section VIII of this proposal). You be the judge.
You must have CONSISTENT COPY QUALITY.	The 3500 delivers consistency for you. In a test performed by Sally, your receptionist was unable to distinguish between the first copy run on our copier and the 1,000th copy.

GOAL 3. Reduce Copier Downtime

Your Requirements	The CPC Model 3500 Solution
Your current document feeder, which automatically feeds to the copier the set of originals to be copied, is the cause of your misfeed problem. To restore performance and productivity, you must have a MORE RELIABLE DOCUMENT FEEDER.	Model 3500 comes with a highly reliable Recirculating Automatic Document Feeder (RADF). The RADF makes all the required copies of one page before moving on to the next page. It is capable of feeding up to 50 pages automatically—and reliably (see references in Section VII).
Machine breakdowns are expensive because of the two-day average time necessary to restore your current copier to working condition. For this reason, OUTSTANDING SERVICE and SUPPORT are crucial. As your business grows, so will your reliance on a copier, so these crucial capabilities will become even more important.	CPC provides the finest service support in the industry. Our service staff is highly competent and arrives in your office, on average, within four hours of your call. We provide a twenty-four-hour service help line and a seven-year parts guarantee. If your machine is down for more than eight hours, we will provide you with a free loaner.
	We back our service with the industry's most comprehensive "Total Satisfaction Guarantee." If for any reason you are not satisfied within the first three years of ownership, CPC will replace your machine, no questions asked.

GOAL 4. Produce Double-Sided Pamphlets and Newsletters

Your Requirements	The CPC Model 3500 Solution
Sally says that double-sided pamphlets and newsletters are now the industry norm, yet your current copier is incapable of accomplishing this. For this reason, you need AUTOMATIC DOUBLE-SIDED COPY CAPABILITY, which allows you to make two-sided copies from single-sided or two-sided originals. Double-sided copying will reduce paper and postage costs.	Model 3500 produces double-sided copies very quickly—in 90+ percent of normal, single-sided 35-CPM speed. Jobs will be completed in less time, with outstanding copy quality.
The production of special-event materials for your clients frequently requires images to be enlarged. That's why you need REDUCTION and ENLARGEMENT capability.	The Model 3500 offers 50 percent to 200 percent reduction/enlargement range, more than enough flexibility to meet your enlargement needs.

GOAL 5. Find a Copier that Requires Less Monitoring and Supervision

Your Requirements	The CPC Model 3500 Solution
Many fast copiers do not complete jobs quickly because of limited paper supplies. Especially in a situation such as yours, where the copier is not in plain view, a LARGE PAPER SUPPLY is important.	The 3500 offer one of the industry's largest on-line paper supplies—two paper trays as standard equipment, one with 250 sheets, another with 1,300 sheets.
Currently, your copier takes 5.5 seconds to make its first copy. Sally says this can be a nuisance, and it would be nice to have a FASTER FIRST-COPY TIME.	The Model 3500 takes just 4 seconds to generate its first copy.

GOAL 6. Simplify Billing Procedures by Tracking Copies per Client/Job

Your Requirements	The CPC Model 3500 Solution
You would like to track the usage of your machine and bill clients accordingly. A copier with ACCOUNT CODES would enable you to track the number of copies per user, and bill your clients accordingly.	The 3500 comes standard with 100 account codes. The more account codes the better. With 100 codes, you will be able to set up project-specific accounts for each client. This tracking will dramatically simplify your accounting and billing procedures.

V. WHY CPC?

CPC Corporation is a $2 billion customer-driven company staffed with people who believe that your complete satisfaction is why we are in business. We are a worldwide leader in high-performance office automation systems and support services. We have helped over 250,000 customers improve document quality, and we would like to achieve the same goal for you.

Why CPC Corporation Is Unique in the Copy Machine Industry

- Our local service staff is highly experienced and knowledgeable. Our technicians have, on average, eight years' experience. Each technician invests two weeks per year in the classroom, sharpening the necessary troubleshooting skills.

- Fast response time. If you have a problem, we get to you *fast*. Our company's average response time is 4 hours. Here in our local office, we averaged 2.4 hours response time last month. Here's what one customer said recently:

  > Our CPC machine is 4 years old and we have "put a lot of miles" on it. Our heavy usage has caused a few breakdowns recently, so we must call for help. My compliments to your management for running such a fine service organization. David Smith, our CPC technician, is SUPERB! He gets here within 3 hours, fixes our machine quickly, and always has a smile on his face. Keep up the good work!
  > —Mary Jones, Office Administrator,
  > Law Offices of Wilson & May, Feb. 14, 19XX.

- Our 24-hour service help line is unique in the industry.

- Free loaner is guaranteed if your machine is down for 8 hours.

- CPC's "Total Satisfaction Guarantee." If for any reason you are not satisfied within the first 3 years of ownership, CPC will replace your machine, no questions asked.

- In-house financing means you make your lease payments to the same company responsible for servicing your machine. Prior to creating CPC Financial Services, Inc., we leased our copiers through an outside leasing company. Upon delivery of the machine, we received a check in full from the finance company, who then invoiced and collected payments from customers. Since starting CPC Financial, many customers have told us that making payments to the same company that services them gives them peace of mind.

Why the CPC Model 3500 Is the Best Choice for T. Day & Associates

- Proof positive of reliability and consistent copy quality in companies with needs almost identical to yours. Fox & Associates Advertising & Marketing installed a CPC Model 3500 copier one year ago. Today, Fox has 35 percent more employees than last year, and their usage of the Model 3500 has increased accordingly. They are a heavy user of the double-sided copy capability and automatic stapler, which they use for newsletters and pamphlets. Their phone number is listed in the reference section.

- Fastest double-sided copy speed available. You will use this capability for the newsletters and pamphlets you produce for your largest clients. A fast double-sided copy speed will improve your responsiveness to key clients.

- The largest on-line paper supply. Capable of holding 1,550 sheets in two trays. This means less administrative supervision.

- More account codes. The 3500 offers 100 account codes standard, which means you can allocate not only by client, but also by individual projects. This will streamline your accounting procedures and enhance the services you provide to your customers. Also, it will prevent lost revenue, due to administrative errors.

VI. FINANCIAL PARTICULARS AND PROFIT IMPROVEMENT SUMMARY

Investment Analysis

Description	Quantity	Unit	Price
CPC Model 3500 copier	1	8,686	$ 8,686
20-bin sorter	1	1,500	1,500
Automatic stapler	1	1,400	1,400
	Subtotal		$11,586

Annual Guaranteed Maintenance Agreement (GMA)		
Seven-year parts guarantee	included	
Twenty-four-hour service help line	included	
Free loaner/replacement	included	
Up-time guarantee—98 percent	included	
($.015 per copy × 9,000 copies/month × 12 months)		$1,620
Five Year Lease Option (includes GMA)		$375 per month

Profit Improvement Summary

Based on the financial calculations described in Section II of this proposal, the estimated profit improvement impact of the CPC Model 3500 would be:

Monthly cost reduction		$490	
Monthly revenue enhancement	1,000		
Contribution to profit (40% of revenue)		400	
Gross monthly profit impact			$890
Less: Model 3500 monthly lease amount			(375)
Net monthly profit improvement			$515

Annual Net Profit Improvement   ($515/month × 12 months) = $6,180

VII. DELIVERY AND IMPLEMENTATION TIMELINE*

Task	Person Responsible	Person Days	Completion Date
Site review (to ensure power and space requirements)	Curtis	.2	May 10th
Deliver copy machine	Jim	.3	May 12th
Program account codes	Kevin	.3	May 12th
Orientation training	Brian	.5	May 12th
Follow-up training/support	Brian	.3	May 17th

Author's note to reader: Delivery for a midvolume copier is straightforward. If your product or service requires a complex schedule, use the above format to document exactly what will be done, by whom and by when. A well-documented implementation timeline will prevent some prospects from experiencing Step 5 (Fear).

VIII. REFERENCES AND RELATED MATERIALS

References

Fox Marketing and Advertising   Contact:
400 Summit Road   Mr. Sam Fox
Skyline, CA 921XX   (916)556-1232

Over a year ago, Fox & Associates struggled with a copier too small for their thriving practice. To better support the needs of their clients, they installed a CPC Model 3500 in May, 19XX. They are a heavy user of the double-sided copy capability and automatic stapler. These capabilities are used for newsletters, pamphlets, and other promotional materials.

McKenzie Communications, Inc.   Contact:
100 Crow Canyon Road, Suite 1010   Ms. Paula McKenzie
San Jose, CA 921XX   (916)559-2141

We have been serving McKenzie Communications' copy needs since 1988. McKenzie began with our Model 10 (10-CPM personal copier), then upgraded to our Model 200 (20-CPM) in 1993. Six months ago, they upgraded to the Model 3500. Since then, McKenzie has averaged 10,000 copies per month, approximately 80 percent of which are double-sided.

Related Materials

Enclosed are supporting documents [not shown here], including:

- Copy sample, current copier.
- Copy sample, CPC Model 3500.
- Model 3500 brochure.
- Model 3500 specification sheet.

NOTES

Introduction

4   The top five sources of customer frustration were taken from "How To Push Customers Away," by Richard Whiteley (*Sales & Marketing Management*, February 1994): p. 29.

Chapter 1   Clash!

8   *Future Shock*, by Alvin Toffler (New York: Bantam, 1970), p. 14.

10   The dramatic increase in international telephone volume was taken from "The Global Free-For-All," by Catherine Arnst (*BusinessWeek*, September 26, 1994), pp. 118–126.

10   Motorola's speed in the construction of a microprocessor plant was obtained from "Motorola: Training for the Millennium," by Kevin Kelly (*BusinessWeek*, March 28, 1994), pp. 158–163.

10   The fact that of the hundred largest U.S. companies in 1900, only sixteen are still in business, was taken from *Searching for the Spirit of Enterprise*, by Larry Farrell (New York: Penguin Books, 1993), p. 7.

11   1994 sales and profit figures for America's 1,000 most valuable companies were taken from "A Bittersweet Year for Corporate America: Profits Zoomed and Productivity Soared. So Why Didn't Market Value Rocket Up?" (*BusinessWeek*, March 27, 1995), pp. 90–95.

11   1993 sales and profit figures for America's 1,000 most valuable companies were taken from "America's Most Valuable Companies: Many Ugly Ducklings Turned into Swans—and Ought to Stay Beautiful," by Veronica Byrd (*BusinessWeek*, March 28, 1994), pp. 72–78.

11   The information on the life cycle of PCs and disappearing middle-management jobs was taken from "Rate of Change Grows Ever Faster," by Judith Hamilton, guest columnist (*San Francisco Examiner*, April 10, 1994), p. C-5. Ms. Hamilton is CEO of Dataquest, a leading research and consulting firm specializing in information technology.

11   The figures on the corporate downsizing of the white-collar workforce and Joseph Cooper's quote were taken from "Layoffs Double Among

Men in Middle-Age," by Chronicle Wire Services (*San Francisco Chronicle*, May 13, 1994), p. A-6.

11 Surveys on layoff survivors' sickness were taken from *Healing the Wounds: Overcoming the Trauma of Layoffs and Revitalizing Downsized Organizations*, by David Noer (San Francisco: Jossey-Bass, 1993), p. 88.

15 Dartnell Corporation research was taken from "How Soon Do Salespeople Quit Pitching?" by Nancy Arnott (*Sales & Marketing Management*, December 1993), p. 17.

17 Information on studies that confirm decision makers who follow a systematic approach stand a better chance of achieving their goals than if they make their decision on "gut feel" alone was obtained from *Decision Traps: The Ten Barriers to Brilliant Decision Making & How to Overcome Them*, by J. Edward Russo and Paul Schoemaker (Garden City, NY: Doubleday, 1989), p. 119.

18 Habit 2: Begin with the End in Mind taken from *The Seven Habits of Highly Effective People*, by Stephen R. Covey (New York: Simon and Schuster, 1989) p. 95.

Chapter 2   The Buying Process

20 The exact cost of a field sales call varies from company to company, but all experts agree the cost is rising. One company, DuPont Corporation, estimates its cost at over $500 per field sales call in "It's Jerry Hale on the Line," by Martin Everett (*Sales & Marketing Management*, December 1993), p. 75.

20 Reorganization of IBM sales, and the high percentage of IBM customers being sold over the phone was obtained from "The Few, the True, the Blue" (*BusinessWeek*, May 30, 1994), pp. 124–126.

23 For more information on consumer buying behavior, see *Why People Buy*, by John O'Shaughnessy (New York: Oxford University Press, 1987).

24 For more information on business buying behavior, see *Major Account Sales Strategy*, by Neil Rackham (New York: McGraw-Hill, 1989).

35 For more information on the sales funnel, see *Strategic Selling*, by Robert Miller and Stephen Heiman with Tad Tuleja (New York: Warner Books, 1985), pp. 234–260.

Chapter 3   Sales Role #1: The Student

37 Mack Hanan's comments were taken from "Selling Profits, Not Products" (*Sales Force: Strategies & Tactics for Sales Professionals*, a newsletter published by the editors of *Sales & Marketing Management*, October 17, 1994). Note: The publication of this newsletter was discontinued in April 1995.

38 Kevin Corcoran's comments were taken from "A Fresh Start for Sales Training," by Beverly Geber (*Training Magazine*, May 1993), p. 46.

40 Information on what CEOs worry about was taken from "The Change Monster" (*Training Magazine*, May 1994), p. 136.

40   The change in corporate focus from cost cutting to revenue growth was taken from "The 'Top Line'; Not Top Drawer: Will Scant Sales Rein in Profits?" by George Koretz (*Business Week*, October 23, 1995) p. 26.

43   The example of authority versus influence with the President of the United States was obtained from *Power Base Selling: Secrets of an Ivy League Street Fighter*, by Jim Holden (New York: John Wiley & Sons, 1990), pp. 17–23.

45   Information on the copier salesperson selling to the ice cream store was obtained from the audiocassette program *State of the Art Selling*, by Barry Farber (Chicago: Nightingale-Conant Corporation, 1993). See cassette side 9: "Selling Beyond the Nine-Dots."

47   The quote from on-line industry expert Wally Bock, of Oakland, California, was obtained during a personal interview in April 1995. Wally is the author of *Getting On the Information Superhighway* (Menlo Park, CA: Crisp Publications, 1995) and the audiocassette album *Doing Business Online* (Kansas City: National Press Publications, 1995).

50   Information on the availability of corporate reports from the SEC via the World Wide Web was taken from "Financial Records On Line," by staff and wire reports (*Contra Costa Times*, October 6, 1995) p. C–1.

52   Daniel Burrus's comments were obtained from "Pleading Their Case," by Weld Royal (*Sales & Marketing Management*, February 1995), pp. 50–57.

59   Letter formatting points were taken from "Better Letters: Beware the 'Ooh, We're Eager' Letter," by Herschell Gordon Lewis (*Selling Magazine*, May 1995) p. 40.

60   Information as to why graphics should be placed on the left side of a page and text on the right was obtained from *The Creative Brain*, by Ned Hermann (Lake Lure, NC: The Ned Herrmann Group, 1993), p. 15.

Chapter 4   Sales Role #2: The Doctor

75   Information regarding the cellular telephone industry's growth rate was obtained from Hoover's Industry Profiles (Austin, TX: Reference Press Inc.) via America Online.

Chapter 5   Sales Role #3: The Architect

100   Research that found an 87 percent loss of selling skills taught in training when there is no follow-up coaching by sales managers was taken from *Managing Major Sales: Practical Strategies for Improving Sales Effectiveness*, by Neil Rackham and Richard Ruff (New York: HarperBusiness, 1991), pp. 128–130.

101   "The Greatest Commercials Ever Made" appeared on the CBS television network on March 15, 1995.

115   The Levi Strauss story was taken from *Levi's: The "Shrink to Fit" Business That Stretched to Cover the World*, by Ed Cray (Boston: Houghton Mifflin, 1978) pp. 2–3.

118   Information regarding Motorola's commitment to training was ob-
      tained from "Motorola: Training for the Millennium," by Kevin Kelly
      (*BusinessWeek*, March 28, 1994), pp. 158–163.

Chapter 6   Sales Role #4: The Coach

131   J.D. Power and Associates information was obtained from "Lexus Deal-
      ers Please Buyers," by James Healey (*USA Today*, June 17, 1994). Money
      section, p. 2.

151   John Madden information was obtained from *You've Got to Be Believed to
      Be Heard: Reach the First Brain to Communicate in Business and in Life*, by
      Bert Decker (New York: St. Martin's Press, 1992), pp. 7–9.

Chapter 7   Sales Role #5: The Therapist

161   The information on price research was obtained from *Major Account
      Sales Strategy*, by Neil Rackham (New York: McGraw-Hill, 1989), p. 116.

Chapter 8   Sales Role #6: The Negotiator

167   Information on win-win negotiating was taken from *Guide to Business
      Negotiating*, by Roger Dawson (Chicago: Nightingale Conant Video,
      1988).

194   Using the martial art of Aikido as a metaphor for handling conflict was
      obtained from *The Magic of Conflict*, by Tom Crum (New York: Touch-
      stone Books, 1987), pp. 40–48.

195   Don't attack the other side's position, look behind it, was obtained from
      Getting to Yes, 2nd edition, by Roger Fisher and William Ury (New York:
      Penguin Books, 1991), p. 109. The difference between a position and an
      interest was obtained from p. 41.

198   Most people are either speaking or preparing to speak was obtained
      from *Seven Habits of Highly Effective People*, by Stephen Covey (New York:
      Simon & Schuster, 1989), p. 239.

Chapter 9   Sales Role #7: The Teacher

205   Information regarding the cost of acquiring customers being five to six
      times the cost of retaining existing customers was obtained from *Creat-
      ing Customer Value: The Path to Sustainable Competitive Advantage*, by Earl
      Naumann (Cincinnati: Thomson Executive Press, 1995), p. 128.

205   Watson Wyatt Data Services information on sales training needs was
      obtained from "Sales Training Hit List" (*Inc.*, November 1994), p. 126.

206   The "Five Phases of Learning," was adapted from "The Five Levels of
      Competence," *Creative Training Techniques Handbook: Tips, Tactics and
      How-To's for Delivering Effective Training* by Robert W. Pike (Minneapolis:
      Lakewood Publications, 1989), pp. 5–6. Used by permission.

211   For more information regarding Forum Corporation's research on customer expectations, see *The Customer-Driven Company: Moving from Talk to Action*, by Richard Whiteley (Reading, MA: Addison-Wesley, 1991), p. 4.

215   Brand awareness information and IDG survey information were obtained from *TechnoBrands: How to Create and Use Brand Identity to Market, Advertise, and Sell Technology Products*, by Chuck Pettis (New York: Amacom Books, 1995), pp. 9–11.

220   Your customer's perception that value is your purpose for being in business was taken from *Competing on Value*, by Mack Hanan and Peter Karp (New York: Amacom Books, 1991), p. 4. Equating sales with banks was adapted from "Equating Investments with Short-Term Loans," pp. 79–81.

222   Information on the M.I.T. study was obtained from *Keeping Customers for Life*, by Joan Koob Cannie with Donald Caplin (New York: Amacom Books, 1991), p. 14.

231   Steelcase case study information summarized by permission, Steelcase Inc., P.O. Box 1967, Grand Rapids, MI 49501.

Chapter 10   Sales Role #8: The Farmer

233   Management Compensation Services study obtained from "More Sales Pay Linked to Satisfied Customers," edited by William Keenan, Jr. (*Sales & Marketing Management*, June 1995), p. 37.

233   Information on the National Fuel Gas sales compensation plan was obtained from "Look Who's in on Your Performance Review," by Lisa Holton (*Selling Magazine*, January/February 1995), pp. 47–56.

237   Information regarding factors that contribute to dissatisfaction being different from the factors that contribute to customer satisfaction was obtained from *Creating Customer Value: The Path to Sustainable Competitive Advantage*, by Earl Naumann (Cincinnati: Thomson Executive Press, 1995), p. 52.

241   Information regarding tape-recorded testimonial letters was obtained from *Breakthrough Selling*, by Barry Farber and Joyce Wycoff (Englewood Cliffs, NJ: Prentice Hall, 1992), p. 149.

244   Referral information was obtained during a personal interview with San Francisco-based marketing consultant David Garfinkel, author of *Referral Magic: 17 Ways to Let Your Clients Do Your Selling* (Rutland, VT: Gemstone Publishing, 1994).

248   Information on the Denver International Airport's baggage handling system was obtained from "Tiny Company Is Blamed for Denver Delays," by Julie Schmit (*USA Today*, May 5, 1994), pp. 1–2.

Chapter 11   Winning the Complex Sale

252   Information on Nike founder and CEO Phil Knight's personal challenges with technology was obtained from "Underlings' Skill Can Give Them an Edge," by Julia Lawlor (*USA Today*, May 16, 1994), pp. 1–2.

Would You Like to Share with Others What's New and Working for You?

I'm planning another book, a field applications guide, that will consist of selling success stories, tools, and methods. A published collection of real-life stories will help us all to learn from each other. The more examples we have of consultative, customer-focused selling, the more effective all of us will be.

To make my next book a reality, I need your help. If you have a story that describes how you applied a new idea learned in this book (or a new idea you discovered elsewhere), I'd love to hear from you. All contributors whose stories are published will be credited in the book and will receive $50.

Please send your story, and the new idea it describes, to:

Kevin Davis
The Kevin Davis Group
4115 Blackhawk Plaza Circle, Suite 100
Danville, CA 94506
Phone: (510) 831-0922
Fax: (510) 831-8677
E-Mail: kdavissell@aol.com

Be sure to include your name, address, and phone number on your submission. Thanks!

INDEX